D1151660

FORD MADOX FORD

Ford Madox Ford (the name he adopted in 1919: he was originally Ford Hermann Hueffer) was born in 1873 in Merton, Surrey. His father, Francis Hueffer, who was an author and musicologist, died when Ford was fifteen. Ford's mother, Catherine, was the daughter of the Pre-Raphaelite painter Ford Madox Brown. Ford quickly took to writing: his first book, a children's fairy-tale, was published when he was seventeen, and his first novel, *The Shifting of the Fire*, came out in 1892. After the death of Ford Madox Brown in 1893, Ford wrote a biography of his grandfather, which was published in 1896. He was therefore an experienced author before (now married to Elsie Martindale) he encountered Joseph Conrad in 1898, and began a literary relationship which proved highly fruitful for the development of both writers' conception of the novelist's task. Conrad and Ford collaborated on *The Inheritors* (1901) and other books, and Ford wrote an instalment of *Nostromo* when Conrad was too ill to meet the deadline. Ford continued to write prolifically on his own account in a variety of forms: art criticism (books on Rossetti and Hans Holbein in 1902 and 1905), poetry, essays and novels. His trilogy of historical novels about Henry VIII and Katherine Howard began with *The Fifth Queen* in 1906, followed by *Privy Seal* in 1907 and *The Fifth Queen Crowned* in 1908. In 1908, he founded the *English Review*, which proved a literary success if a financial failure, publishing works by many major writers (such as Conrad, Hardy, Wells, James, Bennett and Forster) and helping to begin the careers of such as Wyndham Lewis and Lawrence. Ford's complicated private life became a matter of public notoriety when first *The Daily Mirror* and then a magazine called *The Throne* referred to Violet Hunt, for whom Ford had left his wife, as Mrs Hueffer, and Elsie set in train legal proceedings. Meanwhile, Ford's literary output continued with further novels (including *A Call* in 1910), his *Collected Poems* in 1913, and a critical study of Henry James. He wrote the novel which he called his best book, *The Good Soldier*, in 1913–14, and it was published in 1915. In the same year, Ford took a commission in the army. His experience of the battle of the Somme in 1916, during which he was wounded, furnished him with material for his Tietjens tetralogy, *Parade's End*, which began with the publication of *Some Do Not* in 1924. By then Ford had begun a relationship with Stella Bowen, by whom he had a daughter (he had two previous daughters by Elsie Martindale), had moved to France, and had begun to edit the *Transatlantic Review*. This journal published the work of, among others, Pound, Gertrude Stein, Hemingway and Joyce. A book of reminiscences of Joseph Conrad was published in 1924; the second Tietjens novel, *No More Parades*, in 1925; the third, *A Man Could Stand Up*, in 1926; and the fourth, *The Last Post*, in 1928. His critical study, *The English Novel*, appeared in 1929. Having separated from Stella Bowen and had an affair with Jean Rhys, whose work he published in the *Transatlantic Review*, Ford met Janice Biala in 1930, and lived with her until his death in 1939. He continued to publish novels regularly, as well as other works, notably an extended *Collected Poems* in 1936.

ALSO BY FORD MADOX FORD FROM CARCANET

The Rash Act
Ladies Whose Bright Eyes
The Good Soldier
Parade's End
Selected Poems
The Ford Reader
Return to Yesterday
A History of Our Own Times
The English Novel

FORD MADOX FORD

....

War Prose

EDITED BY MAX SAUNDERS

CARCANET

This prose collection
first published in Great Britain in 1999 by
Carcanet Press Limited
4th Floor, Conavon Court
12–16 Blackfriars Street
Manchester M3 5BQ

Texts copyright © 1999 Janice Biala
Introduction and editorial matter
copyright © 1999 Max Saunders

The right of Max Saunders to be identified
as the editor of this work has been asserted
by him in accordance with the
Copyright, Designs and Patents Act of 1988.
All rights reserved.

A CIP catalogue record for this book
is available from the British Library
ISBN 1 85754 396 3

The publisher acknowledges financial assistance
from the Arts Council of England

Set in 11/12pt Bembo by XL Publishing Services, Tiverton
Printed and bound in England by SRP Ltd, Exeter

For there is no new thing under the sun,
Only this uncomely man with a smoking gun
In the gloom...
What the devil will he gain by it?
Digging a hole in the mud and standing all day in the rain by it
Waiting his doom,
The sharp blow, the swift outpouring of the blood,
Till the trench of grey mud
Is turned to a brown purple drain by it.
[...]
And what in the world did they bear it for?
I don't know.
And what in the world did they dare it for?
Perhaps that is not for the likes of me to understand.

[from 'In October 1914', later titled 'Antwerp']

Man is to mankind a wolf – homo homini lupus – largely because
the means of communication between man and man are very
limited. I daresay that if words direct enough could have been
found, the fiend who sanctioned the use of poisonous gases in the
present war could have been so touched to the heart that he would
never have signed that order, calamitous, since it marks a definite
retrogression in civilisation such as had not yet happened in the
Christian era. Beauty is a very valuable thing; perhaps it is the most
valuable thing in life; but the power to express emotion so that it
shall communicate itself intact and exactly is almost more valuable.

['From China to Peru' (on Pound's *Cathay*),
Outlook, 35 (19 June 1915), pp. 800–1]

Contents

Introduction

Ford Madox Ford is now recognised not just as a central modernist author, but as one of the major writers about the First World War. His best-known treatment of war, the sequence of four novels known collectively as *Parade's End*, has been regularly in print since 1948, when perhaps it felt newly relevant after a second world war. It has been achieving broad recognition as the best English novel about the First World War. William Carlos Williams wrote that the four novels 'constitute the English prose masterpiece of their time'. Malcolm Bradbury describes *Parade's End* as 'the most important and complex British novel to deal with the overwhelming subject of the Great War'. He judges it 'the greatest modern war novel from a British writer'; Samuel Hynes calls it 'the greatest war novel ever written by an Englishman'.[1]

It was unusual for a man of forty-two to serve in the line. Though Ford's experience of combat was limited – he was at the Front for about two months – he took part in the Battle of the Somme, and was in the Ypres Salient. He was frequently under bombardment, and suffered from concussion, shell-shock and lung damage. His army experience was varied; and it proved to be the decisive episode in his life.

The shadow of the First World War fell on almost everything Ford wrote after the 4th of August 1914. When it broke out, he was finishing his Edwardian masterpiece, *The Good Soldier*. The date of the 4th August sounds through that novel like the death-knell of the era. The story ends in private devastations – madness, enervation and death – which have been read as metaphors of the public cataclysm. Ford rightly saw the war as the defining experience of technological modernity. 'The world before the war is one thing and must be written about in one manner,' he wrote: 'the after-

---

1 Williams, *Sewanee Review*, 59 (Jan.–Mar. 1951), pp. 154–61; reprinted in *Selected Essays* (New York: Random House, 1954), p. 316. Bradbury, 'Introduction', *Parade's End* (London: Everyman's Library, 1992), pp. xii, xiii. Hynes, 'The Genre of *No Enemy*', *Antaeus*, 56 (Spring 1986), p.140.

war world is quite another and calls for quite different treatment.'[2]

Ford was at Mary Borden Turner's literary country-house party near Berwick-upon-Tweed when war was declared. Other guests included Wyndham Lewis and E. M. Forster. Ford was writing weekly 'Literary Portraits' at the time, and registered his shock at the conflict immediately. His wartime journalism was extraordinarily far-sighted. (Some excerpts are included here.) Within a few days of the outbreak, he was pondering the effects on his mind, on national psychologies, on literature and society. This moving between questions of war and questions of psychology and aesthetics is, as we shall see, deeply characteristic of all Ford's war writings. Even before he saw active service, he realised that the war presented a new kind of challenge to literature, and to his own form of literary impressionism in particular.

Ford's response to the war was as much European and transatlantic as it was English or British. His allegiances were cosmopolitan and complex. He was the son of a German father and English mother. He had tried to acquire German citizenship in 1912 (in order to get divorced). Like his father, Francis Hueffer, and his English grandfather, Ford Madox Brown, he had a deep love of France, and was appalled by the thought of its devastation. His multiple sympathies are evident in many of the pieces here, which remind us that *Parade's End* too is an international work, adopting the techniques of European and American modernism to render France and Germany as well as Britain.

In his journalism Ford took a controversial stand against the prevailing rhetorical hysteria, urging that the war should be fought in chivalric mode: against a 'gallant enemy'. This was brave for someone with a German surname. (He remained 'Ford Madox Hueffer' throughout the war, only changing his last name around the time of the Versailles peace treaty.) His anti-propaganda stance may have suggested that he would be a useful propagandist. Soon afterwards, he was recruited by his friend Charles Masterman, the Liberal Cabinet Minister put in charge of British propaganda. The 'Literary Portraits' turned into sketches of German and French culture, and these were revised into two large propaganda books in 1915, *When Blood is Their Argument: An Analysis of Prussian Culture*, and *Between St Denis and St George: A Sketch of Three*

---

2   Ford to T. R. Smith, 27 July 1931: Cornell.

Civilisations. His propaganda was of an unusually cultural and humane kind. He had a horror of the rhetoric denouncing the enemy as 'mad dog', 'mercenary', 'brute', 'tyrant'. He claimed that his poem 'On Heaven' was circulated by the Ministry of Information to cheer up the troops. Some of the pieces here should perhaps be read in a similar spirit. Yet he soon found himself affected by the tide of popular patriotic aggression. In a fascinating exploration of the origins of hatred (which he characteristically relates to aesthetics and to sexual conflict), he turns his formidable psychological acumen on himself, revealing himself as disturbed to find that after only a few months of war he too had begun to wish Germans dead.

There is thus a large body of work written between August 1914 and Ford's joining the army. Most of it has been excluded here, partly for reasons of space, but also to give a more coherent concentration on the effects and after-effects of first-hand experience of military life and military conflict. But I have included the passage from *Between St Denis and St George* about his state of mind as war was declared; two propagandistic stories that give a sense of the rumours and sentiments that were circulating; and excerpts from his 'Literary Portraits' that were too personal to be incorporated into the propaganda books.

Ford enlisted in the summer of 1915, and got his commission as a second lieutenant in the Welch Regiment (Special Reserve). He probably took an introductory course at the Chelsea Barracks, before joining his battalion for training first at Tenby, then Cardiff Castle. He had to wait until 13 July 1916 before he left Cardiff for France. The journey is described here in the propaganda article, 'Pon... ti... pri... ith'.

At Rouen Ford was attached to the 9th Battalion, and sent to the Somme, where the fiercest battle in British military history had been raging since 1 July. He wanted experience of the front line, but his CO thought he was too old, and stationed him with the battalion transport, just behind the front line near Albert. He described the battle in a letter to Lucy Masterman on 28 July:

> We are right up in the middle of the strafe, but only with the 1st line transport. We get shelled two or three times a day, otherwise it is fairly dull – indeed, being shelled is fairly dull, after the first once or twice. Otherwise it is all very interesting – filling in patches of one's knowledge [...] The noise of the bombardment

is continuous – so continuous that one gets used to it, as one gets used to the noise in a train and the ear picks out the singing of the innumerable larks...[3]

Either that day or the next he was 'blown into the air by something' – a high explosive shell – and landed on his face, with concussion and mouth injuries. 'I had completely lost my memory,' he said, so that 'three weeks of my life are completely dead to me'. He even forgot his own name for thirty-six hours. When the battalion went into rest camp he was sent to a casualty clearing station at Corbie for treatment. He was suffering from what was becoming known as 'shell shock'. His sense of patches of knowledge being blasted away, and the terrors and hallucinations that followed, were to become some of his most compelling subjects.

By 23 August he had rejoined the 9th battalion, which was now stationed in the Ypres Salient near Kemmel Hill. He found it 'quiet here at its most violent compared with the Somme' – even during the 'strafe that the artillery got up for George V', whom he said he'd seen strolling about on a royal visit to the Front. But Ford was still very tense and harassed. He didn't get on with his Commanding Officer, Lieutenant-Colonel Cooke, an ex-Eastbourne Town Councillor who doubted Ford's power as a leader of men. (He thought this unfair, telling Lucy Masterman that the First Line Transport was 'composed mostly of mules'.) He tried using the Mastermans' influence to get transferred to a staff job, where he realised his abilities would be put to better use. But the move was blocked, not only by Cooke, who wanted Ford out of the army, but also by MI6, on the grounds that his German ancestry made him unsuitable for intelligence work.[4]

Ford was sent back to the first line transport, where he found the war exhilarating as well as nerve-wracking: 'it is very hot here & things are enormously exciting & the firing all day keeps me a little too much on the jump to write composedly,' he wrote to his mother. 'However it is jolly to have been in the two greatest strafes of history – & I am perfectly well & in good spirits, except for money worries wh. are breaking me up a good deal – & for the

---

3 *Letters of Ford Madox Ford*, ed. Richard M. Ludwig (Princeton, 1965) – henceforth *Letters* – pp. 66-7.

4 Ford's service record is at the Public Records Office, Kew, file WO 339 / 37369. MI5 blocked Ford's brother's application for Intelligence work in similar terms. Oliver Hueffer's service record is also at Kew, in file WO 339 / 44941.

time, perfectly safe.'[5]

He later said that it was while returning to the Front that he realised he was the only novelist of his age to be in the fighting. This made it all the more necessary that he should bear witness; and he recalled: 'I began to take a literary view of the war from that time'. This is evident in three extraordinary letters he sent to Conrad in September 1916, rendering his impressions of the war – particularly 'notes upon sound'.

The first of the letters describes suddenly finding himself under a table during an artillery barrage:

> Well I was under the table & frightened out of my life – so indeed was the other man with me. There was shelling just overhead – apparently thousands of shells bursting for miles around & overhead. I was convinced that it was up with the XIX Div[n.] because the Huns had got note of a new & absolutely devilish shell or gun.
>
> It was of course thunder. It completely extinguished the sound of the heavy art[iller]y, & even the how[itzer] about 50 yds. away was inaudible during the actual peals & sounded like *stage thunder* in the intervals.[6]

It is these paradoxes of subliminal consciousness and surprised perception that fascinate him. He later gave an example of the converse situation. He heard three of the younger officers discussing who was 'the coolest person on a certain night in Jy. 16 when we were suddenly shelled behind Bécourt Wood'. They agreed that 'old Hoof was by a long chalk & that old Hoof ought to have had the MC only the CO didn't like him'; one of them added: 'But then, one expected it of Hoof!' The rest of the letter is quintessential Ford: ironising the very egotism it risks; attending to the art of the novelist; and unobtrusively shaping a vignette of lethal comedy:

> I remember the occasion quite well: I was so busy looking after an officer who had got very drunk & was trying to expose

---

5 Ford to Cathy Hueffer, 6 Sept. 1916: House of Lords Record Office.

6 F[anny] B[utcher], 'Ford Madox Ford a Visitor Here Tells of His Work', *Chicago Tribune* (22 Jan. 1927). Ford to Stella Bowen, 20 Jan. [1927], identifies 'F. B.'. Ford to Conrad [first week of Sept.], 6 and 7 Sept. 1916: *Letters*, pp. 71–6. There are more accurate transcriptions of these letters in *The Presence of Ford Madox Ford*, ed. Sondra J. Stang (Philadelphia, 1981), pp. 170–7.

himself, that I never really noticed the shelling at all except that I was covered with tins of sardines & things that had been put out for our dinner.

That was really the worst of the Front from the novelist's point of view. One was always so busy with one's immediate job that one had no time to notice one's sensations or anything else that went on round one. H. G. [Wells] w^d. no doubt do it very much better![7]

The novelist of perplexity and displaced sensation was particularly suited to presenting this psychology of battle, in which the obtuseness and subliminal noticings of the protagonist become an index to the mental strain he is under. He told Conrad: 'I have been for six weeks – with the exception of only 24 hours – continuously within reach of German missiles &, altho' one gets absolutely to ignore them, consciously, I imagine that subconsciously one is suffering.' The second letter describes his attempt to buy flypapers in a shop while a shell lands nearby, and the Tommies joke as if the noise was made by the flies. 'No interruption, emotion, vexed at getting no flypapers,' writes Ford: 'Subconscious emotion, "thank God the damn thing's burst".'

Despite all this, he could say with strangely detached irony: 'It is curious – but, in the evenings here, I always feel myself happier that I have ever felt in my life.' It is indeed curious that he can say this in a letter beginning 'I wrote these rather hurried notes yesterday because we were being shelled to hell & I did not expect to get thro' the night.' It was, as often, a sense of death's imminence that made him want to go on writing: a paradox he addresses in the third letter to his former collaborator:

I wonder if it is just vanity that in these cataclysmic moments makes one desire to *record*. I hope it is, rather, the annalist's wish to help the historian – or, in a humble sort of way, my desire to help you, cher maître! – if you ever wanted to do anything in '*this line*'. Of course you wd. not ever want to do anything in this line – but a pocketful of coins in a foreign country may sometimes come in handy. You might want to put a phrase into the mouth of someone in Bangkok who had been, say, to

7　Ford to Stella Bowen, 22 Nov. 1918: *The Correspondence of Ford Madox Ford and Stella Bowen*, ed. Sondra J. Stang and Karen Cochran (Bloomington and Indianapolis: Indiana University Press, 1994), p. 40.

Bécourt. There you wd. be! And I, to that extent, shd. once
more have collaborated.[8]

Violet Hunt, with whom Ford had been living before the war,
sent him the proofs of her latest novel, *Their Lives*. He wrote the
brief preface (included here), signed with a bitter, ironic anonymity
'Miles Ignotus' ('The Unknown Soldier'), in which he described
reading them on a hillside watching the Germans shelling Belgian
civilians in Poperinghe. It seemed an example of senseless Prussian
cruelty, and is described as such in the passage in *No More Parades*
where the protagonist Christopher Tietjens recalls having watched
the same sight. There, as in Ford's other description of the scene –
in *No Enemy* – he records a disturbing conflict between a kind of
aesthetic pleasure in the spectacle, and the thought of the human
suffering it represented.[9] There was also a feeling of joy at the sight
of allied shells bursting over the German trenches. This volatile
emotional mix of awe, pity, excitement and outrage recurs in his
war prose, particularly in the most significant piece he wrote while
on the Western Front: the essay 'A Day of Battle', dated 15
September 1916, and also signed 'Miles Ignotus'.

Always an intense reader, Ford also managed to spend some of
'the eternal waiting that is War' reading. He reread the authors who
had meant most to him: Flaubert, Turgenev, Maupassant, Anatole
France, and his friends Henry James, W.H. Hudson, Conrad and
Stephen Crane. He never forgot the moment of disorientation
produced by *The Red Badge of Courage*: 'having to put the book
down and go out of my tent at dawn,' he remembered, 'I could
not understand why the men I saw about were in khaki' rather than
the blue or grey of the American Civil War; 'the impression was
so strong that its visualization of war completely superimposed itself
for long hours over the concrete objects of the war I was in'.
Rereading James gave him the same disorienting feeling of double
vision.[10] In the companion piece to 'A Day of Battle', 'The Enemy',
he gives another instance of this double vision, and how important
it was to his activity as a novelist. He recounts a near-death experience, when shot at by a sniper. He imagines the German, then

---

8   *Letters*, pp. 75–6.
9   *No More Parades* (London, 1925), pp. 308–10 . *No Enemy* (New York, 1929), pp. 82–7.
10 *Return to Yesterday* (London, 1931), p. 49; *New York Essays* (New York, 1927), p. 30;
    'Literary Causeries: IV: Escape.....', *Chicago Tribune Sunday Magazine* (Paris) (9 March
    1924), pp. 3, 11.

imagines the German looking at him through his gun-sight.

He spent a weekend in Paris for the publication of a translation of his second 'propaganda' book, *Entre Saint Denis et Saint Georges*, and was thanked by the Minister of Instruction. The leave was scarcely less stressful than the line. Ford worked so hard revising the translation that he collapsed, and was told he was 'suffering from specific shell-shock & ought to go to hospital'. But he wouldn't go. He was back in the Salient by 13 September. None of this stopped him writing about the episode, in the article 'Trois Jours de Permission'.[11]

Soon after this he was sent back to the 3rd Battalion's home base in North Wales, at Kinmel Park, near Rhyl. Ford found his new posting a new waste of his abilities, and – without overseas pay – a strain on his financial resources.

When the War Office did eventually order him back to France at the end of November, he tried without success to avoid being re-attached to Lieutenant-Colonel Cooke's 9th Welch. He was given 'various polyglot jobs' such as 'writing proclamations in French about thefts of rations issued to H. B. M.'s forces & mounting guards over German sick'. But he fell ill himself in December. 'As for me, – c'est fini de moi, I believe, at least as far as fighting is concerned,' he told Conrad: 'my lungs are all charred up and gone'. The Medical Board wanted to send him home, but he protested that he 'didn't in the least want to see Blighty ever again'.[12]

Ford said his respiratory illness was due to 'a slight touch of gas I got in the summer & partly to sheer weather'.[13] He has been accused of lying about being gassed; not least because he elaborated the story later, telling a marvellous tale about how, while on leave in a Paris hotel, he opened his portmanteau and inadvertently released gas trapped there since he had begun packing during an attack. But there may be some truth in this. Clothes do give off yesterday's fumes, and someone with breathing difficulties would have been sensitive to even a hint of the lethal chemicals. However, the fictionalised version given in one of the pieces here, 'True Love

---

11 Ford to C. F. G. Masterman, 13 Sept. 1916: *Letters*, p. 76. 'Trois Jours de Permission', *Nation*, 19 (30 Sept. 1916), pp. 817–18.

12 Ford to Masterman, 5 Jan. 1917: *Letters*, pp. 81–3. Ford to Conrad, 19 Dec. 1916: *The Presence of Ford Madox Ford*, pp. 177–8; Ford to Cathy Hueffer, 15 Dec. 1916: House of Lords Records Office.

13 Ford to Masterman, 5 Jan. 1917: *Letters*, p. 82.

and a GCM [General Court Martial]', suggests another possibility. The protagonist, Gabriel Morton, is so furious after being accused of cowardice by his CO that he walks through a low gas-cloud in a shelled building. He is only subliminally aware that it is gas, and his repression of the fact makes the gesture virtually suicidal.

Ford was certainly ill enough for the army to send him to No. II Red Cross Hospital at Rouen, whatever the cause. As he knew, the damage wasn't only physical. 'I wasn't so much wounded as blown up by a 4.2 and shaken into a nervous breakdown,' he told his daughter Katharine, adding that it had made him 'unbearable to myself & my kind. However, I am better now & may go up the line at any moment – tho' I shd. prefer to remain out of it for a bit [...]'. Two days later the Medical Board said he was too unwell to return to the Front before the summer: 'the gas of the Huns has pretty well done for my lungs – wh. make a noise like a machine gun,' he told her:

> Of course it is rather awful out here – for me at least. Of the 14 off[ice]rs who came out with me in July I am the only one left here – & I am pretty well a shattered wreck – tho' they say my lungs will get better in time. And I sit in the hut here wh. is full of Welsh officers all going up – and all my best friends – and think that very likely not one of them will be alive in a fortnight. I tell you, my dear, it is rather awful.[14]

Survivor's guilt only exacerbated his despair. 'It wd. be really very preferable to be dead,' he wrote to his mother: 'but one isn't dead – so that is all there is to it.'[15]

When he had a relapse on Christmas Eve, the terror he had experienced in the Casualty Clearing Station returned:

> all night I lie awake & perceive the ward full of Huns of forbidding aspect – except when they give me a sleeping draft.
>
> I am in short rather ill still & sometimes doubt my own sanity – indeed, quite frequently I do. I suppose that, really, the Somme was a pretty severe ordeal, though I wasn't conscious of it at the time. Now, however, I find myself suddenly waking up in a hell of a funk – & going on being in a hell of a funk till morning. And that is pretty well the condition of a number of men here.

---

14 Ford to Katharine Hueffer, 10 and 12 Dec. 1916: Cornell.
15 Ford to Cathy Hueffer, 15 Dec. 1916: House of Lords Record Office.

I wonder what the effect of it will be on us all, after the war –
& on national life and the like.[16]

It was the kind of experience he needed to write about many times:
in several of the pieces here; in a letter to Conrad; and in *Parade's
End*. When he was well enough, he was sent to Lady Michelham's
convalescent hospital at Menton. The opulence of the Riviera was
a surreal contrast to the war, and he wrote about his time there too,
in the essay 'I Revisit the Riviera'. In February he left Menton, and
took a train to the frozen, snow-covered north. At Rouen he was
assigned to a Canadian casual battalion for three weeks, then put in
charge of a hospital tent of German prisoners at Abbeville. On the
evidence of *Parade's End* he found it 'detestable to him to be in
control of the person of another human being – as detestable as it
would have been to be himself a prisoner ... that thing that he
dreaded most in the world'.[17]

He was back on leave in London in the spring of 1917. The
Medical Board would not pass Ford as fit to return to France, so
he was given light duty commanding a company of the 23rd King's
Liverpool Regiment, stationed at Kinmel Park. He got on well with
his new Commanding Officer, Lieutenant-Colonel G.R. Powell,
whose commendation in Ford's service record must have gone a
long way towards redeeming him from Cooke's criticisms:

> Has shown marked aptitude for grasping any intricate subject and
> possesses great powers of organization – a lecturer of the first water
> on several military subjects – conducted the duties of housing
> officer to the unit (average strength 2800) with great ability.[18]

He was posted to a training command at Redcar, on the
Yorkshire coast, where he spent the rest of the war. Despite the
frustrations of army life, and the increasingly fraught meetings with
Violet Hunt, the life suited him. He never minded frugal living and
hard work. In the spring of 1918 he was attached to the Staff, and
told Katharine proudly that he would go 'all over the N[orth]. of
England inspecting training & lecturing':

---

16 'I Revisit the Riviera', *Harper's*, 166 (Dec. 1932), p. 66. Ford to C. F. G. Masterman, 5
    Jan. 1917: *Letters*, pp. 81–83.
17 *A Man Could Stand Up –* (London, 1926), pp. 186–7. Other accounts of German prisoners
    are in *Letters*, pp. 79–80, 'War & the Mind', p. 47 below, and *Return to Yesterday*,
    pp. 118–19, 329.
18 Quoted by Arthur Mizener, *The Saddest Story* (London, 1972), p. 296.

It is in many ways lucky for me as I was passed fit & should have gone out to my B$^{n.}$ again just the day after I got the order to join the Staff – & my B$^{n.}$ has been pretty well wiped out since then, so I suppose I sh$^{d.}$ have gone west with it.[19]

He was given the temporary rank of brevet major (meaning extra status without extra pay), and was even offered 'an after the war post as Educational Advisor to the Northern Command, permanently', with the rank of Lieutenant Colonel. (He considered it, but thought it would stop him writing.) He lectured on the Ross rifle, on 'the Causes of the War or on any other department of the rag-bag of knowledge that we had to inflict on the unfortunates committed to our charge'. His other topics included 'Censorship', 'War Aims', 'Attacks on Strong Points', 'Salvage', 'Military Law', 'Harmonising Rifle Fire', 'Cyphers', 'Geography and Strategy', 'Hospitals', and – of course – 'French Civilisation' – 'So I must be some sort of Encyclopaedia,' he said. His fictional alter-ego in *Parade's End*, Christopher Tietjens, loses his encyclopaedic memory when shell-shocked. Clearly Ford was beginning to feel himself again.

He had an 'exhausting and worrying time' after he was given the task of defending someone in a Court Martial (an experience which would presumably have gone into 'True Love & a GCM' had Ford completed it): 'the wretched man [...] began to go mad last Sunday,' he wrote, 'was certified yesterday, and the Court-martial washed out. This morning he rushed into my tent, having escaped from his escort: tried to strangle his father, bit me, and has just been carried off to an asylum'. He added: 'If there is anything of that sort going I am generally in it!'

In Yorkshire he again found himself in conflict with his new Commanding Officer, Lieutenant-Colonel Alexander Pope, who appears to have been a less conscious satirist than his namesake:

My rows with the CO are only funny – not worrying, because he is desperately afraid of me and only speaks to me as it were with his cap in his hand. The last one arose after he had said to me at a dance: 'Well, H., I suppose now peace is here you are the great man & I am only a worm at your feet.' And I cordially agreed. The dance, however, lasted to 0400 hours[.][20]

---

19 Ford to Katharine Hueffer, 13 Mar. 1918: Cornell.
20 Ford to Stella Bowen, 22 Aug. 1918; *The Correspondence of Ford Madox Ford and Stella Bowen*, p. 7.

Ford was expecting to be sent back to France with a large draft of troops on 7 November 1918. But he was told he was 'indispensable to the Bn'. Four days later the Armistice was declared. He remained in the army until 7 January 1919, when he took a single room 'studio' in a small London house in the next street to Violet Hunt's in Kensington. They had scandalised London society in 1912 by claiming, without proving, that Ford had divorced his wife Elsie Hueffer in Germany, and that they had married. He now tried to protect Hunt's reputation by appearing at her parties. To abandon her would have cast more doubt on their truthfulness and their marriage. Yet their relationship had been collapsing before he joined the Army. In the spring of 1919 he moved to a cottage in Sussex, 'Red Ford', and was joined by his new love, the Australian painter Stella Bowen.

The aim of the present volume is to assemble most of Ford's unpublished or uncollected prose explicitly about his experience of the war and its after-effects, to produce a new volume of unfamiliar work, but also to form a companion volume to his other important writings about the war, namely: *Parade's End*; the fictionalised memoir *No Enemy: A Tale of Reconstruction* and the autobiography *It Was the Nightingale* (which both deserve to be republished in full); his published correspondence;[21] and his war poetry (the best of which can be found in the *Selected Poems* in Carcanet's Millennium Ford series).

The prose is ordered into four sections: Reminiscences, Fiction, Prefaces, and a Miscellany. Such discriminations by genre are not intended as absolute – indeed, the distinction between autobiography, fiction and criticism is rarely an easy or useful one in Ford's writing, and the parallels to be found here often bring out how the fiction draws upon autobiography, how the reminiscences are fictionalised, and how Ford's critical intelligence is constantly at work in all genres. The 'Reminiscences' are eight pieces ranging from the declaration of war to anticipations of the next war.

The section of 'Fiction' contains the entire novel fragment 'True Love & a GCM' – arguably the centrepiece of the volume – and

---

21 Besides the *Letters*, and *The Correspondence of Ford Madox Ford and Stella Bowen*, sixty letters were published in Carcanet's *Ford Madox Ford Reader*, ed. Sondra J. Stang (Manchester, 1986).

six complete short stories. 'True Love & a GCM' is the first novel
Ford began after the war. Though unfinished, it possesses a form
of imaginative completeness; and it has an arresting quality that the
other unpublished novel of the period ('Mr Croyd', alias 'That
Same Poor Man') often lacks, despite being finished – partly because
in 'True Love' Ford is concerned with rendering states of mind
rather than getting involved in elaborate plotting. Actually the
'True Love' and the court martial of the title hardly figure at all in
the typescript. (The fact that the court martial Ford was to act in
was cancelled may have been one obstacle to completing the novel.)
Instead, the piece reads as a novella about how the disturbing experience of war affects the protagonist's mental processes, and how
this induces a reverie of reappraising his past, and in particular his
relationship with his father, thoughts about sexuality and about
literature. These concerns recur in the short stories too. The first
explores the fear of German invasion. The other five are all
examples of a popular wartime genre, turning on paranormal or
uncanny experiences.

Three of the 'Prefaces' are to other people's books: two written
in war-time, the other, written just after Ford had completed
Parade's End, offering a substantial discussion of the issues
confronting a war-novelist. These are placed alongside the prefaces
he wrote to three of the volumes of that tetralogy. Editions of
Parade's End have indefensibly excluded Ford's dedicatory letters for
half a century. But they are obviously significant documents. Their
omission made it easier for Graham Greene to suppress the final
volume, *Last Post*, from the Bodley Head edition in 1963, claiming
that Ford had 'not intended to write' it; yet the dedicatory letter to
No More Parades shows that from an early stage he intended to present
Tietjens in the 'process of being re-constructed'.

The Miscellany consists of short works and excerpts covering the
entire range of Ford's war experiences. They are drawn from many
published books and articles, as well as unpublished essays and
letters. Some excerpts of the complete but unpublished novel, 'That
Same Poor Man', appear here for the first time.

The war changed Ford's life utterly, as it did the lives of most
Europeans. It affected almost everything he wrote. It is thus hard
to draw a line between his 'war prose' and other writings.
Confining this volume to writing directly about the Western Front

would misrepresent the breadth and complexity of his responses to the war. He wrote in and across many genres: novels, stories, reminiscences, poems, propaganda, letters.

Curiously, what he didn't write was the kind of first-person testimony that became one of the central First World War genres: something comparable to *Goodbye to All That, Memoirs of an Infantry Officer, Undertones of War.* Indeed, the war falls silently between his two major autobiographical books, *Return to Yesterday* and *It Was the Nightingale.* The first ends with the outbreak of war; the second begins with Ford's demobilisation. He did write the fascinating book of war reminiscences, *No Enemy,* but it is strangely oblique and fictionalised. In a sense, the present volume attempts to sketch what the unwritten book of Ford's war memoirs might have covered.

He was above all a novelist, of course, and it is in *Parade's End* that he treats his war experiences definitively. As in that work, in the pieces published here he is preoccupied with the cultural, historical, moral, and literary after-effects of the war.

Even while the war was still being fought, Ford was creating an interpretation of the experience with which the twentieth century finally caught up, in novels such as Pat Barker's *Regeneration* trilogy. Ford's war, that is, is primarily psychological: presented in terms of its effects on the mind, on habits of perception; its terrors, anxieties, traumas; its disturbances of memory, identity, and language. He used two forms of the collective title for the pair of essays 'A Day of Battle' and 'The Enemy': first 'Arms and the Mind', then, 'War and the Mind'. The first has Virgilian echoes, and suggests the start of an epic project (realised in *Parade's End*) to record not the founding of a civilisation, but its foundering. Both versions indicate that this epic is to be a psychological one. In a sense, 'War and the Mind' is the project of all Ford's writing about the war.

His novel *The Marsden Case* asserts the universality of the psychological damage: 'the eyes, the ears, the brain and the fibres of every soul today adult have been profoundly seared by those dreadful wickednesses of embattled humanity'.[22] Ford felt it took him until 1923 to recover, when he told his old friend H. G. Wells: 'I've got over the nerve tangle of the war and feel able at last really to write again – which I never thought I should do.'[23] That was when he

---

22 *The Marsden Case* (London, 1923), p. 144.

was beginning *Parade's End*. Much of the work included here was written earlier, while he was still himself in the process of reconstruction. Its occasional unsurenesses, the sense of a damaged personality, make it revealing about precisely the damage caused by the war.

Ford realised with astounding prescience that the mind's repression of war-suffering made it difficult to exorcise the suffering, and by the same token difficult to convey in prose. About a month after the outbreak he found himself 'absolutely and helplessly unable – to write a poem about the present war', and attributed it to 'the hazy remoteness of the war-grounds; the impossibility of visualising anything, because of a total incapacity to believe any single thing that I read in the daily papers'.[24] But being in the war-grounds didn't make the experience much easier to visualise in words. 'A Day of Battle', which is a key document in the genesis of *Parade's End*, is a deeply paradoxical piece, vividly recreating the predicament of someone who feels he can no longer create vivid representations. It is all the more effective for being one of the few such prose testimonies actually written at the Front. As in his letters, he is concerned with what the mind doesn't perceive – or at least not quite consciously. This comes across in a curious fantasy of protection and exposure that recurs in several of his war works.

> I used to think that being out in France would be like being in a magic ring that would cut me off from all private troubles: but nothing is further from the truth. I have gone down to the front line at night, worried, worried, worried beyond belief about happenings at home in a Blighty that I did not much expect to see again – so worried that all sense of personal danger disappeared and I forgot to duck when shells went close overhead.[25]

Three central aspects of Ford's psychology of war emerge here. First, that war mobilises powerful fantasies of escape: from domestic anxiety, from life altogether, and from war itself. Second, that the doubling of civilian and military suffering recreates the situation crucial to Fordian impressionism, of being in one place with one's

---

23 Ford to Wells, 14 October 1923: *Letters*, p. 154. He also wrote to Conrad: 'I think I'm doing better work as the strain of the war wears off', 7 October 1923: Yale.

24 'Literary Portraits – LIII: The Muse of War', *Outlook*, 34 (12 Sept. 1914), pp. 334–5.

25 'A Day of Battle', p. 41 below. Compare the similar passage from *The Marsden Case*, included in the Miscellany, p. 241 below; and *A Man Could Stand Up–*, pp. 63, 124–5.

mind somewhere quite other: 'he is indeed, then, *homo duplex*: a poor fellow whose body is tied in one place, but whose mind and personality brood eternally over another distant locality'. Hence the 'double pictures' discussed in 'True Love and a GCM'. Thirdly, as he puts it in *Parade's End*'s dedicatory letters, that this 'never-ending sense of worry' produced 'mental distresses' that were as significant as the 'physical horrors': 'The heavy strain of the trenches came from the waiting for long periods of inaction, in great – in mortal – danger every minute of the day and night.'[26] It is not that he ignored the physical horrors. The point is that they were so extreme, so unprecedented, that they seemed beyond the real. One of the most disturbing, apocalyptic passages comes in the piece entitled 'Epilogue':

> We *don't know how many men have been killed* .... One is always too close or too remote. On the Somme in July 1916, or under Vimy Ridge in February 1917 one saw [...] such an infinite number of dead – and frequently mouldering – Huns [...] when you see the dead lie in heaps, in thousands, half buried, intact, reposeful as if they had fallen asleep, contorted as if they were still in agony, the heaps of men following the lines of hillocks, of shell holes, like so much rubbish spread before an incinerator in the quarter of a town where refuse is disposed of ..... Well, you think of Armageddon, and on any hill of that Line, as I have seen it, from the Somme up to the Belgian Coast where you see, and can feel, the operations of counted millions of men moving million against million – you think again of Armageddon.[27]

He would refer to the war as a 'crack across the table of History', and later described its psychological aftermath in equally apocalyptic terms: 'it had been revealed to you that beneath Ordered Life itself was stretched, the merest film with, beneath it, the abysses of Chaos'.[28] He had been haunted by that uncanny vision of the dead since the Somme, and much of his war prose is impelled by the need to exorcise it; and by another vision – of what, in 'A Day of Battle', he calls 'most amazing fact of history': the presence of those

---

26 *It Was the Nightingale* (London, 1934), p. 197; compare *Joseph Conrad* (London, 1924), p. 192. *No More Parades* (London, 1925), p. 6; *A Man Could Stand Up –* (London, 1926), pp. [vi–vii]; both reprinted here. Compare *Great Trade Route* (London, 1937), p. 96.
27 'Epilogue', pp. 59–60 below.
28 *A Man Could Stand Up –*, p. 13. *It Was the Nightingale*, p. 49.

'millions of men moving million against million' in the lines along the entire Western Front. The immense scale of the war makes it seem equally unreal.

He was already beginning to think through the central problems of *Parade's End*: how is it possible to *see* such a vast panorama as a world war? From what vantage point can the novelist gain a perspective? What hill can he stand up on? How can he avoid being 'always too close or too remote'? And how can he make his readers see experiences characterised by a displacement of the perceiving mind from those things so fundamental to the conventional novel: time, place and action?

Ford's impressionism was already well-developed before the war. Its fragmentation of time and plot, and foregrounding of haunting visual scenes, should have been well-suited to rendering war's traumas and hyper-reality. The war could only be expressed in terms of vivid impressions – it didn't make any other kind of sense – narrative, moral, philosophical, historical. But dwelling on those memories is too disturbing: his mind wants him to forget them, to suppress them. The nerve specialist tells the young hero of 'Mr Croyd': 'keep out of the way of what you call vivid words'. Human kind could not bear very much war reality. He found himself in a double-bind.

Which is why Ford approaches crucial memories from several angles in the pieces here. These reapproaches have been left uncut, because the overlappings (both with other material in this volume, and with other books – *Parade's End*, *No Enemy*, *Provence*, and others indicated in the prefaces and notes) give a valuable insight into the creative processes of Ford's memory and writing, and into the intractability of the material. It was partly because he was bravely treating difficult topics – fear, madness, humiliation, guilt, rage – that he needed to return to them.

Ford's writing from 1916 onwards – especially his letters to Conrad from the war, 'True Love & a G.C.M.', 'Mr Croyd', *No Enemy* (on being a 'creature of dreads'), and *Parade's End* – bears the impress of that blind terror he later characterised as his 'Corbie-phobia': above all, terror of losing control of his mind. It weighed on his mind to the end of his life.

There can have been hardly an Englishman who ever expected to engage in actual warfare, so that when he did so his entire moral balance called for readjustments; his entire view of life, if

he had one, was smashed to fragments; and, if he survived the
war, his reaction against all its circumstances resulted in a very
terrible mental fatigue from which he has not yet recovered [...]
The results in the case of myself, with literary training enough
in all conscience, were such that for several years after the
armistice I was unable to write a word that had not about it at
least, let us say, a touch of queerness.[29]

That sense of disturbance to one's sanity, shaken by war's mad
unreality, produces a specific effect in several of the works here; a
disturbance of identity, in which the familiar boundaries dissolve.
Sometimes it is the boundary between the conscious and unconscious minds, as in 'Pink Flannel' and 'The Miracle'. More
uncannily, it is sometimes between one person and another; as in
'The Colonel's Shoes', another eerie story of psychological strain,
concerning a seemingly paranormal experience in which a young
lieutenant momentarily assumes his uncle's identity.[30] Or, more
uncannily still, this slippage of identities can occur between the
living and the dead, as in 'Fun! – It's Heaven'; or 'True Love ...',
at the point when Gabriel Morton 'did not know if it was he or his
father' who has a vision.
    One could say these disturbances anticipate the episode of
Tietjens' shell-shock in *Parade's End*, but they should also be seen
as a development of Ford's concept of the 'sympathetic identifica-
tion' which enables the novelist (think of Dowell in *The Good
Soldier*, saying he loves Ashburnham 'because he was just myself').[31]
They also suggest the impact of Ford's war experience on the
notion of exchanged and mistaken identity which governs his late
novels, especially *The Rash Act* and *Henry for Hugh*.
    These things aren't unprecedented in Ford's pre-war writing,
nor indeed in the paranormal fantasies or science fiction of other
Edwardian writers. Where they do occur, though – in *A Call*, say,
or in *Ladies Whose Bright Eyes* and *The Good Soldier* – the intima-
tions of insanity are precipitated by sexuality. (Freud, after all,
analysed the uncanny in terms of the return of the repressed.) Ford's

---

29 'From a Paris Quay', *New York Evening Post Literary Review* (13 Dec. 1924), pp. 1–2.
30 I discuss these works in greater detail in *Ford Madox Ford: A Dual Life*, volume 2 (Oxford,
    1996), where a fuller treatment of Ford's wartime experiences can be found.
31 (London, 1915), p. 291.

war fiction makes this connexion more explicit, by using a trope central to the history of war literature – that of the 'sex war'. 'True Love and a GCM': that juxtaposition is crucial. The marital and the martial: sex and violence. In the propaganda story 'Fun! – It's Heaven', the innocent love between the dead soldier and his fiancée is supposed to redeem his sacrifice. (That it grants her a vision of him in Heaven is a denial of the finality of his death.) In 'Pink Flannel' the instinct of self-preservation causes the soldier to protect his adulterous liaison with Mrs Wilkinson. In 'The Miracle', the marital conversation frames the memory of war. In these stories, as in 'Epilogue', intimacy between men and women is posed as war's antithesis, as its cure. In other pieces here – 'True Love ...', or the Preface to *Their Lives*, there is a darker suggestion, and one which was to become central to *Parade's End*: that war's violent conflict is somehow analogous to, or even an expression of, sexual conflict. Ford is representative here, too. Many war novels – Rebecca West's *The Return of The Soldier*, Richard Aldington's *Death of a Hero*, R. H. Mottram's *Spanish Farm Trilogy* in the First World War, say, and Norman Mailer's *The Naked and the Dead* or James Jones' *From Here to Eternity* in the Second – turn on comparable contrasts between the Home Front and military hostilities; all bring war and sexuality into relation. And as in many such novels (and indeed in other contemporary ones, such as Lawrence's *Women in Love*), the heterosexual conflicts imply, and are implied by, relations between men. The literature of the First World War is now regularly read in terms of the homoerotic and homosocial bonding between soldiers. Ford's prose is characteristically sensitive to the question of male intimacy, as one might expect from the author of *The Good Soldier*, and as is most explicit in the 'Epilogue' to *Women & Men*. But his war writing (again, like most of his work) is valuable, too, for its exploration of the relations between the sexes, and how they were being transformed.

The fact that it took him nearly a decade to find the right fictional form to make sense of his haunting visions of the war, only impresses on us how disturbing those visions must have been. Several of the pieces here read like first attempts at rendering experiences that recur in *Parade's End*, or in Ford's later reminiscences. Yet his mastery of language and effect means that they are all readable for their own sake. The material here presents a valuable picture of how one of the best writers of his century responded to one of its profoundest crises. Ford often argued that a good writer should be the historian of his own times. 'In the end,' he said of his experience of the war, 'if one is a writer, one is a writer, and if one was in that hell, it was a major motive that one should be able to write of it [...]'.[32] Most of the work here – even when fragmentary or unachieved – gives rare glimpses of that hell.

A NOTE ON THE TEXTS

The texts given here of works published during Ford's lifetime have been based on the texts of the first book or periodical publications, with the following exceptions: 'Arms and the Mind', 'War and the Mind', 'Pink Flannel' and 'The Colonel's Shoes'. These have been based on the manuscripts and typescripts at Cornell, and my readings of them differ in several respects from the versions previously published.

With the previously unpublished material, 'Epilogue', 'True Love and a G.C.M.', 'Enigma', the letters and military lectures, 'Years After', and the excerpts from 'Just People', 'Last Words about Edward VIII', 'O Hymen', 'Pure Literature', and 'That Same Poor Man', typographical errors and other inconsistencies have been silently emended. Any editorial additions or expansion of abbreviations appear in square brackets. Ford uses varying numbers of suspension dots for emphasis, and these have been retained here.

ACKNOWLEDGEMENTS

The manuscript material here is published with the kind permission of Ford's executor, Janice Biala; the Manuscripts Division of the Department of Rare Books and Special Collections, Princeton University Library for 'Epilogue'; the Honourable Oliver Soskice and The House of Lords Record Office for Ford's letters to his mother; and of the Carl A. Kroch Library, Cornell University, for all the rest.

I am very grateful to the following for their help in the preparation of this volume: Lucy B. Burgess, and the staff of the Carl A. Kroch Library, Cornell University; Alfred Cohen; Sara Haslam; Dr Jan

---

32 *It Was the Nightingale*, p. 100.

Willem Honig, Department of War Studies, King's College, London; Bill Hutchings; Professor Samuel Hynes; Robyn Marsack; Ana Mejia; Anthony Richards, Department of Documents, Imperial War Museum; Margaret Sherry, Department of Rare Books and Special Collections, Princeton University Library; Harold Short, and the staff at the Centre for Computing in the Humanities, King's College London; Paul Skinner; Mike Stevens; Dr Rivkah Zim.

Reminiscences

An Englishman Looks at the World

From the second of Ford's two propaganda books, *Between St Denis and St George: A Sketch of Three Civilisations* (Hodder and Stoughton, 1915), Part II, chapters 1 and 2. Ford's heading echoes H.G. Wells's 1914 book of the same title.

Let us attempt to recapture, in as precise a phraseology as we may, what was the British psychology immediately prior to the outbreak of the present war, and what was the state of affairs in England then. So remote does that period seem that the task is one of some difficulty, and the field is singularly open to those who are anxious to prove that Great Britain at that date was a militarist menace to the rest of Europe. So absolutely are our minds now fixed upon the affairs of the present, so bellicose in consequence has every proper man become, that, if Mr Bernard Shaw or Herr Dernburg choose to assert that before July 1914 every Englishman was a raging fire-eater, there are few of us with our minds sufficiently concentrated upon the immediate past to be able to question, much less to confute, those generalisations. And that is partly a matter of shame. Because the necessities of the day are so essentially martial we are ashamed to think that we were ever pacifist; because Germany – the German peoples as well as the Prussian State – have now put into practice precepts which they have been enjoining for the last century and a decade, I am ashamed to think that less than a year ago I had, for the German peoples, if not for the Prussian State, a considerable affection and some esteem. By a coincidence, then, which I must regard as the most curious of my life – though, indeed, in these kaleidoscopic days something similar may well have been the fate of many inhabitants of these islands – in the middle of July, 1914, I was in Berwickshire engaged in nothing less than tentative machinations against the seat in Parliament of – Sir Edward Grey! In the retrospect this may well appear to have been a fantastic occupation, but how fantastic do not all our occupations of those days now appear! On the morning of July 20th, 1914, I stood upon the platform of Berwick-on-Tweed station reading the London papers. The London papers were exceedingly excited, and I cannot say that

I myself was other than pessimistic – as to the imbecility of human nature, and, more particularly, as to the imbecility of the Liberal Party, and, more particularly again, as to that of the editors of the — and the —, which are Liberal party organs. These organs at that date were, in veiled language, calling for the abdication of the King of England. That, again, sounds fantastic. But there it is; the files of the newspapers are there to testify to it.

Those organs, then, reminded the world, the sovereign, or what it is convenient to call the Court Party, that the day for the intervention of monarchs in public affairs was past; that an immense and passionate democracy, international in its functions and one-minded in its aspirations, had taken control of the world, and that the past, with its absolutisms, its oligarchisms, its so very limited monarchies, its dictatorships, and its wars was over and done with. We had had a very tiring London season; I seem to recapture still very well the feelings of lassitude which made me dislike having to turn my mind again to excited political matters. By the middle of July in a properly constituted world the Eton and Harrow match and the Universities' match at Lord's have brought the interests of the world to an end. We seek brighter skies than those of London; the Houses of Parliament may be expected to slumber for a few days more upon their benches and the Press devotes itself to the activities of the sea-serpent or to speculation as to ideal matrimonial states, We do not, as a rule, look for newspapers during August.

Besides, I had got myself into a frame of mind for occupying my thoughts with past things – polished armour, shining swords, fortresses, conflagrations, the driving off of cattle, the burning of inhabitants within their dwellings – all those impossible things of the past which assuredly would never come again. For, on July 20th, 1914, it was impossible to think of war, though it might be desirable to eject Sir Edward Grey from the parliamentary representation of the town of Berwick-on-Tweed. Sir Edward Grey was undoubtedly a nuisance. My own chief objection to him was that in 1909 he had not sufficiently backed up Russia when Austria annexed Bosnia and Herzegovina. I said to myself, and I said frequently to other people, that Great Britain had gained a lasting discredit from this instance of the pusillanimity of its rulers. What credit, indeed, I asked, could ever attach to Great Britain again in the councils of the nations? As it appeared to me, Sir Edward Grey had not backed up Russia, but had ever since been attempting to propitiate that Empire by presenting her with little spiced cakes in the form of valuable spheres of influence – now it was bits of Persia, now Mongolia, now it was some other pin-prick to Germany which Russia asked for. I regarded Sir Edward Grey's chief occupation, since he had lately announced that he never read the newspapers, as being that of delivering ceaseless pin-pricks to Germany. This roused Germany, which had always seemed to me a rather childish Power, to slightly absurd foamings at the mouth and threats of a war that was obviously impossible. People would not go to war; public opinion was against it. Democracy, though it might be a nuisance as a too facile instrument in the hands of party politicians, and even a menace when voiced by the — and the —, would at least have the virtue of its defects, and, with no uncertain voice, would prohibit the firing of a single shot. War, anyhow, was impossible.

I am, perhaps, attaching too much importance to my speculations as to war. For the fact is that I did not speculate as to war at all. It was one of the impossible things that we left out of our calculations altogether. It was like the idea of one's personal death which one dislikes contemplating and puts out of the mind; but it had – the idea of war – none of the inevitability that attaches to the idea of death.

Nevertheless, Sir Edward Grey was a nuisance. By his pin-pricks he fomented the absurd rages of Germany and thus brought Germany into the foreground of things. And, whatever the world needed, it particularly did not need attention drawn to Germany. Germany, at that date, I hoped, was well on the road to national bankruptcy, and going faster and faster in that direction. And the sooner Germany was done for by those pacific means the better I should be pleased, since one might hope that the Germans would then return to their simple pastoral pursuits, leave off sitting in over-heated red-plush restaurants, reading offensive and gross journals, and drinking chemical drinks that were not good for them. But, indeed, except for thinking that Sir Edward Grey paid a great deal too much attention to Germany, I bothered my head about that Power very little. It may even be possible that I am giving you too elaborate a picture of my frame of mind as I stood upon the platform of Berwick-on-Tweed station reading the daily papers on July 20th, 1914. And yet I do not think that I am over-exaggerating what passed through my mind. It is true that I had wanted to think about the Border warfare; about Rokehope, which would have been a pleasant place if the false thieves would let it be; about Edom o'

Gordon; about the Widdringtons, and about the little old bridge
that goes across the Tweed into England from Berwick which is
neither England nor Scotland, but just Berwick. And the quaint
reflection crossed my mind that, if ever England went to war with
Russia as her ally, we might well attainder Sir Edward Grey, since
Sir Edward Grey sits for Berwick, and Berwick is still at war with
Russia, the proclamation of peace after the Crimea having been
omitted in the town of Berwick-on-Tweed, which is neither
England nor Scotland.

At any rate, there I was upon the long, narrow, crowded platform
of the station, and I had an hour and a half to wait for the train that
was to convey me to the town of Duns, in Berwickshire. I was
surrounded and a good deal jostled by an alien, dark, foreign-
spoken population; mariners all, all loud-voiced, all discoursing
rather incomprehensibly of the doings of the *Ann* and *Nellie*, of the
Peter Smith and of the *Last Hope*. They talked, these dusky people,
in the gloom of the covered platform, of singular feats of sailing, of
nets, of rock-salt, and of the gutting of herrings. The situation, and
the hour, were all the more proper for introspection and for taking
stock of oneself, not only because of the intense solitude amongst
that populace from whom I was certainly descended, as because of
the fact that an immense public convulsion was about to overwhelm
the people of at least one of these islands, and because, amidst threats
of revolution in the other islands, a definite step had been taken.
On July 19th, 1914, in fact, His Majesty the King had summoned
a Conference to discuss the Home Rule problem. I was going,
however, to have a good deal of golf, some billiards, some auction,
and, I hoped, some riding amongst the Cheviots, and I am bound
to confess that, if the golf and the auction were not the chief
interests in my existence, for the moment, at any rate, the topog-
raphy of that Border country was really the major interest of a
period in which I was inclined mostly for what is known as
'slacking.' One doesn't know what one will find in a country-house
to which one is going for the first time, so that, during such waitings
at junctions, a certain amount of mental drifting is perhaps pardon-
able. [...]

The reader will by this time be aware that I am describing truth-
fully and as carefully as possible the frame of mind of the average
Englishman of July 1914. I am attempting, therefore, to provide as
exact an historical document as if I were reporting the *procès verbal*
of the trial of Joan of Arc or the speeches and votes during a sitting

of Parliament. I am presenting, perfectly accurately, the workings of a comparatively normal English mind on an occasion which, for personal reasons, remains singularly clearly with me. This seems to me to be a method of controversy much more fair than that which would consist in saying, 'The Englishman is a militarist', or 'The Englishman is a flannelled fool too indifferent to public matters to think of anything other than the problem of getting past "silly point".'

Pon... ti... pri... ith

(translated by Max Saunders)

Ford wrote the following essay in French in the autumn of 1918, when he had returned from the Western Front, and was attached to the staff in Yorkshire, inspecting, training and lecturing. It appeared in *La Revue des Idées* in November 1918 (pp. 233–8). It was probably written as further propaganda for the Ministry of Information. But like all Ford's propaganda, it is oblique. The editor perhaps felt it necessary to say Ford's 'inclinations are clearly anti-German' precisely because the piece doesn't read like an anti-German tract. The Germans are not even mentioned. The fighting is not directly described. What does come across is an intense elegiac poignancy, embracing both the Welsh soldiers and the French citizens who welcome them. Again, like so much of Ford's writing, it is autobiographic, reminiscential, and impressionist: more a personal attempt to render his state of mind, than a public polemic. And, as so often, Ford expresses the effects of war on his mind – how shell-shock disturbed his memory; how grief colours his remembrance of his fellow-soldiers. He does this partly in terms of art: visionary fragments of scenes, works of art, works of literature. The whole piece is offered as a picture. Ford is a man of his times, conscious of tradition and modernity. The editor calls him a leader of the English impressionist school; and certainly Ford often styled himself impressionist, along with James, Stephen Crane, and Conrad. The sight of Flaubert's house meant so much to him because Flaubert had always been one of the writers he admired most. Yet Ford describes his method of composition here in more modern terms: as an exercise in cubism. It was a combination of impressionism and hallucinatory collage that would become the stylistic principle of his post-war writing.

Ford Madox Hueffer was born in 1873. He has been strongly influenced by French literature and is now one of the leaders of the English impressionist school. His inclinations are clearly anti-German; his last book 'Zeppelin Nights' was written in collaboration with Violet Hunt.

Here is the most coloured picture, the most moving vision of the whole war – for me and for so many others who are no longer there!

As for me, I am going to tell you why this vision comes back to me, clear and light, blue and vermilion, in spite of all the shadows of violet smoke, like those touching illuminations, which represent towns, calvaries and people, such as you can see in the book of hours of Mary Queen of Scots at Rimini...

★
★ ★

A flight of linnets passed between the two masts of the vessel which, heavily laden with men, was panting up the calm river. Some cows, white, dazzling, spotted with black, raised their friendly, gentle heads. Their glistening flanks reflected the azure of the summer sky and the grass of the meadows. They watched our laborious passage without astonishment, we who were going up the garlanded river...

For the river was garlanded, in its Sunday best! A whole population was walking in the meadows near the water; in black dress-coats, white dresses, the people were standing in the orchards which sheltered the little green hills; they were leaving the churches waving handkerchiefs, scarves, top-hats; they were leaning out of the windows of the little white and red houses. So many colours, so many cheerful and friendly sounds, were reaching us across the water which refined and softened the human noises, that each of us said, in his own soul:

'Well, they believe in us!'

★
★ ★

It was the 8th July 1916, and I believe it was a Sunday. Because we had left Cardiff on Friday the 6th; we had spend the night at London and left the port of Southampton towards midnight on Saturday.[1] But that is all blackish clouds; all that comes back to me like one of those Futurist or cubist pictures which we had discussed throughout July 1914... July 1914!

Anyway, it was perhaps the 9th July, and Monday... But no, it

---

1 The 8th of July was a Saturday in 1916.

was the 8th... I don't remember any more; so many things were effaced from my memories since the morning when I woke up in the C[asualty] C[learing] S[tation] at Corbie, that I was not able to answer when they asked me my name.

I could perfectly well tell you what I did, what I said, thought and accomplished on the 6th July 1891, a quarter of a century ago; or even in September 1892, when I visited the town of Albert to write an account of its art-nouveau church... Art nouveau! and I remember very well what I wrote about it. But as for what happened to us between the 6th and the ? July 1916 – to we others of the Welch Regiment – it only comes back to me as some fragments, confused, comic or even pathetic, as in a cubist picture...

In a corner of this picture is the menu of a sort of restaurant Duval, in Cardiff; 'sweetbread à la financière, fourpence'; and the left eye of a crying woman; and part of Newport station and the large nose of a Colonel; and then, of Waterloo station – the livid light, the canopy, high and banal; and the mothers, and the wives and girlfriends of the Welch officers; and the little brown Tommies, heavily engrossed; and their wives who were carrying pale babies and the tin badges of their husbands. And all laughing and crying and jostling each other... and the alabaster hands shaking behind the 'photographic representative' of the Northcliffe papers, who has his head hidden under his black velvet hood, and who exhorts us to assume imbecile smiles... Clouds, shadows, pale faces, spirals of violet smoke, out of which loomed the iron columns supporting the station roof – enormous and as it were deathly...

★
★　★

And then this cubist picture effaced itself and gave way to a small canvas, as who should say Pre-Raphaelite, at the flight of the linnets who were escaping; the white cows spotted with black; the good bourgeois in their Sunday-best; the meadows under the summer sun and the small pink clouds which lost themselves in the depth of the blue beyond the Château Gaillard...

We all came from South Wales – and I would like to bet that the reader of goodwill will never have heard anyone talking here of South Wales... Well, the Welsh race is the indigenous race of the British Isles – 'the little, dark persistent race' – of the ethnographers; and I must add, obstinate and a little mystical... and difficult!

When they speak – our Tommies – they have the voices of ravens; with a Chinese accent... Several thousand of them could not make themselves understood in English. They spend their days a hundred metres under the grass of the fields, in an eternal night... they spend their lives mining the coal that is found in all the ports of the world – and in singing! They sing at all times and for all reasons; and they play football – at all times and for all reasons! It was the Welch Regiment that advanced at Etreux in 1914, kicking a football and shouting 'Stick it, the Welch'; and singing in chorus 'Aberyst with', 'Jesu, Joy of Man's Desiring!' and 'Hen wlad fy nadhau, Gwell angau na chwyllydd...'.[2]

But yes, they sing, the Tommies of this regiment, although, when they speak, it is as if you were hearing ravens chatting over some stinking quarry – they sing in chorus like the angels and the prophets... and like men who are about to die...

On the boat there were eight hundred men and two hundred and fifty officers who had all come from South Wales... and as an officer who spoke a few words of French, I was on the bridge, next to the captain of the vessel – or perhaps it was the pilot?

We had sung... and sung... and eaten our rations... and sung... and drunk the water of the Seine... and sung. And then, silence; and the ripples of the river whispering... A large Red Cross steamer came down the river amidst a whirlwind of hurrahs... And then again silence...

The green hills came near; you saw, very near, the handkerchiefs and the top-hats which were waving... And then, all of a sudden, from the whole boat, the voices rose in chorus:

> There is a path, very, very long
> Which unrolls under the white moon
> There is a very long time to wait...

Very long, alas! Go and tell that to Mametz wood.

And then, again silence. And suddenly one voice, coming from the bank, which shouted to us across the whispers of the water:

---

2 'Aberystwith' is printed as if two separate words in the French text, presumably to indicate the phrasing of the singing. The sentence in Welsh conflates part of the Welsh national anthem (which the French footnote gives as 'O Land of my fathers', whereas it should read 'Old land of my father'), with the motto of the Welch Regiment (which the footnote gives as 'anguish is preferable to dishonour', whereas *No More Parades*, p. 39, provides a better translation: 'Death is better than dishonour'). 'Nadhau' should read 'nhadau', and 'chwylldd' should read 'chywilydd'.

'Where do you go from?'[3]

And with one voice, as in an enormous, Aristophanic laugh the boat replied:

'Pon... ti... pri... ith!'

For Pontypridd – which is pronounced Pontiprith – is a small town of pleasure, of coal dust, of potteries; a hideous town, a grotesque town; a town responsible for eighty percent of the regiment's 'crimes of absence'. The 150,000 men who came out of the mines to follow the very long path, have the habit of 'absenting themselves' for six or seven hours to go and taste the delights of Pontypridd. And when you hear 'Pontypridd' said by the fields of France, you see rise up before you the rocks, the fir trees, the waterfalls of the Golden Valley; the castles, Castell Goch and the 'mountains' of Caerphilly; the clouds, the chimneys and the gigantic wheels of the Rhondda; the salt marsh sheep of Porthcawl and Sker...

That is why I told you that this picture remains the most coloured and most moving of the whole war for many of my comrades of that day, for in six days, the majority – the majority, alas! – of them would give their lives in Mametz wood, where more than half the Welch Regiment perished on the 14th July 1916... it was indeed there, on that tranquil river, that they glimpsed civilisation, and the gentlenesses of this bourgeois, friendly, rural, riverside life – for the last time...[4]

In less than five minutes, the captain – or was it rather the pilot? – a kind of marine god, bearded, sombre and silent who had been listening and watching with good will, but without speaking a word, as if we had been all the little mortal children around the throne of an ancestor of the gods – this taciturn but amiable Neptune touched my arm and grunted:

'Look!'

And I looked – at a well-set little house, with geometric

---

3   The question appears in English in the French text.
4   Ford himself didn't leave Rouen for the front until 18 July 1916, so it is not clear whether he means that many of his companions on the boat had died on the 14th, or that they too were to die in Mametz wood where half the regiment had died earlier.

windows, by the side of an enormous wall of some sort of factory. And at my stammering – it is true that I stammered:

'But it is... it is Croisset!'

He answered: 'It is Flaubert's house.'[5]

He added: 'He also waited for help from England – which didn't come – in 1870! I've read his letters to Georges Sand.'

And, for the moment I thought I could glimpse the forehead of a ghost which spied on us from behind the venetian shutters of the little house – and I lost myself in speculations on this country whose Seine pilots read the letters to Georges Sand, from her poor troubadour...

I should add that, the following day, while buying some small items to complete my equipment I had wanted to buy a copy of the *Education Sentimentale* – to read for the fourteenth time, and this time in the trenches. It was impossible to find – it was impossible to find a single printed word of Flaubert's in any book shop in the town of Rouen. I could have thought I was once again in England!

---

5   Ford was perhaps recalling Conrad's *A Personal Record,* which begins with memories of being moored at Rouen, and imagines Flaubert's ghost hovering 'with amused interest' (London, 1975), p. 3.

Arms and the Mind/War and the Mind

Ford wrote on the manuscript of the first of this pair of essays, 'Written in the Ypres Salient: 15th Sep. 1916'. The second was written in the summer of 1917. Neither appear to have been published during his lifetime, but they give important insights into experiences and feelings while on the Western Front that were to loom large in *Parade's End*. In particular, they are concerned with the problem of visions: questions of perspectives, hallucinations, and the difficulties of visualisation; and also with feelings of hostility, not only towards the enemy troops, but towards unsympathetic civilians.[6]

A DAY OF BATTLE
by Miles Ignotus

I: Arms and the Mind

I have asked myself continuously why I can write nothing – why I cannot even think anything that to myself seems worth thinking! – about the psychology of that Active Service of which I have seen my share. And why cannot I even evoke pictures of the Somme or the flat lands round Ploegsteert? With the pen, I used to be able to 'visualize things' – as it used to be called. It is no very valuable claim to make for oneself – since 'visualizing' is the smallest, the least moving, of the facets of the table-diamond that art is.

Still, it used to be my métier – my little department to myself. I

---

6   The first essay was first published as 'Arms and the Mind' in *Esquire* (December 1980), then as 'A Day of Battle' in *The Ford Madox Ford Reader*, pp. 456–61. It was republished, together with the second essay, under the collective title 'War and the Mind', in the *Yale Review*, 78:4 (Summer 1989), pp. [497]–510. All these versions were edited by Sondra J. Stang. The present texts offer several different readings, based on the autograph manuscripts of both, plus a typescript of the second, at Cornell University. That they form a pair is evident not just from the numbering, but from the fact that manuscript of the second bears the deleted title 'A Day of Battle'.

could make you see the court of Henry VIII; the underground at
Gower Street; palaces in Cuba; the coronation – anything I had
seen, and still better, anything I hadn't seen. Now I còuld not make
you see Messines, Wytschaete,[7] St Eloi; or La Boisselle, the Bois de
Bécourt or de Mametz – altho[ugh] I have sat looking at them for
hours, for days, for weeks on end. Today, when I look at a mere
coarse map of the Line, simply to read 'Ploegsteert' or 'Armentières'
seems to bring up extraordinarily coloured and exact pictures
behind my eyeballs – little pictures having all the brilliant minute-
ness that medieval illuminations had – of towers, and roofs, and
belts of trees and sunlight; or, for the matter of that, of men, burst
into mere showers of blood and dissolving into muddy ooze; or of
aeroplanes and shells against the translucent blue. – But, as for
putting them – into words! No: the mind stops dead, and something
in the brain stops and shuts down: precisely as the left foot stops
dead and the right foot comes up to it with a stamp upon the hard
asphalt – upon the 'square', after the word of command 'Halt,' at
Chelsea!

As far as I am concerned an invisible barrier in my brain seems
to lie between the profession of Arms and the mind that puts things
into words. And I ask myself: why? And I ask myself: why?

I was reading, the other day, a thoughtful article in one of the
more serious weeklies, as to a somewhat similar point – as to why
the great books about the psychology of war (such as Stephen
Crane's *Red Badge of Courage* or even the *Débâcle* of Zola) should
have been written by civilians who had never heard a shot fired or
drilled a squad. But the reason for that is obvious: it was not Hector
of Troy – it wasn't even Helen! – who wrote the *Iliad*: it wasn't
Lear who wrote *Lear*; and it was Turgenev, not Bazaroff, who wrote
Fathers and Children. Lookers on see most of the Game: but it is
carrying the reverse to a queer extreme to say that one of the players
should carry away, mentally, nothing of the Game at all.

I am talking of course of the psychological side of warlike operations. I remember standing at an OP during the July 'push' on the
Somme. It was the OP called Max Redoubt on the highest point
of the road between Albert and Bécourt Wood. One looked up to
the tufted fastness of Martinpuich that the Huns still held: one
looked down upon Mametz, upon Fricourt, upon the Ancre, upon
Bécourt-Bécordel, upon La Boisselle, upon Pozières. We held all

---

7   Now Wijtschate.

those: or perhaps we did not already hold Pozières. Over High
Wood an immense cloud of smoke hung: black and as if earthy.
The push was on.

And it came into my head to think that here was the most
amazing fact of history. For in the territory beneath the eye, or just
hidden by folds in the ground, there must have been – on the two
sides – a million men, moving one against the other and impelled
by an invisible moral force into a Hell of fear that surely cannot
have had a parallel in this world. It was an extraordinary feeling to
have in a wide landscape.

But there it stopped. As for explanation I hadn't any: as for significant or valuable pronouncement of a psychological kind I could
not make any – nor any generalization. There we were: those
million men, forlorn, upon a raft in space. But as to what had
assembled us upon that landscape: I had just to fall back upon the
formula: it is the Will of God. Nothing else would take it all in. I
myself seemed to have drifted there at the bidding of indifferently
written characters on small scraps of paper: WO telegram A/R
2572/26; a yellow railway warrant; a white embarkation order; a
pink movement order; a check like a cloakroom ticket ordering
the CO of one's Battalion to receive one. But the Will that had
brought one there did not seem to be, much, one's own Will. No
doubt what had put in motion the rather weary, stiff limbs beneath
one's heavy pack had its actual origin in one's own brain. But it
didn't feel like it. There is so much – such an eternity of – waiting
about in the life of any army on the move or up against the enemy
trenches, that one's predominant impression is one of listlessness.
The moments when one can feel one's individual will at work limit
themselves almost to two types of event – the determination not
to fall out upon the march and the determination not to be left
behind in 'going over'.

Even work that, on the face of it is individualistic is too
controlled to be anything other than delimited. If you are patrol
officer your limits are laid down: if you are Battalion Intelligence
Officer up on an Observation Point, the class of object that is laid
down for your observation is strictly limited in range. And, within
the prescribed limits there is so much to which one must pay
attention that other sights, sounds and speculations are very much
dimmed. And of course, if you are actually firing a rifle your range
of observation is still more limited. Dimly, but very tyrannically,
there lurk in your mind the precepts of the musketry instructors at

Splott or at Veryd ranges. The precepts that the sights must be upright, the tip of the foresight in line with the shoulders of the ⁻V⁻ of the backsight are always there, even when the ⁻V⁻ of the backsight has assumed its air of being a loophole between yourself and the sun and wind and when the blade of the foresight is like a bar across that loophole. And the dark, smallish, potlike object upon whose 'six o'clock' you must align both bar and loophole has none of the aspects of a man's head. It is just a pot. ......

In battle – and in the battle zone – the whole world, humanity included, seems to assume the aspect of matter dominated eventually by gravity. Large bits of pot fly about, smash large pieces of flesh: then one and the other fall, to lie in the dust among the immense thistles. That seems to be absolutely all. Hopes, passions, fears do not seem much to exist outside oneself – and only in varying degrees within oneself. On the day on which I was sent to Max Redoubt OP to observe something, I was ordered further to proceed to the dump of another Battalion in Bécourt Wood and to make certain preliminary arrangements for taking over the dump.

The preoccupations of my mission absolutely numbed my powers of observation. Of that I am certain. It is, in fact, the sense of responsibility that is really numbing: your 'job' is so infinitely more important than any other human necessity, or the considerations of humanity, pity, or compassion. With your backsight and foresight aligned on that dark object like a pot you are incapable of remembering that that pot shelters hopes, fears, aspirations or has significance for wives, children, father and mother ..... It is just the 'falling plate' that you bring down on the range. You feel the satisfaction that you feel in making a good shot at golf.

It is all just matter – all humanity, just matter; one with the trees, the shells by the roadside, the limbered wagons, the howitzers and the few upstanding housewalls. On the face of it I am a man who has taken a keen interest in the aspects of humanity – in the turn of an eyelash, an expression of joy, a gesture of despair. In the old days when I saw a man injured in a street accident or in an epileptic fit by the roadside, I felt certain emotions: I should wonder what would become of him or what I could do for him. Or to put it even nearer home, when by Turnham Green or the Swiss Cottage, in peace time, I have seen dusty 18 pounders, khaki coloured and passing, jingling along behind the brave horses, I can remember to have felt emotions – to have felt that the guns looked venomous, dangerous, or as if they had been peering, like blind snakes.

But, stepping out of Max Redoubt into the Bécourt Road, that day, I came right into the middle of ten or a dozen lamentably wounded men, waiting by a loop of the tramline, I suppose for a trolley to take them to a CCS.[8] I remember the fact: but of the aspects of these men – nothing! Or so very little. They were in khaki: some of them had white bandages round their heads: they grouped themselves on a bit of a bank: they were just like low, jagged fragments of a brown and white wall ruined by shell fire. And they are as dim in my memory as forgotten trees.

And so with the guns that in peace time I had found interesting or picturesque: they rattled past me there in an endless procession: they crushed slowly into the sandy road behind immense tractor monsters like incredible kitchen stoves. Further down in the wood they were actually at it: a dozen converted naval howitzers like enormous black toads that wheezed, panted out flame, shook the earth, and ran back into shelters of green boughs. The shells went away with long, slow whines ....

But it all seemed to signify nothing. One did not think of where the immense shells struck the ground; blowing whole battalions to nothing. One did not think that the RFA guns, hurrying forward, meant that the Push was progressing. Even the enemy shells that whined overhead were not very significant – and the visible signs that, shortly before, these shells had pitched into the new British graveyard, seemed to mean nothing very personal. One *reasoned* that the shells might pitch there again any minute: but one *felt* that they would not. I don't know why. And of course it meant nothing. In moments of great danger I have felt convinced that I was immune: five miles behind the lines I have been appallingly certain of immediate death because an aeroplane was being shelled a mile away. Mainly the reason for these moods is very commonplace. If one has plenty to do one is not afraid: in one's moments of leisure one may be very frightened indeed. The mere commonplaceness of one's occupation, and of the earth and the grass and the trees and the sky, makes the idea of death or even of wounds, seem exaggerated and out of proportion. One is in a field, writing a message on an ordinary piece of paper with an ordinary pencil – '*from* OC no. 1 platoon, B. Coy *to* OC anything...' Nothing could be more commonplace .....

---

8   Casualty Clearing Station.

So the idea of tragedy is just incongruous and death quite inap-
propriate. No! Reason has very little to do with it. For you may
be in a large field – a 40-acre field – and the Huns may be dropping
their usual triplet of 4.2's into it. Your reason – if you are not
employed for the moment – will tell you that your chances of being
hit are 400 to 1 against. But it does not in the least comfort you.
On the other hand I have been lifted off my feet and dropped two
yards away by the explosion of a shell and felt complete assurance
of immunity.

The force of one's sense of responsibility is in fact wonderfully
hypnotic and drives one wonderfully in on oneself. I used to think
that being out in France would be like being in a magic ring that
would cut me off from all private troubles: but nothing is further
from the truth. I have gone down to the front line at night, worried,
worried, worried beyond belief about happenings at home in a
Blighty that I did not much expect to see again – so worried that
all sense of personal danger disappeared and I forgot to duck when
shells went close overhead. At the same time I have carefully
observed angles, compass bearings, landmarks and the loom of
duckboards: and I have worried – simultaneously with the other
worries – to think that I might have neglected some precaution as
to the safety of the men, or that I might not be on time, or that I
might get some message wrong – till gradually the feeling of the
responsibility eclipsed all other feelings .....

Still, as I have said, one's personal feelings do not get blotted out,
or one's personal affections. If, for instance, the wounded that I had
seen by Max Redoubt had been men of my own Bn. or of another
Bn. of the Welch Regiment that was side by side with us, I should
have tried to do what I could for them – and I should certainly
remember them now. For I do remember all the wounded of my
own Bn. that I have seen. The poor men, they come from
Pontypridd and Nantgarw and Penarth and Dowlais Works and
they have queer, odd, guttural accents like the croaking of ravens,
and they call every hill a mountain.... And there is no emotion so
terrific and so overwhelming as the feeling that comes over you
when your own men are dead. It is a feeling of an anger .... an
anger.... a deep anger! It shakes you like a force that is beyond all
other forces in the world: unimaginable, irresistible .....

Yes, I have just one War Picture in my mind: it is a hurrying
black cloud, like the dark cloud of the Hun shrapnel. It sweeps
down at any moment: over Mametz Wood: over the Veryd Range;

over the grey level of the North Sea; over the parade ground, in the sunlight, with the band, and the goat shining like silver and the RSM shouting: 'Right Markers! Stead a......ye!' A darkness out of which shine – like swiftly obscured fragments of pallid moons – white faces of the little, dark, raven-voiced, Evanses, and Lewises, and Joneses and Thomases..... Our dead!

That is the most real picture of war that I carry about with me. And that, too, is personal, and borne along with, not observed in spite of, responsibilities .....

WAR AND THE MIND

II. The Enemy

1.

No Man's Land and what lay beyond No Man's Land always remains in my mind as blue – a blue grey mist; a blue grey muddle of little hills – but fabulous and supernatural. I suppose that one could really call it the territory of Armageddon.

But, of course, I am speaking now of the mind at rest. When it was necessary to be observant one saw the earth, brown, reddish-brown, sandy, dusty, veiled by thistles, or with the long shadows, at night, from globes of light hanging in the blackness. Or, from high points like the OP on the Albert-Bécourt road, or from Kemmel Hill or the Scarpenberg, in Belgium, one saw Martinpuich on high in bristling and ragged tufts of trees; Pozières with trees torn leafless, big and coloured bits of wall and the white lines of trenches in the chalk, below the feet. Wytschaete with the tranquil red roofs and Messines, again, grey and rather upstanding. And little white balls would exist, one by one, at intervals of a second or so, appearing to be an inch to the right, or an inch to the left, all the way between Messines and Wytschaete. One thought comfortingly: 'Our own shells.' And one said aloud: 'Somebody will be ducking, out there!'

But that was the observant – as it were the official observer's mind: say the mind of the Battalion Intelligence Officer. The quiescent mind, that of the Impressionist in Letters, always returned to the blueness and greyness – to the blue-grey muddle of little hills peopled by blue-grey hobgoblins without features – the Huns in their Anti-Gas masks!

I am fairly confident that I am right in this division of the mind. When I used to ride in from the line to Divisional HQ in Albert, for the purpose of copying onto the maps for Battalion use, the alteration of trenches that had been made in the night, I know that the lines that I made with blue, yellow or red pencils, on the map that showed Pozières, Welch Alley, Bazentin le Petit or Mametz and High Wood ...... those lines which represented Brigade and Divisional boundaries, new trenches, the enemy's new lines, MG emplacements and so on, represented nothing visual at all to my intelligence. The mind was too much taken up with the necessity of copying the mark exactly; with seeing that all the squares, from A1 to D3 had each their complement of straight blue, zigzag yellow or curved red lines, Machine Gun emplacements and the like. One sat, at a large drawing board, in a quiet, glass roofed shed, in the large, sunny courtyard of an old French château, with monthly roses climbing up the walls, and one drew fast, changing from pencil to pencil, engrossed and hastening. Then one got on one's horse and hastened back, through the endless lines of slow[-]moving transport wagons, in the dust, over the shoulder of the hill, to where No Man's Land the Lost Territories were once more visible. (On the Somme a year ago, when I was there, it was always summer weather, the sun brilliant and clear over the Sussex-down landscape, the sky translucent, punctuated by the brooding sausages, our 'planes always shining in the blueness, dust underfoot and thistles and swallows and partridges.)[9]

No: the mind connected nothing from the maps, except that we hadn't yet – we had eventually – taken Ovillers[,] La Boisselle and Pozières. For Pozières was a sort of every morning torture. One woke to hear that the Australians had taken Pozières; that the Gordon Highlanders had taken Pozières; that we, the Welch, had taken Pozières: that one or other of the Anzac Battalions had gone clean through the place and got caught between our own barrage and the Huns' barrage. And one rode back to Albert and, from copying the map, one observed that Pozières was not yet taken: and one was impatient, angry; we were all annoyed: puzzled; bitter .... Why didn't we take Pozières and go through to Cambrai? After all that we had done! The Staff never took advantage of advances .... And so on. But, in the visualising mind, 'Pozières' presents no

9 On the relationship between maps, landscape, and impercipience, compare *No More Parades*, pp. 308–10; *No Enemy*, pp. 82–7; and *It Was the Nightingale*, pp. 97–8.

image ...... And once again the idea of the Lost Territories became a painful thought.

That is precisely what it was – a painful thought! A vexation; a harassing annoyance that one did not talk about...... I don't know just why it assumes this aspect always, for me. I don't think it is a purely personal matter...... or perhaps it is. I never, in France or Belgium, felt immediately worried that France or Belgium had lost these lands; and I did not feel dishonoured – or that we were dishonoured – because we had not yet succeeded in retaking those blue stretches that, when we retook them, became the downlands of France or the marshy plains of Flanders. The loss was the fortunes of War; we had not yet retaken Martinpuich, Pozières and all the slopes downwards to Cambrai.

The Fortunes of War! For, at that stage – and ever since – war has so seemed to be the normal state of Europe that questions of Right and Wrong effaced themselves from the mind. We were just at war – and War, the war of millions, of a whole continent, a whole region of the world, seemed to be something dispassionate and universal – more dispassionate and more universal than the sun or the moon. It existed always, through day and night, through summer and winter: dispassionate, precisely, and all[-]pervading, like an ether, like atoms – like God himself. If one hated the Hun it was for specific acts of barbarism; for little things that impressed themselves on the imagination. One did not as a rule hate him for having occupied that stretch of territory – but one did hate him a great deal for what he had done inside that territory or outside – at Scarborough, at Whitby, or for the apparently senseless shelling of churches ....[10] And one would hoot at the name of the Kaiser – but rather officially than with passion. It was only very occasionally that one thought that one was there, in that misery, in that inconvenience, or those fears, or those physical anguishes – all of us! – because of the ambitions – or call them what you will – of the German warlords. No: the feeling was that we were just there,

---

10 German warships shelled Scarborough, Whitby and the Hartlepools on 16 December 1914. For examples of the shelling of churches, see p. 51 ('Trois Jours de Permission'); p. 190 (Preface to *Their Lives*); and p. 57 ('Epilogue'). Ford's letter to Conrad of 6 September 1916, describes the sound: 'Shells falling on a church: these make a huge "*corump*" sound, followed by a noise like crockery falling off a tray – as the roof tiles fall off. If the roof is not tiled you can hear the stained glass, sifting metallically until the next shell. (Heard in a church square, on each occasion, about 90 yds away.)': *The Presence of Ford Madox Ford*, p. 173.

normally, in a normal state of things; one was pessimistic; fatalist! One had forgotten: I daresay not óne in a hundred thousand of us had ever heard of – those attempts of Sir Edward Grey to avert the cataclysm; or the interview of Sir Edward Goschen with Bethmann Hollweg. There did not seem ever to have been a time when British Ministers and German could have met amicably in tall rooms with high mirrors and marble busts and long tables, blotting pads, quill pens.... No: it was predestined ....

The roads in that part of the world were queer and, again, painful things. They were broad, downland high roads, some bordered with poplars, some without, and they ran onwards with that engrossed air that a highroad, to me, always seems to have. They looked just as if they ought to bear farm carts, old carts with tilts: flocks going to market – just like that. But, if one pursued them with the mind – suddenly they ended, in that blue territory.

Of course, actually, they don't end suddenly. It is a gradual process. The road becomes torn with traffic, the pathway makes detours over the edges of fields: little, deep ditches, as if they were cut for drains begin to run beside the road. Trenches! But a trench is such a natural-looking thing! You might imagine it was cut just to receive drain-pipes. That is the queer side of war that so many natural objects look so commonplace.

But, where the trenches begin to appear beside the road, the poplar trees will begin to appear to suffer. They will be broken off like pencils: they will be stripped of all leaves: they will have crow's nest platforms erected on them; they will lean over as if, agonised, they were stretching hands in despair, to the skies! And then, in the road, great pockmarks will be there: for twenty yards no road will exist. Then it will begin again: then more pockmarks, some dead mules, bits of cartwheels, old tins, old steel hats – any old rubbish. And then the road will persist, tenacious and obstinate, like a severed nerve. You will come to a light barrier between hedges with, perhaps, a picket of RMP loafing about – and placards: 'No wheeled traffic beyond this point.' 'No Parties stronger than four in number to proceed at less intervals than 150 yds. between parties.' Then you know that the road is going into the view of Hun eyes. You halt your signallers, or whatever your party is, order them to break up into parties of four, put on your tin hat – and walk round the hedge onto the down. But the road itself looks singularly normal. It won't be torn up by traffic: traffic is forbidden. It won't be pockmarked by shells because the Germans, as a rule, do not expend shells upon parties of four. No, the road will be quiet, preoccupied, as if dreaming, proceeding upon its affairs. I remember riding, rather sleepily, along such a sleepy road behind the line at Kemmel, in Belgium. I had discharged some errand, I forget what, and was going back to RE farm or to Locre. The cornlands sloped down to Kemmel church: BHQ – an old château, peeped out of quiet trees. I was about a mile behind our front line: I didn't imagine I was in any danger: indeed I wasn't thinking of danger altho' I knew that the road was visible from the Hun lines. I was thinking about some place in South Wales, and about Turgenev and that I must tell my servant – 25782 Pte Phillips L., — Welch —, to get some washing done for me. A fair-haired, small, crow-voiced fellow, like most of the lads from the Rhondda Valley, he squatted on his heels all day long and did not get one's washing done automatically but had to be told to get it done – wh. was a nuisance ......

And then: 'Zi ... ipp!' a single rifle bullet as nearly as possible got me. I would swear that it passed between me and my horse's neck! At any rate it cannot have missed me by more than two feet. I found myself saying: 'Four seconds! Four seconds!' and I got over the hill skyline very quickly indeed. 'Four seconds' presented itself to my mind like that, because it would take a sniper about four seconds to load, aim and fire again. And that bit of information seemed to pop up from nowhere and to remain isolated.....

It was a pretty long shot: over 2,000 yards. But I suppose the chap had telescopic sights. The Huns got in some remarkable shots in that way. We had a man killed, by a rifle bullet, in RC Farm that evening. He was sitting, cleaning his equipment, near the cooker-carts – certainly 2,800 yards away from the Hun lines, and under a hedge.

Curiously enough that sniper – if it was a sniper – is the most present in my mind of all the thousands of bluegrey beasts that, in one capacity or another, one saw out there .... And yet I, naturally, never saw him. I *do* see him. He has a black moustache, a jovial but intent expression: he lies beside a bit of ruined wall, one dark eye cocked against his telescopic sight, the other closed. And through the circle of the sight he sees me riding slowly over the down: a small, unknown figure of a man upon a sleepy roan mare. And his finger is just curling tenderly round the trigger. He is a Bavarian. And so he lies, and so he will continue to lie, in my mind, for ever.

I daresay that, really, he was a lean Prussian – it was the celebrated Brandenburgers that we had opposite us there – who let his rifle off at a venture.

But, otherwise, the Huns always seemed to me to be impersonal – blue-grey beasts, as I have called them – except when they had their helmets on, when they became, for me, blue grey hobgoblins. But beasts: never human. I, at any rate, never saw another Hun who struck me as being a man – except one, and he was hardly a man. That was in Bécourt Wood. I had gone down to see about some of our wounded in the château which was turned into a dressing station. Whilst I was talking to a man who had been a gardener near Dynas Powis, an RAMC major came into the courtyard and asked if anyone were there who spoke German. A German officer who was wounded persisted in tearing off his bandages. I went in.

The Hun was a spectacled, bearded, mad-looking brown man. He had been a teacher of mathematics in a girls' school at Hamburg. Sure enough, he had torn his bandages off: he was wounded in the thigh and the blood was dripping through the stretcher. I asked him why he did it. He looked up at me with agonised brown eyes:

'You are the Welch?' he said. 'I am a prisoner of the Welch.'

I said that that was so.

'The Welch,' he said, 'The Welch and the Munsters always torture their prisoners and then murder them. When I have been tortured to extract information, I shall be murdered.'

I laughed.

'Don't talk such b—y poppycock,' I said. 'You will be dressed here and taken to a CCS of the most comfortable kind. And in a month you will be in a lovely manor house called Llanfair Haiadu or some such name in the Clwyddian Mountains: and you will be walking about the town of Denbigh, buying picture postcards of the castle – for the duration of the war.'

He looked up at me, piteously.

'I suppose you couldn't laugh like that if you weren't speaking the truth.['] I don't know what became of him. One loses curiosity out there, and I had had enough of him. As I say, he did not strike me as being quite a man – a teacher of mathematics in a Hamburg girls' school .....

He told me, by the way, that my own Bn., after we had taken La Boisselle, stood 250 prisoners up against the wall and shot them. That was circulated in the official German Comic Cuts.

What actually happened was that after we had got those lamentable ruins a machine gun and its crew came out of a cellar – the MG on a lift – within twenty yards of one of our companies. The men threw up their hands: the officer and the NCO did not. Our company commander and the CSM, thinking they had surrendered, went a pace or two forward; whereupon the German officer and the NCO fired with revolvers, killing the Coy. Sergeant Major. Our people then bombed the whole lot of them to death, except two men who bolted back into the warren of cellars. That of course is war: I don't see that there is anything to complain of on either side. But the German official trench bulletin made us responsible for torture and murder .....

The poor old Welch! We get it in the neck both ways. Yesterday I was on the seashore superintending some of the returned BEF men who were doing PT. A fat lady with a very fat bulldog came along and, as the bulldog appeared to be more excited than was safe by the movements of the men I asked her to be good enough to put him on the lead. I did not wish to see men who had gone from Pontypridd to France in 1914 mauled by a large white dog. She put him on the leash and then she said:

'I suppose your men are all Scotch.'

I said:

'No: Welch.'

She said:

'Oh: but they've got wound-stripes. And I read in the papers that none of the people in Wales have enlisted. Most disloyal I call it: so your men *must* be Scotch.'

I answered: thinking of Mons and Gheluvelt and Belgium and the Somme:

'Oh no, madam. But of course we are all of us conscripts. Forced to do it, you know.'

'Ah: I thought so,' she answered. 'I read it in the papers.' And, large and fat, with her large and fat white bulldog pulling on the chain, she waded off thro' the sand.

They do us rather well between them – the Hun and the English papers.

Miles Ignotus

Trois Jours de Permission

Ford wrote this brief article about his leave in Paris during September 1916 a few days later. It was published in the *Nation*, 19 (30 September 1916), pp. 817–18. A more elaborate account is in *No Enemy*, pp. 153–63 and 261–2. Both works also describe attending a performance of Delibes' *Lakmé* : *No Enemy*, pp. 165–6 and 194–221. (There is also a brief variant in *Return to Yesterday* (London, 1931), pp. 151–2.) But the version here gives a vivid impression of the contrasts between military and civilian life. The ferrets are also mentioned in *Joseph Conrad*, p. 192, and *Provence* (London, 1938), p. 298.

'Une petite minute! ... a little minute'; the words, uttered by a functionary in evening dress with the features, and far more than the gravity of, a British statesman, consecrate one to a long period of waiting in the reverential and silent atmosphere of a palace of high rooms and tapestried panels. A long period of waiting .... Well, the longest period of waiting that I have known in a life that nowadays is characterized by more waiting than I have ever known. Waiting for the transport; waiting for the bombs to come up; waiting for one's unit to move; waiting for one's orders; waiting for the shelling to stop; and, above all, waiting for *the* shell – the solitary whining shell, the last of three that is due from the methodical German battery miles away on the plain – waiting for that to manifest itself in a black cloud, up there; in an echoing crash, and in a patter, as of raindrops .... Yes, one learns to wait. The most impatient temperament, somewhere in France, will be strait-waistcoated into inaction, into introspection.

Nevertheless, that quarter of an hour in the high ante-room, giving on to vistas of other ante-rooms, so that all the noise of the streets, of the city, of the world, and of the war! – no longer exist – that period seemed a lifetime. I don't know why. In the great ante-room sat three officers in festive blue, a widow in a cloud of black; an attractive young woman of twenty-five or so, in a large hat decorated with cherries – all absolutely motionless, drooping, with eyes on the bright and priceless carpet. The walls showed, in panels, the terraces of Fontainebleau, in purples, in bright yellows, in scarlets .... But the atmosphere was that of the eighteenth, the seventeenth, the sixteenth century. One might have been waiting for a scarlet-robed figure to appear between the great folding doors. One might have been waiting for Richelieu or Mazarin ....

Yet: 'trois jours de permission à Paris' – weekend leave in Paris should not be a matter of serenities or the seventeenth century. And indeed it wasn't. One dined at Foyot's, at Prunier's, at the Café de la Paix: one went to hear *Lakmé*, and the melodies seemed to turn one's heart round: one leaned over the balcony of the Opéra Comique looking at the dark streets which after nightfall always seem medieval. And one talked gravely and slowly to a French captain, who talked gravely and slowly – about 'là bas', about the different sectors of the Somme that one had seen – and the marmites and the rum jars and the statue shells. One went to mass at the Madeleine; one promenaded in the Avenue du Bois de Boulogne; one talked literature, philosophy, and the economics of after the war, in the Brasserie Universelle. One even found time to play hide-and-seek with the children in the hotel hall, making a prodigious noise on the marble tiles, and smiled at by adult guests who knew that one had 'trois jours de permission' – the rather strained, precocious, bi-lingual children, with black bows and dead fathers....

And Paris, you know, appeared to be exactly the same as Paris always was in September. Not the same as Paris in May, of course; but then it was September. The leaves were beginning to drift down in the Tuileries Gardens, one saw the Champs Elysées in torrents of rain; the Boulevard Saint-Germain was 'up' in a complicated manner, of which only Paris has the secret. And, except that people who otherwise would not have hurried themselves for one, smiled and did hurry themselves when one said that one had only 'trois jours de permission', and so was a fit subject for a little spoiling one might very well have been in one's mufti of three years ago. And indeed I saw fewer uniforms in Paris than I have seen anywhere since August, 1914. London, when I last saw it, was all khaki; the shires all khaki; Wales all khaki; little Belgium all khaki, and the Somme and Rouen. And you cannot be in any country field of *our* 'somewhere in France' without there being in one corner of it at least half-a-dozen battered men in khaki trousers, performing obscure tasks with shovels under the hedges. Between the immense avenues of poplars go the endless columns of transport waggons, along the uplands the moving notes of platoons, companies, battalions, all dust-colored. And all France of the line south of us is mist-blue.

But Paris seems more unconcerned than any city I have yet seen; engrossed in its daily work beneath the September sun or sitting at the little tables at night, under the plane trees on the boulevards, it goes on, quietly running things. And indeed it is the same everywhere. The French officers are serious, taciturn men, who seldom speak, and when they do speak, speak very slowly. And 'out here', what there is of the French left is always quiet and solemn, the immense long avenues, the heavy trees, the plough moving slowly, the solitary women sitting in empty houses, the churches into which the shells fall. Except in the short space of no man's land, and except for spaces on the Somme where there is no blade of grass, but only shell holes for field on field, France continues engrossed in her daily tasks – right up to the trenches. And even beyond! For, a few yards – yes, a few yards! – behind the German trenches, here one can see men in blue blouses and women in black – getting in the harvest. They are forced to labor by their conquerors ....

And at the heart of it are those silent palaces with the seventeenth-century atmosphere, the functionaries looking like British statesmen in evening dress, who are nevertheless only door-openers, and the great functionaries who ask 'in what they can be useful to you' – the time-honored formulary which is supposed to lead one to fortune. It did not lead me to fortune, since I only asked the Minister if he could procure us some ferrets – our regimental ferrets having all died. But there are no ferrets in France, not in the Ministries, not in the Jardins des Plantes et d'Acclimatation. That is perhaps a defect of France, but I have perceived no other.

It is, in short, we who play cricket with pick-handles under shell-fire, and with uproarious noises stand round rat holes waiting for the ferrets to drive out our prey. And France regards us with solemn eyes. No doubt comprehension will grow out of it.

Epilogue

This intriguing essay was unknown until it turned up in the 1980s among Ezra Pound's papers. It was written after February 1917, and before 7 January 1919 (when Ford was gazetted out of the army). The material was rewritten to form the 'Rosalie Prudent' chapter of *No Enemy* (see pp. 228–57), though some parts, especially the meditation on the war dead, do not appear elsewhere. The essay was almost certainly originally intended as the Epilogue to *Women & Men*, an impressionist study the rest of which Ford had written before the war, but did not publish until 1918.[11] 'Epilogue' concerns two women whose courage and steadfastness had particularly impressed him in 1916.

[1.]

I will now tell you about Rosalie Martin and Emil Vander-kerckhoven.

It was on a very wet evening of the 2d September 1916 in the dusky gleaming streets of Nieppe which lies between Ploegsteert and Armentières. Water fell in sheets; water fell in showers. One was wet to the skin; one had been wet to the skin for hours. One had, in imagination and in the Town Marshal's books, planted A,

---

11 Pound got 'Women and Men' published in the *Little Review* (for which he was the London editor) between January and September 1918. The essays published there were written by 1912. 'Epilogue' was probably written as a late addition to this serial. But Pound had run out of funds by late 1918, which may be why it wasn't included then. Or he may have thought it too different from (or inferior to) the other essays. *Women & Men* was republished in a pamphlet by William Bird's 'Three Mountains Press' (Paris, 1923), in a series edited by Pound, again without the 'Epilogue'. By this time Ford had drafted the book that was to become *No Enemy* (although that was not published until 1929), with its rewriting of Rosalie Martin's story. See James Longenbach, 'Ford Madox Ford: The Novelist as Historian', *Princeton University Library Chronicle*, 45 (Winter 1984), pp. 150–66. He includes several extracts from the manuscript, though my readings of these passages differ in several places. The typed carbon copy of pp. 1–11 are at Princeton, together with the autograph manuscript of pp. 12–16. The top copies of the typed pages are at Cornell.

B, and C, Companies in the long long irregular cobbled, factory street running towards the big town. Similarly one had planted D Company in the Rue de la Gare in dripping, red brick villas, and BHQ in the Château attached to the brewery in Pont de Nieppe. One had identified the field allotted to our First Line Transport, but one had been very dissatisfied with it because the ditches that drained it stank under the rain like cesspits ..... And the Battalion should have been in at four thirty. It might have been seven then.

The rain poured down in the dusk: I was standing outside a commonplace house with a door in the centre, two windows on each side of the door and one above it. It had iron railings and a high iron gate – the house of a factory foreman or head clerk. In a dark window I perceived the gleam of a forehead. A woman was sewing there in the dusk – for there is a certain angle that women's foreheads have when they sew by the window in the dusk. No man ever attains to that angle .....

The street was full of transport, of Highlanders ......

The grotesque figures in khaki belonging to the Brigade Canteen which I had billeted in a small shop just opposite were decorating the entrance to the shop in attitudes of fatigue or of insouciance. One of them, a lance corporal, was writing by a candle at a butcher's meat block. He was writing a one act play for suburban music halls for which they payed him £30 a time – and he had had six commissions since Easter ....[12]

I waited and waited.... A gleaming figure on a wet horse with the water dripping from his tin hat appeared behind me. He was coming from the direction of the station – the Brigade Transport officer; but he belonged to my Battalion. He said:

'I'm not going to put the Battalion Transport in that bloody field. It stinks like a latrine. I'm going to find a field along the Bailleul road.'

I walked beside his horse. My orderly should be sheltering mine in what remained of the church porch forty paces away. He said:

'The Battalion was shelled on the road between Dranoutre and Neuve Eglise. Macadam road: *you* know!'

I said: 'Oh God ..... Who?'

'I don't know,' he answered. 'The bloody Staff... I told them yesterday .... Sixty casualties...'

I was getting on my horse. It ran round and round in my mind.

---

12 Compare *A Man Could Stand Up –*, p. 154.

Who? Who was killed? Which Company had the Hun got? Sixty casualties... A whole company, with our depleted strength... It would ruin the world. Because when your men and sergeants and your company officers go west in the pouring rain at night, in the blackness, it is as if a whole side of the house had fallen out...

'You needn't come with me,' Perceval said. 'The Battalion won't come in tonight. I don't know where it has got to but it won't come in to night. You can send your batman in the morning to see where I shall get to.' But I rode beside him with our orderlies behind us – for company I daresay, and because it is one's duty at any time to be in a position to know where the First Line Transport is in case the CO asks. Besides, one wants to be near someone of one's own battalion when a lot of one's own men have gone West. It is very lonely to be with Highlanders and people of the 15th Division and RAMC johnnies, in strange billets. Anyone of one's own battalion in those circumstances is like a woman .....

We rode in the black shadows of the elms of the high château garden; we could see men of the Wiltshires eating fish and chips behind the windows, in cockly glass, of the little cottages on the left. The Wiltshires had come in, then, ...

Out on the high road, past the elms it was lighter – on the long windy road that leads to Bailleul. A big cloud had removed itself from the sky, the shadows of the trees and of the town were no longer there. Where the secondary road turns righthanded to go to Plugstreet we stopped to ask the traffic policemen if the Welch had come down that way. He hadn't seen no Welch. The Wiltshires had .... Perceval said again:

'There's no sense in your coming with me ..... I've got Spencer and Johnnie and Hill with me... They'll have the tents up and supper ready for me... I saw a field opposite the road to Steenwerck – R7 on the map. You'll find it in the morning.'

Then we saw a fat man coming – the quartermaster of the Wilts, with a large paunch and South African ribbons. He kept a pub and had a grazier's and butchering business in Warwickshire – like Shakespeare's father. He was killed by a shell last January and I can't tell you how it upsets me to think that he was killed. And by a shell. And in January .... Quartermasters ought not to be killed by shells – and certainly not Spencer. He ought to be sitting before the taproom fire with his feet in carpet slippers drinking hot rum shrub ......

We said:

'Where are the Welch?'

'In Bailleul,' he answered. 'They won't be here till tomorrow morning.'

The wind began to get up and the Verey lights to pour up into the sky on the right. A shell whined for a long time and then thumped down about two hundred yards away.

'There's something they're after there,' the Wilts Quartermaster said. 'I don't know what it is .... But that's the third in five minutes .... It's the worst of being in a strange country: you don't know what they're after .....' He added comfortably:

'I got that fish in Bailleul .... Welsh rabbit, herrings and beef for supper.'

'Who have the Welch got killed?' Perceval asked. 'But perhaps you don't know .....'

'We were shelled on the road between Dranoutre and Neuve Eglise,' I said. 'The Macadam road, you know.'

He looked at me rather doubtfully; he always did look at me rather doubtfully as if I were a child or an idiot.

'It wasn't you; it was us,' he said with a sort of triumph. 'After they shelled us they turned you down the road to Bailleul that we all ought to have gone.' He always liked to catch me out in a piece of false information or in going Nap on the wrong sort of hand. 'We've had sixty casualties. Thirty killed.'

I turned my horse round towards the town. And indeed the Quarter, still eyeing me doubtfully, said:

'I don't believe we've got enough fish for you. There's Welsh rabbit and beef enough. But I don't believe we've got enough fish .....' For the transport people are hospitable – still they always regard the combatant officers as slightly interlopers.

And I became once more aware that what was annoying me a great deal – and more than anything else at the moment – was the disgraceful state of my cuffs. I hadn't had my shirt off for twelve days and there were long ragged streamers, uncomfortably wet, round my wrists ...... And the white forehead of the woman sewing in the gloom rose before me ....

You see the Welch were all right... I should see A Company coming in as gay as larks in the morning sun. Perceval no longer had the attraction of woman and home – or no longer had it so much. Besides he was going to eat Welch rabbit and herrings and ration beef and tinned peaches in the company of Spencer and Johnnie and Hill. He was all right and the dark town lay before me.

The Quarter said:

'I don't like this bit of road. Not to really like it. Them shells....'

And sure enough another whined and moaned and fell as before beyond the elms.

As the orderly and I rode back into Nieppe we conversed of Pontypridd and Nantgarw and the state of the billets that we had taken over from the Australians. You couldn't say that they were as clean as a new pin. Indeed we agreed that we had never seen anything like them. And Phillips said that he had found stabling for the horses at a carrier's house where there was one of these Belgian girls just behind the church and handylike for the house outside which he had seen me standing.

A shell dropped into the church desultorily ....

But Phillips made for the carrier's house and I for the one with the iron railings ten yards from the church yard square which the Huns with their imbecile obstinacy went on dropping shells into all night. I don't know what they thought they were doing and nobody bothered. The Wiltshire Tommies were still eating fish and chips in the little estaminets with large women standing, their hands on their haunches, looking down on them ..... That is how it goes in that corner between France and Belgium ......

2.

And that is no doubt how it went in Marathon and Thermopylae and how it went and goes at Mont St Jean and Codford and West Point – and Potsdam ....[13] And there was Rosalie Martin.

For, about ten o' clock that night and until maybe midnight, I was sitting in the washhouse of the house with the iron railing, beside the stove with nothing on but my breeches and Rosalie Martin was mending the cuffs of my shirt which, for its improvement and, as the manner is, had been first baked in the oven. And a young officer of the Wilts and the padre of the Highlanders were learning French from Mademoiselle Eugénie Martin, all in the light of a farthing rushlight. It was just the opportunist domesticity that

---

13 Mont St Jean is near Waterloo. There are two villages, Codford St Peter and Codford St Mary, on the edge of Salisbury Plain, which is used as a military training ground. Ford had stayed in the nearby village of Winterbourne Stoke in 1904. Potsdam was the residence of the German emperors.

the world has to offer the world over. The coffee in a saucepan on the stove bubbled and occasionally jumped when the shells fell into the church. And eventually Mademoiselle Eugénie rose and did the washing up because, as she sagely said, woman's work is never done and a house where the washing up is left overnight never prospers. And she asked if it was not un peu fort that Cecile Someone-or-other should have been seen walking out with a Tommie of the Brigade canteen that evening when everyone knew that she was fiancée to that Sergeant of the Australians. And she had a blue feather in her hat pinned in with a cap badge of the RFA which is well known to all the world. They all went to bed about 11.30. But Rosalie Martin went on sewing and I waited for my shirt ....

The large iron stove glowed red, the light of a tallow candle with a rush wick flickered on the whitewashed walls and the rafters that sloped up into entire darkness. The saucepan continued to jump a little on the stove, as the shells dropped desultorily in the church that was forty yards away.

She sat with her head bent over her sewing, silent and engrossed ......

She was a woman, no doubt of forty but looking older by a good many years and her home was in Ploegsteert, six miles away, so that in Nieppe she was a refugee. On Sundays, once every three weeks she would be given a pass by the British military police to go to Ploegsteert and to look at her home which was every day shaking away as the heavy motor lorries went past or bits of shell struck the walls. No doubt a day would come when she would no longer be given a pass and when the house itself would be no longer there. Her husband had been a cooper and wheelwright employing a foreman and five hands. He had been killed in the Belgian Army on December 15 1914. Her elder son had been a clerk in the Crédit Lyonnais in Armentières: he had been killed in the French Army on January 11 1915. Her younger son had been chief bookkeeper to a restaurateur in Armentières. He had been killed in the Belgian Army on January 10 1915. Her elder daughter had been a lay sister in Namur. It was then the 2d September 1916 and Rosalie Martin had had no news of her elder daughter since September 1914. Her younger daughter had been a dressmaker's assistant in Lille. Rosalie Martin had had no news of her since May 1915 when an abbé had written to her from the Isle of Wight to say that her daughter had found refuge in a convent all of whose inmates were well at that date. Both her sons had given her a great deal of trouble to bring into the world and had cost her a great deal of trouble to keep alive: in the daughters' cases both processes had been easy. Her husband, a great, fair, too jovial man had cost her many troubles before she could keep him to the straight way. She had had a salon with polished and waxed apple-wood buffets, cupboards, tables and chairs all en suite; four bedrooms with mahogany beds, waxed linoleum on the floors, crucifixes and water fonts above the commodes at the bed heads. She had had forty dozen of Burgundy in the cellar ..... All these things had gone from the house that was falling to pieces in Ploegsteert.

She had been one of the bonnes bourgeoises of Ploegsteert. In Nieppe she was like a vieille paysanne. She had been proud of her husband and of her sons on a Sunday when she went to mass in a black satin gown with a lace collar and a cameo brooch representing the Judgment of Paris. Now, dressed in black calico, she went shopping amongst heaps of rubble with her head bare, and wore an apron of blue cotton with black stripes. Only the immense cameo brooch at her neck still represented, between the acanthus leaves of pure gold and on the flesh coloured ground the delicate limbs of Paris who was leaning forward from a seat and the delicate limbs of the three goddesses who obscured each other in a little group.

The house which had been allotted to her was bare on the ground floor. There was nothing in the salon, nothing in the dining room, nothing in the room beyond the passage which had served as an office. The bedrooms were all furnished with everything that is usual in clean French bedrooms of the middle class. I don't know why this was, neither did Rosalie Martin. The owners had fled – to Armentières and beyond the seas.

So, in the years that went by, she established a sort of domesticity. Chaplains to the Forces and stray officers usually slept in the bedrooms. For that she could make no charge because they were billeted there. But she could make a profit of fourpence a day on the food with which she supplied them. The garden was also well filled with vegetables. And then her niece Eugénie came to live with her because the Paris dressmaker for whom she worked had to shut down. Eugénie embroidered cambric handkerchiefs for which she charged five, seven or eight francs and which she sold to British sergeants and officers who sent them home to their bonnes amies .... And gradually it seemed to Rosalie Martin that

she had lived all her life in the washhouse of 27 Rue de la Gare –
that that was her life.

So at least she said in a sudden burst of speech that came from her
when she had nearly finished sewing the second cuff of my shirt. –
And she continued:

'One gives oneself so much trouble to bring men children into
the world, and one gives so much trouble in order to keep them
alive and in the straight road. And the days go on and the years go
on and the fields are there and the troops come marching, over
them. And one's male children are gone ....'

I think that is the woman's figure that has struck my imagination most since the 4th August 1914. I don't quite know why it
should be so. But then ..... I don't know anything any more. One's
glass, heaven knows, was never very big: but one used to drink
from one's glass. Now: *na poo*14 glass! Mamman say No bong!

If, before the War, one had any function it was that of historian.
Basing, as it were, one's mentality on the Europe of Charlemagne
as modified by the Europe of Napoleon I, one had something to
go upon. One could approach with composure the Lex
Allemannica, the Feudal System, problems of Aerial Flight, the
price of wheat or the relations of the Sexes. But now, it seems to
me, we have no method of approach to any of these problems.

We *don't know how many men have been killed* .... One is always
too close or too remote. On the Somme in July 1916, or under
Vimy Ridge in February 1917 one saw, on the one hand, such an
infinite number of our own male dead, or, on the other, such an
infinite number of dead – and frequently mouldering – Huns, that
it seemed as if the future of the World must be settled. There must,
one said, be henceforth three women for every live, intact and adult
male, whether of the Allied Countries or of the central Powers.
That, then, settled the question of the relations of the sexes. – Tho'
of course I did not think about it at these moments.

At any rate, when you see the dead lie in heaps, in thousands,
half buried, intact, reposeful as if they had fallen asleep, contorted
as if they were still in agony, the heaps of men following the lines
of hillocks, of shell holes, like so much rubbish spread before an
incinerator in the quarter of a town where refuse is disposed of .....
Well, you think of Armageddon, and on any hill of that Line, as I

---

14 WW1 slang for 'no more', 'finished', 'dead': corruption of *il n'y en a plus*.

have seen it, from the Somme up to the Belgian Coast where you see, and can feel, the operations of counted millions of men moving million against million – you think again of Armageddon. And the War seems of infinite importance.

Well: it is a long way from Champagne to Ostend and if you piece out the line, at one man per five yards on each side of it, and then add four times as many for the lines of communication – and, if you go all round the ring fence that encloses the Central Empire, and space out the men along it like the upright posts of the fence you will arrive at large figures of male beings all *morituri*[15] – or at least candidates for corpsedom. So that, again, the word 'Armageddon' bobs up somewhere in the consciousness.

And the considerations and the generalisings rise up in the mind ......

If so many men are gone, say, there must be polygamy, relaxed sexual morality and so on: if such wars are to continue male children must be raised and woman must become a breeding machine for male children...... Or again: if so many men experience the horrors of an immense Armageddon will not that make future war impossible ... for every one of those men will be set against war – and their children and their children's children, in saeculum saeculorum ......[16] Then there will be no particular need for male children – so there need be no polygamy. And, after what we have been told is a period of relaxed sexual morality there will probably be a period of reaction towards the ecclesiastical idea of indissoluble unions and the rest of it ....

And then again, one leaves the sphere of war: one is moved say to the Italian border, one goes for leave to Paris, to London, into the Shires ..... In these long days' journeys you realise that the actual theatre of war is very tiny. Out there, in the Somme, or in Belgium, you and your fighting comrades seem to be the whole world ..... But go to London or to Birmingham or to Manchester – and you hear no talk but of the sufferings, composures, heroisms and endurances – of the Civilian Population. But one does not discern that the Civilian Population has at all a bad time. There is plenty to talk about: plenty of excitement in the papers, plenty of junket-

---

15 Presumably from the gladiators' speech, '*Ave Caesar, morituri te saluant*': 'Hail Caesar, those who are about to die salute you'.
16 Ford also uses the liturgical phrase 'in saeculum saeculorum', for ever and ever, in *The Good Soldier*, p. 14.

ting. [deleted sentence] In one's capacity of returned and crocked up warrior one is pushed off buses, swindled by shopkeepers who take advantage of one's necessity for specialised clothes and accoutrements; one is used as a pawn in one woman's social game or another's love affair; one is sweated and swindled by the authorities in the interests of the taxpayer, till the sinister thought surges up in the mind that all these people would *like* the war to go on – and other wars supervene, for the sake of the fun and the talk and the moneymaking and all the rest of it .....

But, mostly, the tired brain refuses to generalise: so that, just as the cataclysm has swept over Europe, blotting out alike the Europe of Charlemagne and the Europe of Napoleon I, so a cataclysm of the author's intelligence has swept over this book. The sense of values has changed completely ..... One has grown sentimental incredibly, coarse in a great measure, hungry, thristy, loud voiced. The pleasures of the drawing room are unknown and not at all valued .... A comfortable billet or a dry tent – that's what one is on the lookout for – and a good long sleep – an immense long sleep, with the men all right in quarters and the rations served out for a fortnight ......

You come back to hear the women talking about housekeeping ...... Well: you have been housekeeping for ninety men, or a thousand – or three thousand two hundred and seventeen, as I am doing at this moment, quietly enough and without any talking at all. And then, Good God, out there on Kemmel Hill, in front of Wytschaete, you had a pal. And he would see to it that at 4 ack emma when you came off patrol there was some hot soup ready for you and he would pass you the matches at just the right moment across the top of the table that was made of bully-beef cases: and you will attend meticulously and anxiously to his physical and mental comfort – and he to yours, and all of it in the shadow of death, with a hell of a noise going on – and thumps and jolts and the devil to fear. And he will smile at you and you at him ......

But as for the love of woman ..... Well, there's a girl in the tea shop, of the Entente Cordiale at Bailleul, and a girl on the platform of the G. W. R. Station at Chester, and a girl at Nantgarw, and a girl at Rouen ... and Rosalie Martin sewing y^r shirt cuffs in Nieppe...

And you are sitting on the firing step one day and your pal has the map and compass on his knee and the OC Coy is sitting on the other side of him. And he gives a little laugh and the map and compass slip off his knees into the mud. And you say: 'Clumsy old b....r!' and bend down... to pick them up. And he will be leaning back, smiling under his dirty tin hat .... Just like that!

So it will be: 'Goodbye Jimmy.' – And you will scribble a clumsy letter to a girl in Penarth and, a fortnight later you will get a letter from a girl in Pontardulais asking for particulars of the decease .... And you will get another pal. But never quite the same!

So it will go on..... And Uncle Gibbs will go, and Arnott and Knapp and Morgan ... and half the Battalion .....[17]

And you will go back into Support and out into the line and to the Mont de Catz for a course and home for a week on leave and so the time will pass ......

So that, I suppose, in time of war men children are most esteemed. It is not only that we who go to France and return and go and return – that we traffic with, fight with and appraise men; but the Rosalie Martins of the world, bringing men children diffi-cultly into the world and keeping them with difficulty in the straight paths of civic virtue – the Rosalie Martins are mostly concerned with their dead men children and comparatively little with their ravished daughters. Of course there are the munition factories with all their women ..... But, say what you will, it is the fighting animal that is more prized.

But, in any case, I can't theorize – and it's a marvel to me that anybody can. Yet they are doing it – all over the shop. I don't dislike or despise the theorists, Heaven help me. But I don't see upon what hill they can stand in order to get their bird's eye views. Of course

---

17 The manuscript contains the following deleted passage at this point:

> And yet it's as true as death ..... just that, looking out on the tents and the smoke and the cooks and the rest of it and at a Morris[sic] Farman that was just coming down over the YMCA hut I started to take out a cigarette to aid my meditations. After all, one might arrive at *some* clue to the endless riddle. But, instead of a cigarette I pulled out a cigarette card from the packet..... And it shews – propped against my wire post – a deep gorge with a river running between green woods and old granite cliffs . . . . And the back of the card states: "This is one of the most beautiful river gorges in England"..... Well: it is one of the most beautiful river gorges in England and its memory went with me out to France, and it survived in under the thoughts of the deaths and the shells and the shadows – and the memory of it survives stronger than all the visual appearances that surround me . . . . . *C'est toi qui dors dans l'ombre, ô sacré souvenir!*

A Maurice Farman was a French aeroplane. The French quotation, from Victor Hugo's 'Tristesse d'Olympio', was one Ford and Conrad had used as epigraph to Ford's poem that was itself epigraph to their collaborative novel *Romance*.

there are remote persons who stand aloof from humanity – but if you stand aloof from humanity how can you know about us poor people?

Or perhaps it is that one has learnt out in France, above all things – humility. There, one is like a grain of sand, drifting here and there, downwards as the sands run out of an hour glass – and it is all nothing and all weariness and that is all there is to say about it. Yet I suppose that, in the long dull days on parade, during the long dull days in company offices, during the long terrible days and the long fearful nights under fire, one is achieving..... heroism! One is one of a great band that shall be remembered as the fighters of Marathon are remembered, and the Ten Thousand .....[18] I suppose so. And our women – like the women of Greece – shall appear to the historic imagination, splendid of limb and beautiful of feature – so many Dianas and so many Wingless Victories. No doubt .....

But, indeed, one couldn't ever really theorise worth twopence. Just as every human face differs, if just by the hair's breadth turn of a nostril, from every other human face, so every human life differs from every other human life if only by a little dimple on the stream of it. And the hair's breadth turn of the nostril – the hair's breadth dimple on the stream of life when they come in contact with the lives of others just make all the difference – all the huge difference in the fates of men and women. Perhaps as one's eyes close in death one might be qualified to write a book entitled 'Women and Men'. But one won't be able to.

---

18 In 490 BC, 10,000 Athenians achieved the first Greek victory over the Persians at Marathon.

from *I Revisit the Riviera*

This essay was written for *Harper's* magazine, 166 (December 1932), pp. 65–76. When Ford later reworked it into his book *Provence* (London, 1938), pp. 271–5, he excluded the account of the Rouen hospital.

Red Cross Hospital No. II at Rouen during the winter of '16–'17 was in the old priests' seminary that the Prussians had used as a hospital in 1870. We occupied small white priests' cells, two to a cell, a camp bed in each corner. Diagonally opposite me was a Black Watch second lieutenant – about twenty, wild-eyed, black-haired. A shell-shock case. He talked with the vainglory and madness of the Highland chieftain that he was, continuously all day. Towards ten at night he would pretend to sleep.

As soon as the last visit of the VAD's was over he would jump out of bed and rush to a wall-press with sliding doors. He took out a kilt and a single shoe. His face assumed a look of infinite cunning. He would fix his black, shining, maniacal eyes on me and, stealthily stretching out an arm, would extract from the press a *skene dhu*. A *skene dhu* is the long, double-edged dagger that Highlanders carry in their socks. From the creasing of his lips you could tell when he had put a sufficient edge on that instrument. He would be sharpening it on the sole of his single shoe. He never removed his eyes from mine. He would run his thumb along the edge of the blade and with a leering, gloating look he would whisper:

'*We* know who this is meant for.'

I never ascertained. Delirium would then come on. I was delirious most nights.

One night he had disappeared, and the convoy whistle blew – towards four. It was always disagreeable to be awakened by the convoy whistle. It meant that the Enemy, far away in the black and frozen night, had been pushing an inch or two farther towards the Mediterranean. Wounded were coming down.

Tweedledum in a steeple-crowned hat burst in. He had two fleeces bound round his khaki stomach. He pitched his hat onto a nail in the wall and exclaimed disgustedly:

'H'our caows 'as better 'ouses in Horsetrileyer!'

That was tragedy. I said, 'It is all over. They are putting Tommies in with the officers. The Germans have burst through. They will be here any day. They will be on the Mediterranean in a week.'

That was not snobbishness. It was despair at the thought that there had been such slaughter. There had been no time to sort the wounded. But even in those shadows my first thought was for the inviolability of these shores where now, if the beaches are fringed with foam, the foam is made by human limbs – and the human limbs are mostly German ones. For there are easy ways of getting to the countries of the Sirens ....

Well, next morning, after a night of delirium, I saw across the cell a little, fat, rumpled dumpling of maybe forty, leaning over the end of his pillow, looking with disgust at his breakfast. He spat out to my pet VAD:

'We gets heggs from h'our 'ens in Horsetrileyer.'

He was an officer all right. The line still stood. The Côte d'Azur did not need to tremble. He was a field officer who in civilian life supplied milk to a great city where they walk upside down and have retained since 1840 the purest Cockney language. In the same way in the Kentucky Highlands you still hear the most ancient versions of the Border Ballads ....

It was a relief to be sent down, convalescent, to the Red Cross Hospital at Mentone. There all we poor devils lived like gentlemen.

Yesterday I passed through Mentone station. It is an unadorned building in ferro-concrete. I felt incomprehensible despair – unprepared and incomprehensible. I had been reading one of Georges Simenon's detective stories and had looked up unthinkingly .... But on the 2d of February, 1917 I had stood on that platform. There had been an icy wind and snow falling. I was going up into the line again. If you had asked me then whether I felt despair I should have denied it – mildly. I had been conscious of being dull and numbed in a dull, numb station. All France up to Hazebrouck in Flanders was deep in snow. I was going to Hazebrouck in Flanders. Yesterday the ferro-concrete dullness of the station made me aware that I must have been in despair at going to Hazebrouck when I was certain that my real home was on these shores. I had just been seen off by 'Horsetrileyer', for he had followed me down the line in about a fortnight. He had embarrassed me a good deal, poor

fellow. He stuck to me like – a shadow when I was in the mood
for elegant acquaintance amongst the staid opulences of Mentone.
But he saw me off. He went rolling like a porpoise to the bookstall
to buy me a *Vie Parisienne*. One of my own books was in those days
covering the whole of France. 'Horsetrileyer' came running breathless back to me, his eyes sticking out of his head. He squeezed my
fingers into jam and shouted:

"Ooffer, if ever Hi'd known you'd written a book I'd never'f
spoken to you as I 'ave!'

It was typical that the sincerest of all tributes to literature should
come from an Antipodean mouth beneath the palms of these shores
....

And we had lived like gentlemen. A peeress of untellable wealth
and inexhaustible benevolence had taken, for us alone, all the Hôtel
Cap Martin – staff, kitchens, *chef,* wine-cellars. We sat at little tables
in fantastically palmed and flowering rooms and looked, from the
shadows of marble walls, over a Mediterranean that blazed in the
winter sunlight. We ate *Tournedos Meyerbeer* and drank *Château
Pavie,* 1906. We slept in royal suites; the loveliest ladies and the
most nobly titled elderly seigneurs walked with us on the terraces
over the sea .... You looked round and remembered for a second
that we were all being fattened for slaughter .... But we had endless
automobiles at our disposal and Monte Carlo was round the corner.

It was then that I tried out poor Marwood's system.[19]

We used to get taken into the Principality of Monaco about two.
We changed into mufti on the frontier. Allied officers were
forbidden to use the tables. Half a dozen of us tried the system. It
worked. We played about a dozen times from about half-past two
till six. It never let us down.

The snag is that it is infinitely boring. And the rooms are airless
and, if they are no longer heavy with patchouli they are just as
redolent of the odor of the day. That is what saves that Principality
– that and the fact that if you win steadily and slowly they take your
ticket away. On the other hand, if you have any sort of name at all,
they will lend you money to break the bank with – for the sake of
the publicity!

In our case in the three and a half hours that we used to play we
never made less than one hundred and fifty dollars. Sometimes we

---

19 Arthur Marwood was the pre-war friend whom Ford used as a model for aspects of
Christopher Tietjens' character.

made a few dollars more. But towards six we would get tired of paying attention. It seemed a mug's game to sit there making pennies whilst fortunes were being lost all round us. We would abandon the system and punt on numbers, and it would all go before half-past six when we had to leave. We had to be back in hospital at seven. One day we made quite a lot – sixteen or seventeen hundred dollars in that half hour. But it all went the next day.

In the evening we would walk with the Duc de Sabran-Guenevere, who had served in the French Navy with Conrad; with the Baron Alfred de Schwarzhelmstein who was some general's chauffeur; with Lord Polehampton who had never done anything but live in Mentone. The Duke looked like an aged and tuberculous d'Artagnan; the Baron looked like his name, but as if blown up with a tire-pump; Polehampton was like a washed-out white hen with a solar topee and the white goatee of Uncle Sam. We would pass in the moonlight M. Anatto of the Paris Bourse with his women folk and Senator McPigie of the Dubuque Chamber of Commerce with someone else's. And one and all we would agree that the world was going to the devil, but that if we were in the Higher Commands we could save it. Then we would go back home to bed. We should pass through the lines of the French Senegalese who were all dying of consumption. The spectacle of several thousand moonlit negroes lying tuberculous, motionless, and fatalistic along the shores of the Mediterranean sometimes made us not sleep too well.

I had a disagreeable affair one day coming back from Monte Carlo – in a tram. There were two very very senior officers in that vehicle and a number of French civilians. The senior officers did not belong to any fighting branch: they were civilians given rank so as to have authority when making inspections of military stores. But they were just as bedizened in scarlet and gold as if they had commanded in chief all the troops of the Principality of Monaco. They had with them a lady whom each in turn addressed at the top of his voice. They said, '*Mwor cooshay avec voo!*'....The French civilians mostly got up and left the tram.

I took the view that my own fortunes were relatively unimportant. I was witnessing the sort of thing that makes us Anglo Saxons not so popular on these shores. It is the duty of junior officers to put their seniors under arrest when they have exceeded. So it became a disagreeable affair.

To console me, I suppose, I was put in charge of a body of my comrades a day or two later. An incredibly inaccessible town in the high mountains of the hinterland had asked to be allowed to receive a deputation of British officers. We were told that that town would send conveyances. I was to make a speech in Provençal. It sounded very nice.

Before the lordly steps of that hotel waited six very small donkeys. Behind each donkey was a meager and dishevelled peasant woman. They were our conveyances and there was no avoiding them. It was a military order. All six of us were portly and too weak to walk much more than a mile on the level.

We climbed the inaccessibilities on those valiant beasts. On the hand-breadth paths we had to shut our eyes so as not to see the precipices below. The indefatigable, lean woman ran behind my microscopic mount. She brandished an immense cudgel. Every few steps she brought it down on the flanks of the poor donkey. Each time she cried :

'*Courage*, Montebello!'

It seemed to me to be an allegorical affair – as if poor Montebello, the microscopic donkey, were poor humanity climbing the inaccessible peaks of destiny with the whole load of stupidity of its rulers on its back .... We reached that mountain fastness and were singularly well entertained. They gave us wine that they swore was made as the ancient Greeks made it and that was four hundred years old – or, in the alternative, as old as the days when Hannibal passed that way, crossing the Alps. Napoleon also had passed by there on a similar errand. The wine was thick, golden, glutinous, and perfumed – like an enchanted hair oil. One understood why the ancients used to dilute it with sea-water.

On our return we all had to be medically examined. The Military Authority had heard that every inhabitant of that city suffered from a syphilis that was to them innocuous but that was extraordinarily malignant to anyone else. It was said to be an inheritance from Napoleon or, in the alternative, from Hannibal. The Military Authority had neglected to inform us of the fact before we started.

Preparedness

When Ford visited America at the end of 1926 to promote the third volume of *Parade's End*, he was invited to write weekly articles as visiting critic for the *New York Herald Tribune Books*. He continued to write occasional pieces for the magazine over the next four years. The following essay was published on 6 November 1927, and was illustrated with Stella Bowen's portrait of Ford playing patience.

The Armistice Made the English, French and Americans All One People, and a Few More Years of Unpreparedness Will Make War Between Them Impossible, Says This New Style Pacifist, Who Admits That He Can Enjoy A Good War as Much as Any One
By Ford Madox Ford
Author of 'No More Parades' and 'A Mirror to France'

It gave me something of a shock when, as it were at the pistol's mouth, I was ordered by the Editress of this journal to write on 'Why I Have Changed Front on Preparedness'. I could not think what Preparedness was. I occupy myself from time to time nowadays with preparing to meet the Recording Angel and hoping that his impressions will square with my own. I am also, whilst loafing about this city, preparing to write another book... But as for military preparedness! I do not remember to have thought about that since August 4, 1914 (on the 4th of August, 1914, the Germans crossed the Belgian frontier at six in the morning near a place called Gemmenich). Anyhow, at that date we English had done with preparedness; we had to muddle through.

And I do not know that even before the 4th of August in that year I ever thought much about military preparation. Englishmen didn't. With the apparent exception of my friend Mr H. G. Wells, they still don't. My countrymen prefer even yet, to muddle through. That is a good thing. So apparently – if General Summerall is to be believed – do the inhabitants of this country. That is another good thing. It is almost better. For, with the greater efficiency of American newspapers considered as excitants and energizers of this nation, supposing that some large section of the people or some important interest took it into their heads to organize war-like feelings it would be disagreeable if the United States were already an armed camp. But, as it is things are fairly satisfactory. And, with every minute of unpreparedness that we can manage to gain things grow more and more satisfactory. It is like compound interest applied to peace insurance. The further we get from the late war the more disinclined we grow to contemplate another.

I think that is a true statement. If you come to think of it, for a week or ten days after the Armistice of 1918 most of us still saw red. But once we settled down to the nuisances of after-war conditions we fairly shrieked at the notion of war. Till Christmas day, 1918 let us say to be liberal, we were all of us ready to have a go at anybody anywhere. But a very short time afterwards when Mr Lloyd George's ministry threatened Great Britain with war against Turkey, such an outcry went up from my nation that those gentlemen dropped the idea as if it had been a red-hot halfpenny.

Normally we do not count – we, the decent quiet subjects or citizens of great empires. We are in the hands of politicians over whom we have no influence, they being unable or disinclined to know what we are thinking. For those immense creatures the toys are the lives, streets, city blocks, automobiles, waterways, railways, cornfields, stockyards, purses, speakeasies and corner stores of untold millions. Immense toys, as befits demi-gods. Or is it demagogues?[20] At any rate they have toys enough. So it is of importance that they should not be provided with the enormous toys that kill ... of enormous importance that Preparedness should be blotted out from the world and that the thing and the very name should disappear from human consciousness. For it would be a terrible thing if the United States were an armed camp and if, say 'Big Bill' Thompson were its chief wirepuller. Or Mr Mencken ...[21]

Mind, I like soldiers and soldiering. I like to make men jump to it and dress by the left and number off from the right. I have long

---

20 The following week Ford was to begin the novel about Ney and Napoleon, *A Little Less Than Gods*, under the provisional title 'Demi-Gods'.
21 William Hale Thompson, 1867–1944; Mayor of Chicago from 1915-27, and again from 1927-31; a demagogue, supported by Al Capone. The journalist, critic, and essayist H.L. Mencken, had written a belittling review of Ford's book *Joseph Conrad: A Personal Remembrance*.

said – and as to that it is unlikely that I shall change front – that the British regular army is one of the two most perfect organizations that humanity has produced. The other I will not name, for I have no mind to poke myself into the political problems of the United States. And I am quite ready to believe that the United States regular forces are every whit as efficient as those of my own country. I am indeed sure that they are, only it seems to me, from what I have seen of it, that discipline in the United States Army is too infernally strict ....

And I don't mind fighting or regard it as ignoble, nor do I frightfully deplore physical sufferings or deaths. I was personally happier when I was somewhere in France between August 1914, and November 11, 1918, than I ever was previously, and I could contemplate a personal repetition of that period with great cheerfulness. I do not mean that I could contemplate it cheerfully for others and their dependents. (And I only express these frightfulnesses in order to let the reader feel assured that what is here written is not from the pen of an old-fashioned, peace-at-any-price pacifist of the wool-next-the-skin, vegetarian type.)

Nevertheless, I would without any reluctance join or found an international secret society, every one of whose members was pledged to assassinate any human being who declared any war or was instrumental in promoting one or who used a bellicose threat of any kind. Or who even suggested that today war is possible .... We would train footmen and female domestics and through trusted agencies introduce them into the intimacies of War Ministers, Emperors, heads of Munition Trusts, Publicists .... I have, as you perceive, my eye on my friend Mr Wells. One day he may see his major-domo replaced by one larger, blonder, of bulk and port more majestic. Then let him look to his weekly notes ....

For we are all one people – we races who dwell on the shores of the north Atlantic Ocean. If November the Eleventh did nothing else for us it made us all one people – we English, French and Americans. That is an accomplished fact: may that leaven spread to the farthest limits of the globe! And with that as *chose donnée* it becomes the blackest of crimes even to speak of war between us – as black a crime as to speak to a child of cancer! And, although my Secret Society of the paragraph above may seem a thought fantastic, it is nevertheless a useful symbol. The great defect of American public life is still that decent people do not interest themselves in politics. That is here nothing new. And the same phenomenon is beginning to be very markedly observable in Great Britain. Until lately if the Englishman saw an abuse he would say automatically: 'Something ought to be done about it,' and he did it. That is how the United States came into existence. But the tendency today in England, as here, is for gentle people – *homines generosi* – to say that the Machine is too vast, the effort overwearying. That is true to a point.

But you can deal death-blows nevertheless at the hearts of politicians as well as of papers. I have in my time seen a quite considerable demagogue driven nearly crazy by the receipt of half a dozen letters from quite uninfluential constituents who objected to a point in one of his speeches and I have known the same thing happen to the editor-owner of the most widely circulated newspaper in the United Kingdom and the world... In their hearts these people are crass cowards walking in darkness. A very small sign will fill them with fear, an infinitesimal writing on the wall will cause them to amend their ways. It is then up to us to worry these people out of their lives in order to enforce the final lesson of the Armistice.

For this, I understand is an Armistice Day number. Well, the original Armistice Day was a sort of fever. For myself, I remember Armistice Day very well because I was kept so busy with military duties that I was on my feet all day until I fell into bed stone sober, at 4 next morning. We barbecued whole regimental pigs for the civilian population in the market-place, we organized mixed banquets, concerts, heaven knows what. But I have yet to find anyone who was in a great city and today remembers what he did. You might call that a puerperal fever: the world was being reborn.

Being an impressionable sort of person I never fail to be deeply moved by the two minutes' silence of this day wherever I meet it. For once action is suspended universally so thought must come into play. I wish that the universal thought could be that one thought – that we are all one people and that war between us is as unthinkable as war between Hoboken and Manhattan. And further: the passing of Armistice Day, the ending of our determination to kill, made apparent to us that what we had been fighting was not Germans or even Germany; it was an atrocious ideal.

People are accustomed to ask what we have gained by winning the war or to assert that the whole product of the late war is disillusionment. But that is not true. We died at Givenchy – I am speaking naturally of my own regiment, or you on the *Chemin des*

Dames – in order that the ideal of the shining sword and the flashing helm might die forever as an active symbol of relationships between peoples. No nation ever any more will use such metaphors for the overawing of other peoples. The world today is an infinitely better place than it was before August 4th, 1914, because as an international factor jack-bootism is gone. Neither demagogue nor demi-god will ever employ that metaphor again. No German Emperor, nor 'Big Bill', nor yet Mr Wells, nor yet Mr Mencken. They would find no followers – and what is more important, they know they woud find no followers. And we, who are one people, achieved that by dying together.

And you can very much extend the range of that benefit right into the depths of private life. The spirit of the bully received then so signal a public check that private bullying has a great deal died down. Before the war bluff was enormously applauded and every man aspired to be his own Napoleon. You had everywhere Napoleons of the Press, of the Stage, of the Sanitary Appliance, of the Collar-Stud. Today the locution is hardly any more employed and bluff itself is regarded as something discreditable except in the game of Poker, where it is innocuous. Swank is checked. Parade is gone – we become more and more just people, dependent on individual effort for personal advantage.

We are settling down and every day we are settling more and more down. It is today as unlikely that the people of the north Atlantic seaboard will act aggressively one against the other as that the engrossed rabbits nibbling in the fields of Worcester, in England, should march against the cottontails of Worcester, Mass. If we can see a few years more of Unpreparedness it will be as impossible as that the trees of Gramercy Park, out upon which I look at this moment, should discharge clouds of poison gas over the foliage of the Champs Elysées. Militarism has been scotched; it is for you and me to see that now it dies. For militarism is the antithesis of Thought and the Arts, and it is by Thought and the Arts alone that the world can be saved.

Mrs Meloney, then, asserts that at a dinner, at which I sat beside her, I talked some sort of nonsense about Preparedness. But one talks through one's hat at dinners – I was under the impression that we discussed with acrimony only whether Mysticism and Catholicism were compatible, and I call upon Mrs Padraic Colum and other publicists there present to confirm me – for I have a remarkable memory for conversations. Still I may have forgotten words that then pierced my headgear. In any case you have the above main lines – all that is possible in the space vouchsafed for what they are worth of my thought when it employs itself on these kindred matters.

Fiction

True Love & a GCM

Ford began this novel back in England in September 1918, and worked at it until March 1919. He didn't complete it. The manuscript stops only two pages into Part II, before developing either the 'True Love' or the General Court Martial. But what we do have is an extraordinary document, which combines two powerful elements, both clearly based on Ford's own experience: an account of a war veteran struggling with the mental after-effects of battle trauma; and his reminiscences of his youthful awakenings to art and sexuality. Some of the material was later reworked into *Parade's End* and his books of reminiscence. For example, if Ford's claim that 'chartered accountants are unusual people' may strike us as unusual now, we can recognise that the protagonist Gabriel Morton is an early version of Christopher Tietjens. Like Tietjens, he combines some of Ford's war experience with the mathematical training of his friend Arthur Marwood, who, according to Ford's other sketches of him, certainly had Morton's 'aspect and point of view of Senior Wranglers', his 'demeanour and voices of Judges of the High Court', and who was 'cultured', and 'as sceptical as you please of this poor human nature of ours'.

'True Love & a GCM' was written when Ford was still anxious about the damage the war might have done to his mind. Its experiences are raw, often disturbing, as he courageously investigates his fears. It begins with a headache, and ends in existential crisis. It was possibly this feeling of Morton's – 'that *he* hardly existed' – that made it difficult for Ford to complete the story. In *It Was the Nightingale* (London, 1934), pp. 92–103, he recounts overcoming a comparably suicidal despair when he is demobilised, and arrives destitute and alone in the dilapidated cottage Red Ford. It was at this point – April 1919 – that he abandoned the novel. Perhaps he needed to avoid dwelling on such episodes if he was to reconstruct his life. Or he may have simply felt the material was too painfully self-exposing.

However, we can speculate about how the story might have developed. One possibility is that it could have drawn upon Ford's experience of defending in a court martial the man who went mad. But the persecutions of his Commanding Officer, and the elabora-

tions of Morton's mental disturbances, make it more probable that
he was to have been the accused himself. Certainly that sense of
unjust persecution is the mainspring of *Parade's End*. Tietjens is not
court-martialled, but Ford may have realised (and this may be
another reason for its incompletion) that an actual unjust court-
martial would be too contrived an expression of persecutory feelings;
and that the more effective accusations are precisely those that are
not required to stand the test of legality and proof, but which exist
merely at the level of innuendo and gossip. The 'true love' would
presumably have drawn upon Ford's romance with Stella Bowen,
whom he had met in 1917, and who came to live with him at Red
Ford in June 1919.

Like Tietjens, Morton is another of Ford's visionary characters.
As in many of the pieces here, Ford finds the war has left his impressionism in an impasse: the sheer vividness of his memories, combined
with the sense of powerful repressions, disturbs his sense of identity
and its coherence.

PART I

1.

The sinister brushing of a headache across his forehead – and he
had not suffered from headaches since July, or say, December, 1916
– made Morton think the immense mass of the Cathedral a mere
heaping together of distasteful ornaments.[1] He was walking towards
it over windswept asphalt with a disastrously limping and not very
intelligent officer by his side. He had therefore to walk slowly and,
look at the great building how he would, he could not get it to fuse
into anything but, as it were a monstrous spillikin heap of fretted
and crocketted gargoyles and foliage, too outlined by the soot of
the great Northern city. He did not try.

Instead, he let himself go in a denunciation of all Gothic architecture. He let himself go, more and more, when he felt that he
was re-acting with cruelty on the nerves of the wooden-legged,
tottering brown figure at his side. This officer, with a harshly
beaten, but sincere face, had attached himself to Morton, discerning
him to be what he called a 'judge of Architecture'. He had thus

---

1   The dates are those of Ford's two spells in Red Cross Hospitals in France in 1916.

attached himself during the course of a 'Conference' at Army Headquarters of the X Command. Exactly forty two of them – one from each Unit in the Corps – and a smooth, bored, red-tabbed, GSO2[2], who protested at intervals that he knew nothing of the subject of the Conference but that WO[3] *would* have them – forty three souls, then, had passed two hours and three quarters, packed shoulder to shoulder in a tall, grimy room, with all the sooty double windows closed, all with pipes going, whilst a depressed Major with a dark blue hat band had read, as if he didn't like doing it, interminable paragraphs from some sort of typewritten sheets. He lost his place from time to time and then a voice would be heard asking to have a window opened. Nobody had opened a window. And it had been an August morning.

For the life of him, a month afterwards, Morton could not remember what the 'Conference' had been about. Tall quiet, thirty-four, but looking older, and reputed to be – for no valid reason – an Intellectual, in his Regiment, Morton was the sort of officer whom Orderly Rooms[4] usually send to HQ Conferences. A hurried Adjutant, always a Regular and, as such inclined to be suspicious of Intellect, says:

'Command HQ want an officer for a Conference on' – Gas or Old Tins – or S S 43[5] – as the case may be 'on the 30 8 18.'

An assistant Adjutant, generally an ex Time Serving Orderly Room Sergeant answers hastily and with ill temper:

'They can't have the Gas Officer or the Salvage Officer or the OiC[6] Training. The GOC's[7] coming on the 30 8 18.'

Then the Adjutant says: 'Oh, Send Morton' because, though Morton is a trustworthy officer the Adjutant with his distrust for all men who are reputed to have read books other than Infantry Training and sevenpenny novels or looked at pictures other than those of M Raoul Kirschner, has never been able to bring himself to recommend Morton for a job on the permanent staff of the battalion or for the command of a Company.

The Assistant Adjutant then attacks, hastily and with ill-temper, another problem.

---

2 General Staff Officer, second class.
3 War Office.
4 Room in the barracks where Company business is conducted.
5 S S 43: possibly Ford's fictive militarese.
6 Officer in Charge.
7 General Officer Commanding.

In that way Morton, tallish, fairish, loose-limbed and, except on CO's parade, slightly lounging of figure, had been sent to many Conferences and had got to know quite well the City of X and its Cathedral which, as a rule, he admired.

Wanting to re-capture points of his first seeing the lady who was so profoundly to influence his next few months, he once turned up in his diary the records of his movements on that day; but he found there no more than the words:

'Conference at GHQ... Cathedral a plaster of Paris fraud... Merchant Adventurer's Hall a mad, untidy dream... Or the old woman with the torn lace collar.'

He was accustomed to argue with himself – and with the lady – that he must have been stirred to the soul by the meeting, since she herself had been the attendant of the 'old woman with the torn lace Collar' who had shewn him and the wooden-legged officer over the Merchant Adventurers' Hall. – He must have been deeply stirred by the meeting or he would not have made a three line entry in his diary.

His entries limited themselves usually to something like:

'30 8 18. Reported XHQ.

31 8 18 Returned Bn HQ'[8] He made these notes for the purpose of applying for Detention Allowances that he was as a rule too indifferent to claim.

2.

The reader is not asked to accept the affair in which Morton found himself entangled as in any degree supernatural. Not in any degree! For who of us has not known what we will call states of exaltation which have no apparent physical or circumstantial causes – wearinesses very intense which have been caused by no labours or excesses; discouragements that have no relation to our circumstances; elations when we might very well have had all sorts of a hump? That is precisely it. You will get the hump when you have been as sober as a penniless tramp; as continent as an English born Cardinal; or again, you will wake, clear-headed, active and sparkling after such a night as ....

So no doubt it was with Morton.

---

8   Battalion Headquarters.

He was temperate enough and his temperance had, the night before, been enhanced by arriving at his inn in the ancient city at 9.38 p.m. – eight minutes too late for a legal drink. And, if his impressive respectability had permitted him to get out of the barmaid a single whiskey and soda, his natural delicacy had prevented his pressing the young lady for his usual second. He had been unfortunate lover enough to be more than usually chaste for a Young Officer and, again, the lateness of his arrival in the city had precluded his having any of the vagrant adventures that are so open to the Junior Officer in cities – very ancient and dominated by tall fanes, or in very new towns cloaked in the fumes from tall chimneys. No, he hadn't drunk; he hadn't whored; he hadn't even unduly exerted his brain.

His experiences in France were no longer very recent. He had been pretty bad eleven months before; but, no longer, the moment he shut his eyes in bed did he hear the picks and drills of the German mines going beneath him; he didn't, any more, feel a vague but very real malaise at the droned sounds of aeroplanes in the summer evening skies, and all the doors of a house could slam in a draught without making him spring out of an armchair. Latterly wine, women, work and High Explosives had all spared him their more violent manifestations; so that his annoyance was all the greater that morning to find that he had all the symptoms – irritability that had no apparent cause; a clearheadedness that usually preceded depression and bad pains in the head; a flow of language that was incautious in a junior officer – and the threatening of a headache. Equally causelessly, it appeared to clear off, later in the day.

That day, as has been said, had opened normally enough after a normal night. Or perhaps it had not been so normal. He fancied that he had had a sudden leaning towards a frame of mind that, for four years or more, he hadn't been in – towards the ancient, the mediaeval, the picturesque, the easy going.

The train, in approaching the ancient city of X winds spectacularly round the pile of the cathedral. So that, as, the night before, Morton had been drawn along, he had seen the high and sacred fane, at first purple against a flaming sky, and then, livid, and as if pointing a finger upwards, against a lowering East. When the great bulk had been purple against the profusion of orange and scarlet, the houses of men had seemed to crowd upon, to climb up the heights of, the building of God. Windows had glowed in the blacknesses, reflections flashed out from steeples. So that the city had appeared as an immense, mediaeval ship – a black Unit of the picturesque, voyaging stably down the waves of Time with its freights of burgesses, earls, Archbishops, affairs, intrigues, embraces ....

Yes, it was an old frame of mind, coming anew. Formerly, in that mood, he had approached Chartres at sunset, or Tours, or Vendôme, or Carcassonne or Cologne – or even Rye! – with the feeling of approaching, of plunging into, romances, intimacies, adventures of the cloak and the stiletto. Of course he had not ever contracted the intimacies or tasted the romances. But he had spent summer holidays in many historic towns and had acquired a lazy but persistent habit of enquiring into the more intimate details of local histories – and a quiet taste for domestic and unelaborated styles of architecture .....

Morton had been a chartered accountant.

And chartered accountants are unusual people. They have the chance of being donnish; of being cultured; of being of the stock-broker type or of the type of poets. Theirs is a sedentary and contemplative existence, very often, making for clean white hands and pink nails; it goes far enough into mathematics to let its prac-titioners acquire the aspect and point of view of Senior Wranglers; it deals sufficiently with Law to let them have the demeanour and voices of Judges of the High Court; it permits a man to see enough of villainies to be as sceptical as you please of this poor human nature of ours. So it has – this occupation – its possibilities.

And, 'before', Morton had taken advantage of them. He had seen some life. Early on, for instance he had managed a large Emporium in a South Coast Town – the proprietor being in difficulties. he had administered for a time, a London periodical; he had assisted in winding up and keeping going, the affairs of a great Glasgow contractor and he had spent six months in Paris in control of an English-owned corset business. After that he had been taken into a qualified partnership by an uncle in the firm of Tredgold, Herapath and Morton of Shaftesbury Avenue.

He had been on the road to fortune. That had been in 1911.

From his appearance, diction, voice and conversation, at that date, he might have been anything – anything clean, polished, and nothing in particular. The Emporium; the London periodical; McMinnes and Co of Glasgow and the Lutetian Corset Co of Paris had shewn him enough of greed, villainy and cosmopolitan licence to let his glance be sceptically speculative, whilst a complete personal probity and a normally more than sufficient income, most of which he had to earn, let that glance be direct and his head upright. Two unfortunate love affairs – one with a married woman had modified a tendency to arrogance. He had made his mark on women's hearts, but he hadn't been able, as yet, to retain any sufficiently attractive woman for long enough to make a final sacrifice of goods, position, repute, and the rest of it. He had devoted a considerable amount of time to field-sports, since both he and his uncle [Hera]path had the assurance that a clear brain was the result of an exercised body; so he was a fair cricketer, still; played a moderate game of tennis; rode passably[,] was not much good at billiards, was a fair, third-class shot, played a goodish hand at Auction and appeared clean and healthy. He had studied old buildings with attention and had read a good many books on the Renaissance and so he believed that a kind scepticism and generosity in impulses would eventually save him from the devil. He had read something of the sort in a sentence quoted by John Addington Symonds from Pico della Mirandola or someone of the sort – and the sentence had influenced his whole life in the profoundest manner.

Let me dwell upon the fact for a minute.

In England – at any rate in the England that Morton knew – a man so rarely comes upon moral speculations that are any other than trite and un-striking, that any striking and unusual dictum in ethics, encountered by chance, may well have this profound sort of influence on whole careers; since, so rare are ethical impulses and questionings in a world so settled and unquestioning in its ideals, that, if you have encountered one unusual point of view it is a thousand to one that you will never encounter another to shake its influence. So it had been with Morton. He remembered to the end of his days the day on which he had read for the first time that queer fish of a life-doctrine – or rather he remembered the night after that reading.

It had been a sopping day, a week after he had left Westminster for good – it had been, that is to say, on the 24th December 1892. His father had been an architect inhabiting Kensington – an architect who had designed small public buildings and large private houses in the Renaissance manner. This manner being more comfortable and cushioned than the austerer Gothic that was still rather dominant, Mr Morton had made a very comfortable income – nay he eventually left what passed for a fortune in the 'nineties

of last century. Renaissance architecture in those days attracted and
brought Morton senior into contact with comfortable people –
warm city men, the municipal leaders of large Northern cities and
the like – people who liked cushions, smoking rooms with
arabesques and so on. But this had not prevented his being serious,
anxious to do his duty to a State most of whose churches are Gothic.
If he had not had many of the attributes of architects of his day,
who were austere when they were not Bohemian, he had had all
those of the good citizen. So he had been all the more careful in
the choice of a career for his eldest son.

On the day that Morton had left Westminster for the last time
the father had introduced the son for the first time to his Library.
This was a very large room in a house in South Kensington – a
room large enough to boast Corinthian pillars, dividing it into
three, four real pieces of Grecian statuary – and innumerable books.
It was not of course the first time that the son had been in the
apartment – but it was the first time that he had been given the run
of it. His father then told him that, it being the octave of Christmas
the boy might read for seven days in the Library and, on Christmas
day he might choose any book that he liked, however valuable –
and there were some very valuable books there. He was to have,
in addition, a cheque for ten pounds which – or at any rate a part
of which – he was expected to spend on furnishings, pictures, or
other necessaries for his rooms at Oxford. For to Oxford he was to
go next Easter unless in the meantime something in his character
should transpire that should give his parents a hint as to what career
he really *ought* to follow. His father, having been much away from
home, had had little opportunity of observing his son; and at the
same time he had no predisposition towards any special career for
him. His son might become a politician; a soldier; a physician, or
set his ambitions on the woolsack. The one thing that Mr Morton
did not wish Gabriel to become was – an architect, since he shrank
instinctively from, rather than disliked, the idea of any other soul's
entering his own office. The only thing, on the other hand, that
Mrs Morton wished her son to become, was precisely an architect.
This was because she wanted her son to have an eye kept on him;
but she wanted this only languidly.

So the father decided to give Gabriel the run of the library for a
week. In the spring he was to take the boy to Italy for two months.
He felt, himself, the need for a rest and the need to refresh his mind
with the sight of some of the Renaissance originals in whose spirit

it was his ambition to work. He felt that he had grown stale – and he wanted, too, to make his son's acquaintance.

Mrs Morton rather trembled at the idea that her son should have that run – of a Library and the keys of locked drawers! For there are books – and books! She would much have preferred that the father should supervise his son's reading. But when, whilst retiring for the night, she had mentioned this aspiration to her husband, he had replied that that was exactly what he didn't want. He had that morning received the intimation that he was to be mentioned in the New Year's Honours and that fact had affirmed in him the notion that he knew at once what he did want and how to get it. And he pointed out to his wife that if Gabriel manifested an undue liking for books that are usually kept locked up, his father would in that way have an inkling of tastes that he could afterwards do something to eradicate. Mrs Morton had sighed and said that no doubt it was for the best.

Just at that date – the Octave of Xtmas 1892 – Gabriel Morton, aged little over eighteen,[9] had been suffering from a period of languour. That was no doubt due to a tendency to collapse after rather hard work – Westminster had at that date a distinct trend towards pushing on boys who were docile, obedient and reasonably industrious. Thus, a vigilant mathematical master had singled out Gabriel Morton as one of two possible Wranglers, so that, without any disciplinary action Mr Mreddith, the master in question had seen to it, by hints and persuasions, that Morton had spent more time than the normal over his books at home. At the same time, though Morton had not been actually in the fives team, the Influenza had kept out so many of the regular players that Morton had been kept pretty hard at work over Fives as well as the Binomial Theorem. Such a coming together of exhortations – from Master and Team Captain – is apt to put a pretty fair strain on a growing boy so that, school being done with for him, and, having the prospect of a long holiday, he was already inclined to let himself go – to rest for hours. The run of the Library made him still more inclined to rest.

It was really a sumptuous and closed in room – the more closed in since the windows which might have shown the dull streets of South Kensington were, in the first place double, so that even the sound of hansoms rarely penetrated the stillness; in the second place,

---

9   Ford himself was nineteen on 17 December 1892.

the inner casements were of light coloured glass. So that there was no looking out and the large, tall rectangular room was like an evening section of the British Museum. It was moreover heated by steam pipes – at that date an innovation for private houses, but Mr Morton was the architect of Comfort in the 'nineties – so that no footman penetrated the place for the purposes of putting coals on a fire. The Library was dusted before breakfast; after that meal no servant penetrated its stillness. Over the great Renaissance fireplace of elaborately carved yellowish marble which came from the Palazzo Melondina there was a single large painting by Burne Jones – Sir Edward Burne Jones ARA, at that time a fashionable but 'advanced' artist. It represented a lady in a bluish grey gown, with a bluish, bistre, face and hands. She sat, it was difficult to say how, in a greenish-grey olive tree whose foliage filled the whole canvas, and for ever held in non-muscular fingers, a greenish-yellow lemon – or it might have been the apple of Genesis, a shaddock, or even a pomegranate.

Standing in front of this picture, Mr Morton, a tallish, still lean and active man of forty-eight or so, with a grizzling but carefully cut beard, in a woolly ulster with a belt and a deerstalker cap with ear flaps – Mr Morton, so soon to be 'Sir Edward Morton, FRIBA, RA etc'. delivered to his son a short lecture on this work by Sir Edward Burne Jones ARA. He had intended to devote to his son a few words on Literature as divided into Memoirs, History, Travel and the works of fiction of Mr George Meredith; Mr Thomas Hardy; the author of *Lorna Doone* and the moral works of the then late George Eliot. But, since he found it difficult to begin on a ten-minute syllabus of all the more cultivated Letters of the world he knew, Mr Morton suddenly fell back upon the picture.

Of what he said his son retained little. The impression remaining to him was that, in his early youth Sir Edward Burne Jones ARA had been a little of a heretic, perhaps a revolutionary and certainly a devotee of the Gothic 'which, in my own boyhood,' Mr Morton said with a tolerant laugh, 'I was inclined to admire.'

He gave the impression that the 'Gothic' was revolutionary, youthful, and slightly bad for his own trade. But he asked his son to observe that the lady plucking an apple from an olive tree was decidedly Renaissance – or, if *she* wasn't, the conventionally rendered foliage certainly was. And again, Mr Morton asked his son to observe how admirably the leafage which filled the picture harmonised with the carving on the yellowish alabaster carvings that had been let into the yellowish marble fireplace from the Palazzo.

'And that, dear Gabriel, I may tell you,' he finished, 'is the finest piece of domestic Renaissance work outside Italy.'

He was about to dilate on how, at comparatively no expense, he had secured both the fireplace and the picture, because he would like his son to know how – in his son's interests – he had practised remarkable, though gentlemanly and refined, economies and sharpnesses. But he refrained from dilating, since he did not seem to wish to appear boastful. Instead, he drew from the waistcoat pocket of his brown Norfolk jacket, a wash-leather bag from which, in turn, he extracted with long fingers, a very shiny gold watch and a very shiny sovereign purse. He looked at the watch and said;

'I have just time to catch my train comfortably,' he opened the little spherical golden receptacle which pushed sovereigns automatically upwards against the thumb and he said: 'Do you think you will want three guineas, or had you better have four, to buy your Christmas presents with? You will get something for your mother, for your cousin Olive,[10] and for any of your schoolboy chums you like. A polite letter would be more appropriate for your uncle Herapath than a present as he is so wealthy a man.'

Mr Morton drew three sovereigns from the golden receptacle and then as deliberately replaced them.

'On second thoughts,' he said, 'a five pound note may be more useful to you. You are now growing up and you will soon have to do your own shopping. I seem to notice that you could do with more grown up collars and ties. And there may be charities you are interested in. I should like you to be interested in charities. It is rather a duty in a young man who will probably inherit means. And also...'

Mr Morton looked at his son keenly and humorously, his red upper lip lifting slightly over his right canine tooth:

'Also there is, I believe, Mary Leatham.'

Gabriel, in a little vision of Mary Leatham with dark and shy eyes, thought he should have felt shy – but he did not:

'I should like to give something nice to Mary Leatham,' he said.

'Well, give her an amber necklace,' his father answered. 'Not jewellery. You are too young and not gloves – they are too commonplace.' He paused and then added:

---

10 Ford's cousin Olive was a daughter of W.M. Rossetti.

'When I was a boy, at Christmas, one year, I wanted to give a present to a young lady of my own circle. I even bought the present, but my mother found it in my collar-drawer – and I was very severely punished. Very severely...'

He added meditatively: 'I don't know that it did me any... I daresay I should have been a better man if I had been allowed to – to keep my eyes in my own boat, you know... Yes, keep your eyes in your own boat,' he repeated slowly, 'It's a good thing to do.'

The queer emotions that Gabriel felt to be passing between himself and his father, though they delighted him like first love, prevented his giving his father an assurance that he would endeavour to avoid entanglements outside his own class. He did not know what words to use.

His father kissed him.

'Good-bye Gabriel,' he said, 'I wish I knew you better. I believe you're a good boy. But one works so hard one hasn't the means of knowing. It's stupid rather. Cut throat competition! I hope you'll live into better times...'

He added:

'Don't come down, now you're just here.' He was going to Manchester where labour troubles had broken out amongst the men employed by the contractor for a suburban Free Library.

Gabriel said:

'Good-bye, sir... You're a splendid father to have.'

II

Gabriel Morton was walking beside the wooden legged officer with the tortured face, along the narrow street of the city of X – the narrow, dark street, that, in its narrowness and darkness, suggested at first to the deceived eye that it might contain treasures of a dusky brick-brackery kind, but that, when you came to examine it, you found to consist of mere untidy shams, dusted and begrimed by the war-years. There sham corbels, of cement instead of stone or timber, made bosses under sham bow-windows and over mechanical, diamondpaned shopwindows that had the air of being devoted to eighteenth century coloured prints but that really contained cheap postcards showing regimental badges, cheap tinsel imitations of grenades, crossed machine guns, plumes, horrible sweets, cheap walking out canes – disorderly rubbish heaps of sordid and overcharged objects meant for extracting the meagre pay extortionately from the pockets of poor Tommies. The Tommies went past slouching sideways, saluting endlessly with yokels' gestures; the wooden legged officer returned his salutes shufflingly as if he had meant to blow his nose but changed his mind. Morton walked stiffly and returned his salutes like a machine with a bad-tempered face. His companion, like a lamed partridge, snuffled and panted, as if desperately and pathetically.

And then, suddenly, and more clearly than had ever happened to him before, he found himself again in the Library with the softened air, the Grecian bits of statuary on truncated, dark marble columns, the Renaissance fireplace of alabaster set into yellowish marble and the picture with the lady by Sir Edward Burne Jones, ARA. Heaven knew where the books of the Library were now, or what the Library itself looked like – but he was there; his father had just gone out of the room; he himself had just dropped down into a very comfortable and deep leather armchair. He was continuing to look at her as it were, out of a sense of duty to his father ....

He exclaimed irritably to the limping officer:

'You couldn't. It's all balls. You couldn't have the one without the other.'

For the man with the face transfigured by suffering had been maundering on about better cathedrals than the one at X being built as tributes to the new communistic spirit of brotherhood that should come on the world after the war was finished and dogma and cruelty should be gone too. Morton had wanted to say that the man's own face with the painful smile of a tortured brotherliness was the product of faith and cruelty.

But the sense, the atmosphere, the spirit of the Library settled down more warmly and more stilly upon him and what he wanted to think about was his father's personality and the picture that showed the lady picking a shaddock from a blue-grey olive bough. That picture had been sold to Birmingham or Leeds. Possibly Manchester. It had gone anyhow ....

He had never really got to know his father. He remembered that, on that day, the 18 12 92, the first book he had looked at had been a large copy of *Men of the Time*,[11] to see who his father really was.

---

11 Ford's own father, Francis Hueffer, figured in *Men of the Time: A Dictionary of Contemporaries*, twelfth edition (London: George Routledge and Sons, 1887), as did his grandfather, Ford Madox Brown.

By then he had already remained sunk in the comfortable chair for a long time – quite a long time – getting over the emotions that his father's being and words had caused in him. It had struck him that his father would like him to regard attentively a work of art that was in itself admirable and one which was, like the Renaissance fireplace, a sort of tribute to his father's skill in making a bargain. For he was, in a queer way, very conscious of his family atmosphere. Words dropped during lunchtimes and the explanations that his mother frequently asked for, since her acquaintance with the marvels of the Renaissance or the ways of Town Councillors was equally limited, had made the young Gabriel know quite a deal about his father's affairs. Thus he knew the names of out of the way but progressive northern municipalities and the fact that his father hunted out what he usually called 'pieces' with a keen avidity. From the fact that, when he spoke of things like tallboys that had come from Yorkshire farms and cabinets from ostler's saddle-rooms, his father would take the air in sharply through his keen nostrils, Gabriel had the feeling that he discovered these pieces by the scent of them.

Coming home from school he would see workmen with green baize aprons removing one great piece of furniture and replacing it by another, more sumptuous, more carved, more soft in look and colour, until he seemed, as it were, to grow up into a house that grew into a museum. This was particularly the case after his father had come back from a holiday in Spain.

Yet he knew that his father was not intent on merely commercial speculations; less clearly he felt that his father was not even keen on collecting. Comfortable old gentlemen with very hooked noses, wide shirtfronts and enormous white eyebrows would lean sideways beside the dining table cloth to examine Tanagra vases which his father handed to them during the cigar stage of the meals. They would go out past marquetrie cabinets taller than themselves and would draw in their breaths hissingly. They would talk about gaps in their series of this or that – but his father always had a deaf look when they spoke in that way. He would describe in the air, with his lean, strong hands, the curve of a vase or of [a] musical instrument. No; he wasn't a furniture dealer; he wasn't a collector. One day he saw him leaning a little back on his feet, looking with half closed eyes at a very beautiful woman, with frizzy black hair parted in the middle, with red lips and a great throat, standing against an immense black lacquer cabinet on which the scarlet of conventionalised peacocks showed like the dripping of blood. Then he knew his father for the dreamer that he really was in spite of the frieze ulster and the deerstalker cap.

A dreamer! That remained such a strong conviction in him in all his after life that he never much questioned that conviction. He seemed to see into his father's mind – to see into a region where it was always twilight and there were silver trunked birch trees with their thin leaves against a dusky sky – and a little, thin stream, its waters level with the banks. That picture – or rather it was a feeling more than a picture – came into his mind whenever, afterwards, he thought of his father. It wasn't that he ever thought of his father often.

But, at odd times, long after his father had been dead, the thought of that energetic figure, with the keen nose, the keen eyes, the sharp beard, would come up into his mind. He would be sitting in a Tube; he would be punting on the River; he would be drilling on the Square. And the words 'A dreamer!', and the twilight feeling would come strongly into his mind.

It is doubtful if the words carried much to him. He had probably heard them at school, spoken, perhaps contemptuously of some schoolfellow inept at his lessons – or perhaps spoken respectfully of someone like Keats, a poet who died young. No, the words had no special significance – they meant probably, a man usually very energetic who would have lapses when he just looked at beautiful things and marked time. He would not covet them.

For it certainly didn't till long after come into his mind then to imagine that his father coveted the beautiful lady. It did come into his mind at odd moments in after life. He would wonder if his father had had an intrigue with Mrs Minshull; he noticed that a pamphlet of his father's on 'The Employment of the Acanthus Leaf in Decoration after the year 1600' was dedicated to 'E.G.M.' – which might have been Mrs Minshull. Once he happened to ask his mother who Mrs Minshull was. His mother answered that she had not known the lady very well; she had been a lady of rather doubtful origin, a barmaid perhaps, or a shop-girl, married to a sculptor – 'Sculptors sometimes did that sort of thing' – who was at one time rather a protégé of Morton Senr. Gabriel gathered that his mother did not consider that the Minshulls were quite the sort of people to be in their 'set', though they were invited to dinner at long intervals.

But that, again, made little impression on Gabriel, either as a boy or a young man. The essential idea of his father was always that of a keen man with lapses into dreams that he did not seek to realise. So he considered his home as less of a home than a landscape. The great beautiful things that filled it were less possessions that you collected or by which you made profits, than backgrounds for your imaginings. He had that feeling.

He had it indeed very strongly on that afternoon of the 18 12 92 when he sat in the deep chair in the Library. He felt somehow that he must hurry to take advantage of being there because at any minute the Library might dissolve. The great books with their calf bindings, their red and gilded labels, closed him like a tranquil wall; the Greek fragments on their dark marble plinths seemed to lean back against the high square pillars and just to wait till they were removed. Only the lady by Sir Edward Burne Jones ARA seemed to have any permanence about her – as if he would carry her in his mind for a long time. So he began on the books.

He roused himself from his lethargic posture and went round the walls; he felt small and a little apprehensive, like a child going from pillar to pillar of a vast, solitary cathedral. It was such an immense prospect. He touched with one finger the backs of Robertson's *History of Charles V*; of Mrs Lucy Hutchinson's *Memoirs of Colonel Hutchinson*; of Clarendon's *History of the Great Rebellion*; of Lockhart's *Life of Sir Walter Scott*. He took down an immense scarlet and gilt volume called *L'Art du Moyen Age*; but the plates seemed to him to be hard and he put it back. Finally he came on John Addington Symonds' *Renaissance*.

He took that to the sofa because he had so often heard the word 'Renaissance' on his father's lips and because he had frequently seen John Addington Symonds in their house. He did not find it heavy reading, though it struck him as disconnected. It wasn't of course a story; he had not expected that, though it was more full of stories than he *had* expected. But what a little teased him was that he didn't get from it any connected idea – or indeed any connected idea at all – of what the Renaissance really was. The writer took it too much for granted that the reader would know. And Gabriel had begun with the third or fourth volume. He had intended to dip into it so that he could begin at the beginning if he liked the sample; but he came at once to some passages about assassinations in Venice and he went on reading in that volume for the whole afternoon. It seemed to be full of assassinations and the reasons for assassinations. Queer reasons! Loves, jealousies, the desire to be Cardinals, the desires to prevent other people from being Cardinals. His mother looked in on him once during the afternoon to tell him that she was going calling, and when, in answer to her question as to what he was reading about, she heard him say in an engrossed voice: 'Vittoria Accoramboni', she felt satisfied.

The book profoundly influenced his life. When, years and years afterwards, he picked up one of the volumes, he was astounded to discover how much it had influenced his whole life. It wasn't the moral attitude of the late John Addington Symonds; it wasn't even the culture, the reflections upon mediaeval and later literature and art. No; it was simply the stories of lives and deaths. He re-read Volume 6 in No II Red Cross Hospital in Rouen in the winter of 1916[12] – and it was amazing how, for that day the war disappeared, and his past lived again. For it was *his* past, his own personal past, he found, far more than anything he had actually lived through as a boy. Westminster was dim to him with its buttresses, its fives courts, its grimy square where they kicked footballs in rough mists, it etiquettes in dress and its vicissitudes of classes and athletics. He could hardly remember a master except Mr Mreddith with his brown curly beard, his spectacles and his manner of always swallowing before he spoke; he could not really remember one single boy by name, though he could remember the looks of one or two. But when he re-read this book he knew that a great crowd of splendidly or singularly dressed shades had always peopled his world. He recognised suddenly names, rocky landscapes, small hill towns with crumbling walls, weapons, wells into which bodies were thrown beside church doors – and names and names and names.[13] Lucrezia Malpigli, Lelio Buonvisi, Vincenzo di Coreglia, Sister Umilia, the Chancellor Vincenzo Petrucci, Amilcare Orsini, bastard of the Count of Pitigliano. 'Two hired *bravi*, Olimpio Calvetti and Marzio Catalani, entered the old man's bedroom, drove a nail into his head and flung the corpse out from a gallery, whence it was alleged that he had fallen by accident' – the Cardinal Montalto, Pope Gregory XIII, the Duke of Bracciano, ... 'The Prince Luigi Orsini walked attired in brown, his poignard at his side, and his cloak slung elegantly under his arm. The weapon being taken from him he leaned upon a balustrade and began to trim his nails with a little pair

---

12 Which is where Ford was then.
13 The quotations which follow are indeed from Volume 6 of *Renaissance in Italy* (London, 1909), pp. 271 and 287.

of scissors he happened to find there. On the 27th he was strangled in prison by order of the Venetian Republic'. They were endless.

The influence of the book was profound. When he looked back on that day of reading from between the sheets of the little cell in No II in Rouen he realised that it had been a matter of extraordinary first experiences. He had been used to reading far into twilights, close to windows so as to catch upon his book the last rays of the declining day; and then he had been engrossed. He would be so engrossed that no sounds from the encircling world and no voices were able to make him move. He had read in *Ivanhoe*, in *The Scalp Hunters*, in *Percival Keene*, in *Lorna Doone*, in *Copperfield*[14] – reading coiled up in a window seat as a dog sleeps. If you had touched him then he would have complained inarticulately as a sleeping dog complains. It had been something rapt, like that. He had read also Waterton's *Wanderings in South America*; *Bates on the Amazon*; the *Life of a Scottish Naturalist*.[15] Once a big, dark man with a soft voice had been at one of his mother's afternoons. He was called D.G. Rossetti.[16] This big man saw him in a corner of the large room and asked him what he read. So he answered *The Scalp Hunters* which he was just then finishing. 'Oh, well,' said Rossetti, 'Tell your mother to let you come round and see me and I will give you a much better book. Twenty books in one.'

His father and mother had very willingly hired a fourwheel cab for the afternoon, next day, to send the young Gabriel round to Chelsea. They impressed on the boy that he was going to see a very great poet painter, after whom, as a matter of fact he had been called;[17] for in the early married days of Mr and Mrs Morton the young couple had entertained an almost swooning admiration for that then little known artist. But the idea of a man as being memorable because he was a poet or a painter was so unfamiliar to the little Gabriel that he thought little of it. He went in a cab, slowly, to Chelsea. He was introduced into an immense, gloomy, coloured and dusty room, where gilded sunfishes hung from the ceiling, and

---

14 Mayne Reid, *The Scalp-Hunters: or, Romantic Adventures in Northern Mexico* (London, 1851). *Percival Keene* is by Frederick Marryat (London, 1842).

15 Samuel Smiles' *Life of a Scottish Naturalist* made a deep impression on Ford. He discusses it in 'Stocktaking [. . .] X', *transatlantic review*, 2:5 (Nov. 1924), p. 504; also In *Return to Yesterday* (London, 1931), p. 48, where he says: 'the writer whose cadences have most intimately influenced me were those of Thomas Edwardes [. . .]'.

16 Ford's uncle by marriage. Ford's mother's sister had married William Michael Rossetti, the poet-painter's brother.

17 As Ford had been named after his maternal grandfather, Ford Madox Brown.

immense pictures of ladies stood on easels, so that whole spaces of the room were hidden, and the big dark man stood there wearing what Gabriel took to be an overcoat.

And his recollection rather ended there. He couldn't remember what Rossetti had said or what he had answered, he was wondering what was behind the easels. The man in the overcoat had ordered another, smaller man, in a velvet coat to go and fetch something and presently the young Morton was driving away in the four-wheeler, holding a large, square, rather thin book of very odd appearance for it was bound in a bit of blue of blue cardboard and had on its cover, in gilt letters the words 'Novelists' and Romancists' Library'. It contained, in the smallest and cheapest type you could imagine, *Guzman d'Alfarache, or the Story of a Rogue, Lazarillo de Tormes*, by Lope da Vega; *The Mysteries of Paris* by Eugène Sue; Defoe's *Captain Singleton* and *Moll Flanders*; *The Man of Feeling* and the *Mysteries of Udolfo*, as well as at least twenty other romances, mostly of the picaresque order; that is to say they were mostly about celebrated rogues of the seventeenth and eighteenth centuries.

He read in this book for years. He returned to it again and again; some of the stories he read five or six times, notably he read one called *Lazarillo de Tormes* and Defoe's two books. Yet it was a fact that in after life he remembered nothing of these books. Of *Lazarillo* only one incident came back to him; that unfortunate Rogue whilst still a child had come into the employment and the power of a terrible, blind man, a beggar, whose hearing was so acute that Lazarillo went in constant danger of his life, and whose cruelties were so diabolical that his life was unbearable. How he got away from his master was as follows. It was his province to lead the blind man about, not by holding his hand – that was unnecessary – but by the voice, saying, 'A step to the right, here', and so on. One day they had to cross a little brook, by jumping; and the blind man was a mighty jumper. Lazarillo led his master to a point where, upon the opposite bank of the stream there was a large tree. 'Now jump, master,' he said and the beggar gave a mighty leap. His forehead hit the tree and he fell back into the brook.

Perhaps he was drowned; perhaps he had only fainted. Morton could never remember. At any rate the young Lazarillo escaped. Of *Captain Singleton* Morton could remember nothing; of *Moll Flanders*, nothing. Of the *Mysteries of Paris* there came back to him only the merest silverpoint of a scene where some disguised German prince went into some estaminet somewhere in Paris and ate – or perhaps he only saw – sausages that his guide called 'bags of mystery'.

Yes, he had read in 'The Novelists' and Romancists' Library' for years. He had been thirteen when he had been given the odd looking book; he took his last look at it, as a boy, at close on seventeen when he re-read *Lazarillo de Tormes*.

His mind worked curiously, but always in the same way, when it imagined the backgrounds for the characters of these works or for the anecdotes in Symonds' book. As for Defoe, there had been in 1889 or so an exhibition at South Kensington called 'Old London', with narrow streets, green doors arched, marked with a red cross to indicate the Great Plague – and this little indication was enough to set him imagining a whole city of darkness peopled by stout rogues and merchants in black. Similarly, a single picture by Murillo in the National Gallery, set whole plains, mountains and orange groves in Spain before his eyes. And there were enough pictures of Italy in his father's house to let him create for himself a whole country in which the desperadoes of the Renaissance could live their haphazard and hairsbreadth lives. And the curious thing was [that], when, next spring, he went with is father to Italy, the Italy of his imagination was stronger than the country ruled over by il Re Galantuomo. It was much stronger.

I do not mean to say that, when he stood on the Corso, or higher up on the Pincian Hill, his own intimate Rome, obscured or did not let him see, the fiacres, the blackly and shabbily dressed women of the Roman nobility, or the immense blocks of the Via Nazionale. Or, if he talked to a lady at a party in later years, about Rome he could talk about the Rome of the Hotel Quirinale or the Rome where electric trams ran in a shinily-tiled tunnel under the royal gardens. He had noted enough of modern Rome to be able to talk about it sanely. But, when, alone with himself, he thought of Rome, it was a place of great granite, black, palaces where pikemen with immense steel hats moved amongst courtesans, cicisbei[18] and cardinals in the smoke, and to the light of the flames of scented torches that would be guiding a Cardinal Nephew to the palace of an Ottavia someone or other. Or he would see a Coliseum and a Tivoli in a twilight like no twilight that you will really find in the City of the Seven Hills.

And these were the real things for him.

---

18 The recognized gallants of married women.

III

It was sometimes startling – it was sometimes, indeed, even a little alarming to him – to notice how much these things were the real things to him, whilst what was actually going on round him was hardly even apparent. Indeed, in Red Cross Hospital No II, he asked himself once or twice if he wasn't a little mad – if he hadn't been a little mad all his life. He lay there, for long periods, sometimes quite alone – and he thought a great deal, and generally about his own past.

His past came back to him in waves. It came back to him in waves of an extraordinary intensity; it was as if they took hold of him and overwhelmed him; as if they blotted out the VAD[19] – whom he liked extremely – and the two or three nondescriptly dressed, slippered, untidy-haired officers who from time to time would take a look at him round his door. They would say a rather forcedly hilarious word or two and then drift away. What they said hardly ever penetrated to his inner brain, but he seemed to answer them coherently enough. So he lay there and things came back.

He was aware that he might die. Influenza following on pneumonia caused by neglected gas is a dangerous thing to have. But the fever went away at last; it wasn't fever that made him see the things.

No II Hospital, as so many of us know, was the seminary attached to the Palace of the Archbishop of Rouen. It was therefore divided into little cells, suitable for the studies or cubicles of budding monks, but very unlike the wards usually found in hospitals. During the Franco[-]Prussian War this seminary had been used by the Prussians for their own sick and wounded. It stood high and there was a great deal of light and, during Morton's time there were a great many patients there, the majority of them being chest cases, since the weather up the line was very severe that winter. Innumerable whispers seemed to sound from all sides, though the VADs moved very quietly and the Sisters seemed to move more quietly still. They would be there, looking at you with friendly, enquiring and impersonal eyes, but you would not have heard the door open. Sometimes there would be a doctor there too, in khaki, of course.

It was a little rough luck on Morton that the first patient to share his cell with him should have been a captain of the Black Watch

---

19 Nurse of the Voluntary Aid Detachment.

who was certainly a little mad. It wasn't so much that Captain Fraser
got up every night towards four and began to sharpen an immense
dirk on the sole of one of his slippers.[20] He had the air of doing it
clandestinely, but he seemed to think that Morton would sympathise and he seemed to have no idea of attacking Morton himself.
No. The aspect of madness came from his incessant talking. He
talked without ceasing about unknown and surely unimportant
places in the West Highlands. It was like a long strain in Morton's
forehead and he thanked God when the Black Watchman went
away to Blighty with a convoy. Then the Huns came.

They were the Huns of 1870, mild faced, brown bearded men,
wearing silver helmets topped by eagles, and they were dressed all
in white. Some of them were surgeons, some dressers, some were
senior officers who appeared just to come in to talk.[21] There was a
patient in the other bed of the cell; perhaps there were several
patients, for stretchers came in and out. Sometimes women in black
came in and wrung their hands or stretched them over their heads.
This went on for a long time.

They never noticed Morton. At times he was tormented by
sudden dreads that they would notice him and would do 'things'
to him. But they never did. Nurses came in and fed Morton, but
the Huns were always there, several, leaning over the other bed. It
went on for days. Once a RWF[22] officer with a weak jaw, rather
vacuous eyes and wearing a dilapidated army overcoat, came in
with some cards and proposed to teach Morton the game of
Piquette which he said was an excellent game for two. He went on
giggling all the while that he was dealing the cards and explaining
the game – all the while the Hun surgeons and dressers went on
whispering in consultation over the patient in the other bed.
Afterwards the RWF officer said that he had never known any one
pick up the game so quickly. But Morton, two days later, could
remember nothing of its rules.

At two in the morning on New Years' Eve when the cell was
absolutely full of Germans all in white, with one immense bearded
Hun – Morton took him to be the Emperor Frederic – his top-
booted legs stretched wide apart, his clasped hands resting on the

---

20 Compare 'I Revisit the Riviera', p. 64.
21 Compare the passage from *Mightier Than the Sword* excerpted in the Miscellany, pp. 222–3
     below.
22 Royal Welch Fusiliers.

hilt of his silver sword gazed expressionlessly at the other bed ....
the Convoy whistle sounded and the Hospital seemed like a
building that had come alive. A great convoy of Wounded was
coming in and the nurses were running down to meet them. It had
been very quiet and black.

The door opened and, visible in the light from the corridor a
round man stumped into the room. He wore an immense high-
crowned hat and appeared to have on a Tommy's tunic over a
couple of bolsters. His lungs rattled extremely audibly and he
exclaimed with an expression of deep disgust:

'Hour caows 'as better 'ouses hin Horsetrylier!?'[23]

Morton was very irritated. He imagined that they had put a
Tommy into his cubicle with him. There was no knowing what
they would be doing next. Then anguish came to him at the
thought that we must have been losing horribly heavily. The Huns
must have got through or there would have been no need to put
a Tommy in with an officer. Sweat stood out all over him; he began
to question the wheezing man, but he got no news; the man had
only come from Abbeville. There was nothing doing there.

He turned out to be an Australian Infantry major – but he seemed
to drive away the Huns. At any rate Morton never saw them again.
And he did not remember much until about six o'clock next
evening.

They were giving, at that time, a concert in the Huts that had
been erected in the Quadrangle below his window. – All the
windows of the cubicles faced inwards on the Quadrangle; no
doubt that was to prevent the seminarists of peace time taking
glances at young women in the streets and houses that gave onto
the building. – Strains of drawn out instrumental music poured
upwards in bursts and died down again. No doubt that was when
doors opened or shut.

He lay listening. He wondered why he was not at the Concert?
The MO,[24] or possibly it was Sister Grey, had promised that, if he
went on making progress, he should descend and hear it. But he
hadn't descended. He wondered what he had been doing during
the last twenty two hours. It must be about twenty two hours since
the Australian major had come in...

---

23 Compare 'I Revisit the Riviera', pp. 64–5.
24 Medical Officers.

The Australian Major was snoring heavily in the other bed; it was pretty dark. Morton fell to wondering again why they had not awakened him so that he should go down to the concert. Then he remembered dimly – or rather he remembered vividly – a minute of that morning; just a single minute of light like something seen between the crack of a door. He remembered that he was lying flat with a thermometer in his mouth looking at the Australian major. The Australian major, extremely unshaven and tousled, was leaning upon one elbow, and looking at his breakfast with an expression of intense disgust. Hot rage came over Morton when he heard the Major say: 'Hour 'ens lay HEGGS in Horsetrylier!'

His VAD was standing beside him, silent, her hands dropped before her, one within the other, waiting for the thermometer. And it seemed to Morton that the Australian Officer was complaining of the personal hospitality of his, Morton's VAD. His own personal VAD! It was true that he almost loved his VAD. She was a little faded; tired. She did not cut a hell of a lot of ice in the way of looks; but when she came in and turned over a book on the table at his bedhead to see what he was reading it was as if he were suddenly looking at the angle of an old wall, in the warm sunlight, with wall-flowers and cats' valerian growing out of it. Peace and sunlight and no War!

No WAR! All around him, even there, he could feel the long strain. He couldn't feel that he was really lying down; he seemed to be floating on currents of the war. The transport wagons were crawling on over the heavy roads; crawling; jolting; towards There!... And there, suddenly, the air, the clouds, the fields, the ponds were alive with malignity; the air was threaded with monstrous fragments of flying iron, laced with hissing threads of lead-filled nickel, alive with hatreds and maledictions and strains and murderous vigils and intense listenings. He felt these things were his real preoccupation all the while he lay in his white bed. He belonged to them; so did all the other officers who, generally with unbrushed heads and wearing old army overcoats, looked in at his door. They might have chessboards under their arms; but they did not belong there!

They were beasts being fattened for the slaughter. That was why the Sisters and the MOs looked at them with such impersonal eyes – because they had no more real or personal hold on life than chickens in a farmyard upon whom you looked down and said: 'They are coming on nicely!'

But his own VAD looked at his book to see what he was reading! And she was the most real person there – because she had a name and a home. She was a Miss Wilson and she came frôm Wilmslow – near Liverpool. Or perhaps it was nearer to Manchester! At any rate it was a real place. And she gave him the feeling of an old garden, with old-established plant stocks, and sunlight. And no War! He wondered if this was love! His heart jumped at the thought that this again might be love! He felt immense joy at the thought that it might be love...

He remembered to have felt all these emotions and to have thought all these thoughts whilst he had had the thermometer in his mouth – on the 31 12 16 at 8.0 ack emma.[25] He remembered too that from down there in the Quadrangle, the sound of music had come up. Some sort of instrumentalists finished playing 'My Old Kentucky Home'; then a female voice began to practise: 'Ev'ry Little While!' ....

'For the Concert this evening!' the VAD said, 'If you're good, Mr Morton ....'

She took the thermometer from his mouth; and he remembered nothing more except the strong feeling of pleasure at the tone of her voice when she said: 'Mr Morton'. He had at least an individuality for her ....

'It must,' he said to himself, when his mind again took hold and circumstances irresistibly forced him to go through his biography seriatim from his earliest days, 'it must now still be the 31 12 16; but it is about 6.0 pip emma!'[26]

And he considered that, in his own mental words, there was a bloody big chunk of his life – ten hours – that he would certainly never re-capture.

He had no doubt eaten meals; taken medicine; said things. Possibly things he had said would have influenced Miss Wilson of Wilmslow towards liking or disliking him... But it was just gone. He lay there, nearly in the dark; only the light from the windows of the Huts in the Quadrangle where they were holding the Concert, fell upwards on the ceiling. The Horsetrylain Major from time to time gave out an immense snore from his invisible end of the cubicle. And Morton's head felt clear; his limbs were easy; he was in a light sweat.

25 a.m.
26 p.m.

He knew that the fever had left him; he knew that he was himself again; his normal, natural self. he could afford to think; the thoughts that he then thought would be normal; fitted to be permanent and to influence his permanent life. It was moreover New Year's Eve.

He began, as you might say, to feel himself all over the mind, as a man feels his limbs after a toss from a horse. He wanted to know if his mind was injured anywhere; if there were any permanently painful spots, as there were on his body. For his left wrist wouldn't come right. He had come down on it – off a horse, precisely; in Bécourt Wood when a beastly Naval Howitzer had pooped off almost under the mare's tail. The thing had been so jolly well camouflaged, with rabbit wire and strands of old ivy and rust. Or perhaps it was yellow paint. At any rate he couldn't raise his left thumb so as to make a bridge at billiards. It did not worry him, though the doctors said he never would be able to make a bridge at billiards.

He knew Una Willams [sic] did not play billiards; he had asked her. He couldn't imagine how he had come to ask her – how he had contrived to bring the subject round. But he knew that she did not play billiards. She was not even interested in watching the game. The villa in which she had always lived at Wilmslow near Manchester had not contained a room large enough to hold a billiard table though her father had often wanted to have one because billiards was such good exercise. Her father was a land agent – or an estate agent, perhaps. Miss Wilson had ridden to hounds ....

So there he was; aged ... he could not quite remember his own age; but sound wind and limb, if you excepted the flaw in his wrist bone and whatever injury this show might have done to his lungs; with no doubt a sufficient income, if the War had not fatally depreciated his mother's shares which he would one day inherit and the business of his Uncle Herapath with whom he was in partnership still.

He laughed rather ironically at the thought of what sort of a figure he would present before a solicitor engaged in drawing up settlements on the occasion of his marriage with Una Wilson .... He, Gabriel Morton, was either quite a 'warm' man... or he might be nothing!

Look at his age! He didn't – upon his soul has mind was too unable to attempt figures to let him know whether he was over forty or still in the thirties – he didn't then know whether he would come out of this Show – this hospital – an inactive, plump, wheezing, goggle-eyed man of the dug-out major type, or active, enduring, alert, sober, capable of begetting lovely children. That was probably a toss up.

His father again had left his mother just two thousand a year in gilt-edged securities. His mother had lived in quite great comfort at Tunbridge Wells and had always allowed him four hundred a year, the capital being settled on Gabriel. But what had happened to gilt-edged securities during the War? He hadn't followed them much. Nevertheless, from time to time, his mother had written to him complainingly about the difficulty of living on her income in the comfort to which she was accustomed and which she found necessary. She had had to put down her one-horse brougham and one of her maids. Taxation, too, was terrible and terrifying. Moreover, what revolutions might there not be after the war was finished. And if we lost .... That was all a toss up ....

He then considered his position in the firm of Tredgold, Herapath and Morton – but he did not know what his position in the firm of Tredgold, Herapath and Morton was or would be after the war. For years before 1914 he had been his uncle's partner on probation as you might call it. But both he and his uncle were extra-ordinarily unbusinesslike; nothing like a deed of partnership had ever passed between them and when he had been granted his commission in the early days of 1915 nothing like even a verbal agreement to keep open a place for him had passed between his uncle Herapath and himself. It was very singular, if you came to think of it.

And yet, there it was. His uncle was a splendid, generally smiling uncle, but he treated Morton always as if Gabriel had been a little boy – or rather that seemed to be his attitude to his nephew. It was as if he still looked on Gabriel as if he were the little Westminster boy of twelve over whom he towered whilst he inserted two fingers, smilingly into his waistcoat pocket – his waistcoat had been of black silk with minute blue sprigs! – and extracted a sovereign tip. Morton's first sovereign!

His uncle lived in a large house at Highgate and had a daughter, Olive. So, probably Morton would not be his uncle's heir. But, probably, again, Uncle Herapath would leave the whole of his invested estate to Olive and the business to Gabriel, with perhaps a charge on it in Olive's favour. That might be it – but of course, it mightn't. That too was all a toss up.

So Morton imagined himself going to Miss Wilson's family

solicitor and rehearsing his prospects. He had always had four hundred a year from his mother's estate of two thousand – but he did not know whether his mother would be able or inclined to keep it up after the war. He had had for many years five hundred a year from his uncle as partnership allowance and he could draw a bit extra if he wanted to. But he didn't know whether his uncle would be able or inclined to keep *that* up after the war. Unbusinesslike!

Yes, Morton had always been extraordinarily unbusinesslike. He practically never looked at his own pass-book; he went from time to time to his bank and asked what his balance was. He kept no personal accounts and he generally had a fairly large sum owing to one tradesman or another. Now and then he had been in the habit of trying to get all his bills together and pay them off with an extra cheque from the firm – but bills always cropped up afterwards. And his uncle was just the same. Morton knew for a certainty that Uncle Herapath had not the least idea – to within a thousand or so at any rate – of what his personal income might be. He spent a good deal on his establishment and on Olive and there was always money to draw on and usually a tidy bit at the end of the year to invest and interests came in from those investments – which were always prudent and usually very profitable. He did not suppose that his uncle had ever dropped a hundred – at any rate until the War came.

'An extraordinary position!' Morton said to himself as he lay there in the nearly dark cubicle. The instrumentalists muted and sweetened by distance were playing, rather slowly the part of the air that goes to the words:

> 'So pack your grip and we'll take a trip
> To the little one horse town...'

Or that was as near the words as he could come.

But he knew that it was not an extraordinary position, that of his uncle and himself. They were like the country when war came – they had great resources; they knew that they had great resources and they knew that they lived well within them. They didn't speculate; they lived well. For the rest they were too tired of businesses to attend to their own when the ends of the days came round. They were tired of other people's businesses. They went through endless figures and figures; they gave sound, severe, even Rhadamantine, advice to firms of all kinds. They censured – and they were dreaded when they censured – the slightest tendency towards wild cat finances of Limited Companies to which they

stood as surgeons or physicians. They were capable of advising
Bankers, Discount Houses, Mining Companies, Shipping
Companies, firms of Solicitors or Departmental Stores. But when
they went home at night – Mr Herapath to Highgate and Morton
to his flat in Whitehall Court – the idea of figures became painful
to them. They knew that the books of their own firm were all right
for they had them checked twice a year by a friend who was also
a Chartered Accountant. It was common, public honesty to have
their business books checked – but there it ended. They knew that,
between them, they might have spent say five thousand a year, or
say, six; or a little more. And they knew that between them they
did not spend four, if so much. Possibly, by rigid scrutinising of
tradesman's books, they might have saved a couple of hundred a
year – but it was not worth the trouble. Because it would have been
Work – the usual work of the day.

So, just as Solicitors are bad at making their own wills and just
as Authors are extraordinarily bad at answering letters, Herapath
and Morton were absolutely neglectful of their Accounts and their
personal agreements. Morton had always felt in his bones that he
would have nine hundred a year whilst he was a bachelor; that he
would draw a little more if he married; that he would have another
sixteen hundred a year when his mother died; perhaps a couple of
thousand in addition when his uncle did. But he was extraordinarily shy of talking business. It affected him as the contemplation
of extreme indecencies affected other men. He *couldn't* have gone
to his uncle – just as his uncle *couldn't* have sent for him – and have
said:

'Look here, about the future of the business ....'

Why, it would have meant talking about what would happen
when his uncle died! It would have been unbearable. His uncle had
not even said, when Morton had joined the army, whether he
intended to continue Morton's allowance – and by a similar almost
fantastic exaggeration of delicacy he had never examined the credit
side of his passbook to see whether his uncle paid that allowance
in to his bank or did not. He knew he had a good balance, but he
had never let his mind rest on the figures.

His expenses in the Army had been extraordinarily small – particularly since he had been in France. He imagined that he lived well
within his army pay; but he never knew what his Army pay really
was. He thought he got 11/6 a day – but there were field allowances
and fuel and light and ration and other allowances which he didn't

know whether he did or didn't get. For instance, he was then in hospital; what, in consequence, did the paymaster stop? He didn't know. He knew that his mess account – his battalion messed by companies – his mess account averaged three francs a day. He was his Coy's PMC,[27] that was why he knew that – and he knew that his Coy officers were very satisfied with his exertions as PMC. He knew that they boasted about 'old Morton's' economies and managements to the officers of 'B', 'C' and 'D' Coys and to the officers of other Battalions where messing would cost as much as 7frs 50 a day, in the line and out. He remembered a great many quiet rides over fields far away from great main roads – fields where there was none of the soiling of khaki and over which no Archies[28] pooping off at planes dropped showers of heavy invisible things like raindrops that left no marks of wet – to farmhouses where old men and active women laboured in tranquillity and had geese for sale and vegetables that they would dig up out of hidden clamps and give away for nothing to the 'Angleesh Of cer' who spoke to them slowly, gently and persuasively in their own tongue. He remembered these excursions with real pleasure; they were like oases in a weary life ....

Weary!... Yes, he was dog-tired; he was dog-tired then, after a month in bed. For he had worked himself out. No-one had thanked him for it; no-one would every thank him for it. Yet, for months on end he had never known a moment's rest; he had been always on the go, doing as often as not, other people's work. His Coy pay and mess books were the best in the Bn, in the Brigade, in the Division – yet he certainly was not the Coy QMS.[29] He wasn't even the OC Coy[30] – except that he was generally acting OC Coy without the pay or the kudos. Worked out ... and generally with doing other people's work. And he would not ever even get a Coy – because he was always getting up against his CO. He had defended at a Court Martial, on his first getting attached to the Bn., two officers that the CO, a jaundiced, nervous, thin man, too elderly for the job, had set his heart on getting rid of. It wasn't really Morton's job to defend the fellows; he hardly knew them; they were rowdy and profane and certainly liked hooch; the Bn would

27 Company's President of Mess Committee.
28 Anti-aircraft guns.
29 Company Quartermaster Sergeant.
30 Officer Commanding the Company.

have been better without them – the Army too, probably. But a boy who admired them for their swank – and Morton for his quietude – had worried Morton into getting them off. It hadn't been a difficult job, though it had meant a lot of reading up in King's Regs and the MML[31] because he liked anything he did to be letter perfect. So he read the rules of Procedure over and over again – for hours and hours in a wet dug out. It had not been in the least necessary. A Court really likes a Prisoner's Friend quite as well if he isn't extremely up in the RP – because a Court, being human and usually benevolent, likes giving a Prisoner's Friend kindly advice, particularly if he is quiet and of gentlemanly appearance. Morton was both. So he managed to shut up the Adjutant who was prosecuting, over and over again, by means of objections. The Adjutant, indeed, could hardly open his mouth without making a technical mistake. Practically all the evidence he brought was hearsay and badly elicited. The offence was that of being asleep in huts at 11.30 ack emma on the day of a GOC's parade and the CO had ordered the Adjutant to produce as much evidence as possible of the previously unsatisfactory exploits and alcoholism of the two prisoners. Morton, on the other hand, had a strong card in the fact that the two officers' batman whom they shared had been killed on the Amiens road the night before by a RAF automobile so that he had not been there to waken the two officers – and he made it fairly plain to the court that the CO's proper course would have been to send in to Brigade an unfavourable report on the two officers instead of trying to break them altogether. So they got off and were transferred to other Bns.

It didn't do Morton any good. It gave him a certain notoriety in the Bn; it got him called 'old Morton' by the young officers who came to him incessantly, after that, to get them out of scrapes over cheques, women, absences and to wangle leave for them. It also got him into quite bad odour with the CO – whose jaundiced, slightly unbalanced mind conceived the idea that Morton was one of that type of older man who sympathised with drunkenness and disorder and whoring. He said as much to Morton one day after Bn Orderly Room in the School Room at Pont de Nieppe. He said he should keep his eye on Morton.

It did not worry Morton, for immediately after the CO had gone on to the Kitchen of the Brewery where HQ mess was established

---

31 King's Regulations and the Manual of Military Law.

the Adjutant had said to him: 'You see, old bean, what comes of
shutting my clumsy old jaw over those two perishing squits. You
may be a damn brainy ol' bird, but you'd have been in a soft mug's
job with the gilded ones before now if you hadn't been so
highbrow. Now you never will. See Sonny?'

Morton didn't care, as he would have said, such a Hell of a lot.
The last thing he wanted was a staff job unless it had been one with
a lot of riding. He was afraid of his liver more than of most things
– still it irritated him to think that old Judas, as the CO was called
in Mess, had put up a bad mark against him to brigade. A week
after the CO nearly got him – or he got the CO, if you like.

The Division was moved up next day into the Salient[32] and the
Bn went in, rather hurriedly, to relieve a Bn of the Wiltshires who
had been badly wiped out by a misfortune with gas – the affair was
not made very plain to any one in those regions, only there were
hysterical injunctions to Bns to attend to gasdrill in Divisional
Orders for the next ten days and the men were driven into a state
of sulky disgust by having to put on and pull off their gas helmets
all day long and by having to spend hours over changing helmets
that they did not believe were defective. Anyhow, there the Bn
was in the line, all right.

They were bad trenches, but it was a quiet sector – or it had been
for a month or two – nearly opposite Wytschaete; so the Division
got busy. The parapets were only sandbags and there was no parados
– which made it nasty if anything burst behind you. The outgoing
Division said you couldn't dig because you found lots of water –
however this Division was a digging Division and they began to
dig. They found lots of water at a foot under the ground.

Then the Division took to wanting samples of Hun wire.
Morton was deputed to get a sample. He went over on a gusty,
rainy October night, having with him a corporal and two men,
each of whom carried six Mills bombs and their rifles; he himself
had four and two revolvers and a new trench knife that a young
Lewis insisted on lending him. It was a long journey to the German
wire – a quarter of a mile, say – but things were quiet. That in a
way made it seem a longer job, because there was little to take off
the attention and you had to hold your breath. On the whole
Morton liked that sort of thing better than most other jobs .... It

---

32 The 9th battalion of the Welch regiment was stationed in the Ypres Salient near Kemmel
   Hill when Ford rejoined it in August 1916 after his recovery from concussion.

was like hunting; there was a definite quarry, the little bit of wire.
When the rain held up he could feel his three men creeping beside
him; they were intent; interested with a breathless interest; they
lifted up their heads to the full lengths of their necks to get a view
of a foot or two more of ground in profile. It was extraordinary the
feeling he had towards those three men. He was the father to whom
they came for advice; he was taking his three tiny, toddling boys
out for a walk on a dangerous cliff. He had to say – in whispers –
'Don't run there.' They appealed to him for advice as if he were
infinitely wise. Yet they were dirty swabs with blackened faces
whom nevertheless he had to bear on the palms of his hands as if
they had been thin-shelled eggs. It was breathless anxiety.

It was pride; it was responsibility; it was unity; it was love! And
what worried him excessively was the apprehension that never left
him – that he would put his hand, when he was creeping, into
something nasty. Once, on the high land behind La Boiselle he had
dropped on his hands and knees amongst the six-foot high, dusty
thistles, to avoid the burst of a shrapnel shell – and he had stuck his
hand right into a dead, putrid, Hun's ribs. He didn't want to do it
again – in the dark. It was very dark; the rain stopped; it was extraordinarily still. There did not seem to have been a sound for hours
since a machine gun, to the right, had stopped some slumberous
ejaculations like snores. But when he looked at the watch on his
wrist only two minutes had gone by since then. He jumped to his
feet and said: 'Hell! Oh Hell!' and his heart beat fifty to the minute
and he felt sick. It was because there had been a loud rustle just
under his invisible left hand. A bird had got up from a tuft in the
darkness and fluttered away. He caught a glimpse of it against the
pale sky – for there were some Very lights going up sleepily away
towards Messines and in consequence there was a pale glow on the
sky in that direction. You could see a bird; you could recognise the
form – like the lower half of an iron cross. It had been a skylark.
What the devil was a skylark doing there; frightening you out of
your wits.[33]

He wasn't in the least conscious, otherwise, of fear. That was the
odd thing. Early on, he would have calculated the chances of
stopping something – seventy to one against HE[34] bits; sixty to one
against shrapnel; less or more against a rifle bullet. But he had got

33 The episode was reworked into *A Man Could Stand Up* –, pp. 66–7.
34 High Explosive.

out of that habit. He would have said that he was feeling nothing
– nothing more than if he had been sitting on top of a bus in
Kensington High Street. Yet the skylark had frightened him out of
his wits; there must be something stretched taut inside his mind.
And he was rather desolate.

He was rather desolate because he did not much like his
Battalion. When he had gone forward to the German wire and back
to the British trenches, it wouldn't be like going home; there
wouldn't be any couchy feeling. It wasn't his own Bn; he was only
attached.[35] He didn't know the fellows in the mess well and they
were not his sort, much. Too much hooch! And no mess manners
to speak of. Ah well...

He congratulated himself on the steadiness and the luminosity
of the spirit compass that had reached him from Blighty the day
before. It was a real luxury, like Turkish baths and saddle-bag chairs.
The little fillet of bluish white below his nose hardly swayed; the
figures glowed with a friendly and consoling light. Consoling – it
was as if his compass had very superior mess manners; it would be
a companion. When the Bn. Intelligence Officer dropped every H
in his head and talked about the street girls of Oswestry Morton
would be able to think of his superior compass. He would have
good company, *somewhere*, to fall back on.

His thoughts went on thinking themselves – and he let them
frisk irresponsibly. He could let them, he imagined for about ten
or twelve minutes when they ought to reach the shell-hole from
which he intended to operate. He was a very careful officer – he
had spent hours that day with a telescope poked through a loophole
in the sandbag parapet, studying the track about five yards wide that
he would have to take his men along – an imaginary track. He had
not only seen and selected a shell hole, the further edge of which
went right under a new Hun apron of wire; he had made a little,
squared map of his whole imaginary track. He had marked little
landmarks – three very old bully beef tins, a broken wheel... He
had missed the tins – but his right foot just then caught in the old
wheel! He felt great pride and tranquillity. He was all right. He was
a careful officer. The three men were right in looking up to him.
He would bring them through alive, all right.

His mind – which always worked in double pictures – gave him

---

35 Ford was in the 3rd Battalion of the Welch regiment, but was attached to the 9th while
   in the battle of the Somme and the Ypres Salient.

at once a double picture. He seemed to see the desolate, dry, tufted untidy grass, rendered more desolate and untidy by the wire – as he had watched it for so long through his telescope that day. It seemed to blaze with the light of the October Flemish sun; and the tins; and the old wheel and the two wooden posts of the Hun wire under which he was going to creep. And at the same time he had an image of that piece of No Man's Land like a stretch – a hand-kerchief square – of black satin over which there crawled, with delaying pauses, four brown ants... But it was an easy job. His Coy Officers had said they didn't envy him it. They said a Hun strafe was about due. Brother Jerry hadn't done anything since he had strafed the Wiltshires about five days before. It was about time they did something; Morton would look pretty silly if they put up a barrage whilst he was on his belly under the Hun wire. One particularly odious subaltern, a quack dentist in civil life, with bad adenoids and a snuffle had said: 'Pore ol' Morton! You're too old for these b—y jobs. They ought to make you an RTO,[36] down the line, pore ol' b——r!' It seemed to him rather infamous that he should have to be exposed to – should have now to go back to – such a perishing squit. But he was shewing them.

His right hand, pushed forward, went suddenly down; at first into nothing, then against wet clay. They had come to the shell hole – a pretty big one. There was a lot of water in the bottom of it.

His mind suddenly ceased its wanderings. He had to be sharply professional now. It was beastly dark; but there was just a feeling of a blue-black shadow, half[-]right, not against the sky, but against the loom of Wytschaete Hill. That would be one of the wire-supports. If he halted his men ... And then a vexatious thought came to him. All the morning he had been meaning to ask the L/cpl[37] detailed to him whether he was any good with wire-cutters. He himself was not very good with his hands. And he had clean forgotten to ask the L/cpl! He couldn't do it now; it would be too complicated a thing to ask; it would mean too much whispering. He would have to cut it himself – and he hated cutting wire.

The L/cpl gripped his shoulder:

'Gawd, sir!' he whispered into Morton's ear. 'What's that noise? What the 'ell's that noise?'

A sound like a portentous, prolonged and continuing cough

---

36 Railway Transport Officer.
37 Lance-Corporal.

from a very rattling chest, was coming from in front – it was obviously made by the invisible enemy. A new Hun stunt! Morton could feel L/cpl Meggett's hand tremble on his shoulder. In those days they were desperately afraid of new Hun stunts – things that would annihilate you from unsuspected and unimaginable directions. And indeed, even to Morton, the thought of minds working away, just a few yards off – working, working, working, the little thoughts running around in the industrious and tensely malignant minds – the thought was queer and exciting.

He whispered back:

'It's a saw. A big two-handed saw. They're sawing something.' And he could hear the corporal whisper:

'Orfcer ses its a saw. A big saw. They're sawing something!'

And a deep sigh – of relief. And the words: 'Gorblimey! Sawin! Whatter they sawin'?'

It was to Morton an inexpressible relief. The idiotically loud noise was like an answer to his prayers. The silence had been, as he then realised, a blessing to his nerves – but the noise would save their lives. He could whisper to the corporal. Moreover it resolved a doubt – a fear that he now realised he had had all the time. It meant that the Hun wouldn't be putting up any strafe that night – at any rate not from those trenches. If they had been going to they wouldn't be sawing; every man would be preparing. So again, Providence was with him.

He whispered to the corporal:

'Have you got the gloves and the wire-cutter? Give them over?' And the corporal whispered back:

'You going to cut the wire, sir?' – and Morton felt infinite pleasure in the absolute reliance that man's voice betrayed. He answered:

'Yes ....You three stay here, just inside the lip of the hole. Don't go too deep. You're covered enough unless they dropped a Very Light on to you and saw you. And you don't want to get wet through ....'

The machine gun to the right started wukka-wukka-ing but this time another answered it. Morton was crawling on the ground round the top of the shell-hole – it was a matter of thirty yards to the outside of the wire. More machine guns began to come in. A solitary rifle bullet whirred over his head with a long sound like a hurrying and insistent bee; another followed it. He was glad that he had told his men to keep down in the shell hole. Noise was also beginning – and he was glad of that – the usual senseless noise of someone getting the wind up. It came into his mind that, strictly speaking, he ought to have taken one of the men along with him in case something happened to him. It was at any rate a technical mistake. But he did not think anything was going to happen to him; he felt safe under the mantle of sound. What he most wanted to avoid was going down into the water of the shell hole; he would hate the sudden feel of the deathly chill on his skin. He was trying to keep along the edge of the hole so as to be above the water.

The senseless noise grew into a tremendous thing. There seemed to be a hundred machine guns at it; then the eighteen pounders woke up; shells with high notes went overhead. He knew the whole programme; he recognised it with a sense of boredom; his mind seemed to see the whole country like a map. Some old Hun had got the wind up in the imagination of a non-existent raid; had pooped off with machine guns. Our machine gunners answered; then some infantry Bn asked the RFA[38] chaps to silence the Hun machine guns. So the 18 pounders woke up. Then the Germans would put on something heavyish to shut up the 18 pounder – and there, sure enough they came, the 4.2 shells that seemed to be intending to say 'WE...ARY', until, a long time afterwards they changed their minds and said 'WHACK'! And indeed that type of shell always appeared to him to be tired – as if indeed, they resented the fact that the time for their last journey had arrived and as if they resented their unwilling disintegration when they fell.

And then, sure enough, the really heavy pieces on the top of Kemmel Hill, or near it, spoke with endless reverberations all through the woods. They woke up to silence the German heavies; and great shells went over, slowly, with intermittent changes of note, like immense, bass singers whose voices had a tremolo. At last it was as if half a dozen immense trains were going together through the night a hundred feet up. The usual strafe. Old Brother Boche would be shut up in a minute or two. They never could stand the real heavies. Nothing could.

The earth seemed to shake; the air to be riven; an immense torrent of rain began to fall and continued for the rest of the night. Morton got to the wire – and that was all that Morton remembered, in that acute way. The rest was sketchy.

---

38 Royal Field Artillery.

IV

That curious quality of his mind was always a cause of speculation to Morton. He would wonder if his mind differed in its action from that of other men – but he never had the courage to ask other men. He never had the courage because he suspected that it might mean that he was a little mad – it might be a symptom of brain disease; so that if he revealed it by questions to others it might be put about that he had queer brain symptoms. Besides, at present, any sort of questions to his brother officers as to introspections wouldn't be good for him. If they did not think him mad they would certainly think him highbrow to the very verge of effeminacy. The most you could afford to say as to your mental state was that you had got the wind up like Hell. You could say that to any extent; indeed it was an assertion of courage to be able to say with extravagant emphasis that you *had* got the wind frightfully up on occasions. It meant you had been in the devil of a tight place.

But that was no help to Morton – because when he did get the wind up it was always in circumstances of comparative safety. He had been horribly frightened by the skylark; and, if the saw had not frightened him as it had frightened the men, that was only by a happy coincidence. For, once, about a month before on the road from Locre to La Clyte, well behind the line, he had been frightened out of his skin – by a machine saw that suddenly began to squeal, while he was going to the Divisional Follies in the little town. It had been a sunny afternoon and the machine saw was in the RE[39] dump just beside the road – but for two seconds he had the most incredible panic. He would have thrown himself down on the road – for he had had just the idea that thousands of men had there at that date. The Boche had got hold of some new and devilish engine of annihilation – and if he did not throw himself down on the road it was because death might just as well be coming up through the earth, or along the ground as from the sky. Yes, he had got the wind up then ....

But, in tight places, as he figured it out, he generally had too much to do to attend to his thoughts – and as he was slow and methodical in his duties they generally occupied him longer than other men. That was probably it. So that, on the whole, as he lay there on that New Year's Eve, in the dark, in the cubicle of No II

---

39 Royal Engineers.

Red Cross, he thought rather comfortingly that he had got hold of a theory that would account for the queer way his mind worked. It wasn't incipient madness – it was just that his brain didn't lay hold of thoughts or landscapes when he had something to do. It was particularly like that during the war. He had seen quite a deal of active service; he had certainly seen an immense number of queer things; huge engines; great catastrophes; hideous wounds; a good deal of death. But it was only queer, longish stretches of incident that were really vivid in his mind. He lay there thinking...

Of course it was not only the War that had [a]ffected him like that; the whole episode of Hilda, which had been the agony and the ruin of his life, just before the war, came back to him horribly as he lay there – but only in just such patches. And those patches of memory did not record especially agonising incidents. For instance: once she had parted from him outside the Marble Arch Tube Station. She had got into a taxi and whilst she told the driver to take her to Holborn Circus the driver had pulled down his flag. Morton remembered the ting of the little taximeter bell and the action of the taxi-driver's arm more vividly than he remembered anything of the frightful interview in the park that had preceded their parting. It was as if the bell hit him ....

That was no doubt because, during the whole of the interview he had been talking – talking madly. In those days, before the war, he remembered, talking was the only form of action that was open to a man. And he didn't remember a word of what he had said – any more than he could remember how he cut the wire. Of the interview he had no more than a sense that he had leaned forward, on a penny chair, on the grass and talked and talked, whilst desultory people walked before them over the expanse of grass and that Hilda had sat, rather rigid, like a Gothic Saint with fair, thin features and an unchanging, silent, and enigmatic smile. In just the same way, of actually cutting the wire, he only had a general sense of wetness, noise, laboured breathing – and elation. Yet, while he lay there, listening to the sugary orchestra sending up drawn out chords – and to the snoring of the Australian major – who was a grocer from Sydney in private life – he could not for the life of him remember anything of how he had actually cut the wire. Yet he had undoubtedly cut it. He had reported to the Adjutant that morning before stand-to with two specimens. He remembered the Adjutant's interest in them – for one piece – a sort of guide rope of twisted wire, like a cable, had been the first specimen of the kind they had

seen. Its obvious use was to keep strands of barbed wire, cut by
shrapnel or HE, together in a very arresting tangle. It had been
looped not very tightly down the centre of the Boche apron –
which, except for the two wooden supports had seemed very much
like one of our own.

The Adjutant, a little, pleasant, rather Jewy man, had looked
down at the specimen of cable in his hand and said:

'You must have had a job to cut that. Cut it yourself? Guess you
didn't do it with the bally old bayonet fixture? Any sign of electri-
fication?'

Morton replied that he hadn't thought much about it at the time;
but he couldn't remember any sign of electricity. He was pretty
sure there wasn't any. He had been using the new insulated cutters.
The Adjutant said: 'Good for you, old bean!' and Morton had felt
pleased with himself. The Adjutant began to shave.

That was the queer thing – that he couldn't remember anything
of how he had cut the thick cable – or of how they had got back.
He remembered that he *had* taken one of the men's rifles with the
old fashioned cutting attachments, like a fork attached to the
bayonet. But it had been no use at all for securing a specimen of
wire. If you jabbed with it it cut the wire, but you lost the end. He
had had to drop it and find it again when he went back to the men.
It had been rather a bother. He had forgotten finding it – but he
remembered the bother. And he remembered restoring his rifle to
Private Cedara, because he was just putting it into Private Cedara's
hand, as he lay just at the top of the shell-hole when he saw the
Huns.

They were within five yards of the edge of the shell-hole – six
of them, bunched together and all in profile, standing still, looking
at something up the valley. There were several Very lights going
up behind their own trench, and there was one star-shell over
Mount Kemmel – and against the light the six Huns looked excessively mournful, reflective, silhouettes.

They just stood, looking at something. And whilst Morton could
feel private Cedara's elbow as he fumbled in his pocket, no doubt
for a bomb, it struck him that the six Huns with their iron helmets,
looked exactly like a Duerer etching of mediaeval Lansknechts.[40]
Exactly! They remained motionless, their helmets were like iron
hoods – it was the first time Morton had seen the new Boche tin-

---

40 A *Landsknecht* was a mercenary or hired soldier.

hat – like iron hoods, arching up over the eyes, with an angle above the brow, and a curved place that sheltered the neck. Mediaeval! That was what they were – whereas our things were like shallow vegetable dishes.

The Lance Corporal whispered in his ear: 'Shall we kill the b—rs?'; and Morton remembered answering, like a flash, as if his subconscious mind had worked for him:

'No, our job is to get the specimens back. Take your first pressures and mark a Hun each; but don't fire unless they come towards us. No bombs; the rifle's better.'

That had been his undoing.

And, yet, consider the matter how he would, he could not see that he had done the wrong thing. If he had bombed the Huns or fired – they were within forty yards of the Hun trench. They would have been machine-gunned and trench-mortared out of existence in two seconds. And he considered that the specimens of wire and the lives of three men were more valuable to the Intelligence than the mere lives of six Huns. They wouldn't have been able to rifle the bodies for papers. Besides the Huns carried no papers on raids at that date. They were too precious slim. And Morton, though he was a footslogger, valued a new piece of matter for the Intelligence more highly than the life of a Hun or two. So the lights had faded out and the mediaeval silhouettes, with the rifles and fixed bayonets at bad slopes, had wandered unharmed down the valley.

'Damned cowardice!', the CO had called it, and he added that he was humiliated or mortified or something of the sort that an officer of his should have exhibited such damned cowardice.

He had to take the words back, of course, but that had not helped matters much! He always had his confidential reports to fall back on.

For two or three days Morton had felt elated; he had done all right. But then Williams, the quack dentist, had said to him: 'Pore ol' Morton. The CO's got it for you that you didn't kill those Boches.' Next day little Lewis had said: 'Old Judas doesn't like you a bit, old dear. But don't you mind!'

It had annoyed him, but not much. Two days later the Adjutant had sent down a chit to say that the CO wanted to see Morton at once, at Battalion Headquarters. Morton was in a bit of a rage. He had to wait ten minutes in the HQ Mess; Major Hill, a comfortable, baldheaded bonvivant, with a round stomach was reading *La*

Vie Parisienne. He said, 'Hello, Morton' and, about five minutes later: 'He saved others; himself he could not save!'

Morton took that to mean that the Major had observed his efforts to keep subalterns on the right path; he was pleased on the whole. He imagined that he did not care twopence about the Colonel.

Colonel Littleboy was an Eastbourne Town Councillor. He was thin, too nervous, getting on for fifty with a greyish brown, very wrinkled skin and a very prominent Adam's apple that he appeared to be making violent efforts to swallow. He was sitting behind a kitchen table covered with a blanket in a bare room of the château. Slightly in front of him stood the little, friendly Jewy Adjutant called McGrigor. Morton was standing at a very stiff Attention in front of him.

The CO cleared his throat, looked at Morton for a moment with eyes that Morton took to be yellowish, and then looked away.

'Mr Morton,' he said, 'I understand that you went cutting German wire on Thursday night. You obtained specimens?'

Morton did not speak. He saw nothing to say.

'You obtained specimens?' the Colonel repeated. 'You should answer when you are asked a question.'

Morton answered:

'I did not know it was a question. I obtained specimens, sir.'

The Colonel looked at his thin, nervous, very brown hand.

'What occurred?' he asked.

'I cut four pieces of wire and brought them back without casualties.'

'I know there were no casualties,' the Colonel said. 'You cut the wire yourself... with your own hands. You did not take a man forward with you?'

Morton began:

'It might have been a dangerous job, sir ....'

The Colonel repeated:

'You did not take a man forward with you?'

Morton answered that he had not. Then it came.

'I understand – you told Captain McGrigor – that whilst returning you saw six Germans and you did not attack them?'

Morton looked at McGrigor who was looking at him with an expression Morton could not understand. It would have pleased Morton to be able to understand; McGrigor was evidently trying to telephone some message with his large dark eyes. A rat came out of a hole in the corner under the dusty window; it ran round apparently without direction. Nothing happened. Morton did not speak. He had nothing to say.

'I wish you would answer,' the Colonel said impatiently.

'You made a statement, sir,' Morton said, 'I do not wish to comment on it.'

The Colonel never looked up.

'You agree then that, on your return, you saw six Germans whom you did not attack?'

'It was not during our return, sir,' Morton said, 'It was before we had started.'

'It is a distinction without a difference,' the Colonel said. Morton answered listlessly that there was a difference; they were in a shellhole, under the German wire; at most thirty yards from the German parapet. He hadn't any image at all in his mind. He knew that what he was saying was true – but it was rather as if he had read of his own actions in a police report. He could see the six Huns, looking up the valley, all right. The CO looked up at him, balefully. His eyes were certainly yellow. Morton knew that the time had come when the CO was trying to beat down his glance. He looked into the Colonel's glance, as if he were looking down a searchlight, whilst he counted seven. Then he looked respectfully at his own boot. He wished to indicate that he was not ashamed and at the same time to show that he knew that a Colonel in his Orderly Room is entitled to the respect due to a God. He hoped he had succeeded ....

He heard the Colonel's voice say:

'I never thought to live to see the day when an officer of mine would fail to attack the enemy when he saw them!'

Morton continued to look at his boot. He noticed with annoyance that there was a tiny crack beside the toecap under the dried mud.

'I don't understand, Mr Morton,' the Colonel said, 'Wherever I come upon you you are unsatisfactory... It, it it .. worries me... I expect my officers...' His voice grated. Morton could not help looking up. The Colonel looked down. Morton would have liked to ask him what instances he could give of his unsatisfactory behaviour. It interested him. He knew that his behaviour had been perfectly satisfactory. It was interesting. The rat ran down the hole, his tail in the air. It was a very old rat. Morton was tired of standing. But he rather liked to be there and to hear the Colonel; he didn't want the interview in the bare room to end by any means; but he would have liked to sit down.

'There are always these troubles with you, Mr Morton,' the CO went on fumbling. 'Always. Why didn't you take a soldier with you when you went forward. You know it is in King's Regs. Haven't you read King's Regs. Just answer me that...' He stuttered for a second. And then he brought out the words 'D...Damned cowardice!'

He struck the kitchen table with the thin hand that he had clenched.

It came suddenly and ridiculously into Morton's mind that Colonel Littleboy, DSO – he was familiarly known as Judas in the mess – must be dressed in black velvet and have at his side a very long, thin rapier, with a cut steel hilt. He couldn't at the time think why this should have come into his head – he was respectfully looking at his other boot – but that was it; black velvet and a long, thin rapier! And the name Alessandro Farnesi, Duca di Parma...

'Damned cowardice!' the Colonel repeated.

Morton was suddenly glad that the CO had plucked up the courage to say that – it seemed to give him, Morton, his chance. He drew a deep breath of relief, but he did not say anything. The CO was a desperately pushing Bn Commander; he was always volunteering to shove his Bn in. He would have wanted Morton to bring the specimens in *and* kill the six Germans; he wanted advertisement for the Bn. He did not care much about the Army; it was the Bn; *his* Bn! But Morton was more interested in the Army. The Army needed the piece of cable for its information; the Bn could do without that little piece of advertisement. Besides, it couldn't have been done! Nobody in the world could have killed those Germans with the mediaeval hats and have brought back the specimens and the men. That was an end of that.

The Colonel was nagging on; he repeated the word cowardice several times. He was, Morton was quite aware, trying to affirm himself in his own mind, by the repetition. It was a serious step to take. And Morton felt that, if he had been one of Col. Littleboy's own Bn. instead of being merely attached to it, Col. Littleboy would have got his advertisement by sending in the specimens with a memo calling attention to the specially difficult nature of the enterprise and to the skill and tact of the officer who had conducted [it] in a terrain swarming with Germans. And Morton was quite aware that Col. Littleboy was aware that he knew this. Therefore Col. Littleboy was trying to browbeat him into non-resistance. So he continued to look at his boot. As long as he did that the CO could not tell what he was feeling – and he would get the wind up...

The little Adjutant, standing with his hands clasped before him gave a little cough. He might have been merely clearing his throat – but the CO jumped. He hesitated for a moment and then gladly picked up the idea that Morton had committed a serious offence by not taking a man with him when he went forward: 'You might have been seriously wounded in the wire. All the men might have been killed in trying to extricate you and so your mission would have been frustrated. I suppose you were trying to curry favour with the men; but let me tell you that the men do not respect that sort of thing... You expect to make yourself popular with the Bn. at the expense of me, very possibly. I don't know. It's possible. But don't you know that an officer's life is the property of HM the King. It's not your own, do you understand? Your duty was to obtain the specimen; you hadn't any other duty. Haven't you had sufficient experience as an officer to know that? How much service have you? Who was responsible for training you, I should like to know? It wasn't I. You ought to know better than to risk your life in such foolhardy exploits .... You understand; I will have an end of the insubordination in the Bn. It has got to be put a stop to. I will not be made a laughing stock. If I do not find some sort of amendment in you, Mr Morton I shall...'

He paused.

Morton was very well aware that he was hesitating as to how far he could go. And suddenly he felt sorry for the poor old man. His harangue was mysterious; it was incomprehensible. All that Morton could understand was that the Colonel suspected him of fomenting disorders amongst the younger officers and was trying to frighten him. The Colonel finished:

'I have a good mind to send a report in to Division to the effect that you are an incompetent and undesirable officer unable to control men!'

Morton went out into the HQ Ante Room, where there was an ormolu table covered by a grey Army blanket. On the blanket were two old, pink and yellow copies of the same number of *La Vie Parisienne*, Field Service pocket book and three empty glasses that showed traces of having contained stout. The windows were all broken and there were three deck chairs. In one of them sat Major Hill, whose stomach looked larger than ever. He was now reading a third copy of *La Vie Parisienne*, his face and bald head being hidden by a picture of a lady in blue whose skirts came well over her white and pink knees and who was eloping, in great strides with a young man in a blue tin hat and a spiky moustache. Morton stood in front of the table.

He was so quivering with rage that when he pulled the Field Correspondence Book out of his right pocket the button came off and rolled to the Major's feet. His breath was snorting through his nostrils. He knelt down at the table and began to write with care a memo to the Adjutant. He still had the copy in the flap under the cover. He wrote:

'Sir, I have the honour to request that you will lay before the CO ....'

Major Hill was looking down, past his shining leggings, at Morton's button. He gazed quizzically through an eyeglass and his bald head shone like his boots.

'You'll want this,' he said, and he pushed the button with his boot tip. 'Himself he could not save? Eh?' he chuckled.

'To hell can't I?' Morton snorted. He wrote on:

'This my application to be taken before the Brigadier commanding the —th Brigade with reference to the charge of cowardice in action attributed to me at 11.45 ack emma this 17 9 16 by the CO ....' and so on.

Major Hill, the second in command, was reputed in the Mess to be the laziest man in the BEF[41] in France. Seconds in Command as a rule do little, Major Hill did nothing. Colonel Littleboy would see to everything himself. He said:

'Cheer up my boy, it's all in the day's journey.'

'It's a little outside the journey,' Morton answered. He finished writing and stood up. The Adjutant came in. He looked at Morton as if he were shy, then he looked away.

'The CO says' – He stuttered a little, 'You'd better stay to lunch. The Bn will be coming out this afternoon, so you can take the rest of the day off.'

'I can't,' Morton answered between his teeth.

'I say,' McGrigor uttered painfully. 'I say...'

Morton who had been standing side face half-turned violently towards the little man with the large eyes.

'Do you mean,' he said from his chest, 'That I'm not to go back to the trenches. Is that the CO's orders? Orders, you understand?'

---

41 British Expeditionary Force.

'Good God, no,' McGrigor answered. 'Who'd have thought you had such a temper... Such a quiet chap...'

'Well, I have,' Morton answered. 'You may as well take that now...' He held out the fluttering leaf.

Major Hill wiped his bald head with a purple and brown bandana. He leaned over his fat stomach towards Morton.

'My boy,' he said, 'Don't forget that the Ante Room isn't the Orderly Room... A man may strafe you to Hell in the Orderly Room but you've got to drink his wine next minute, you know.'

'Oh, I know,' Morton said... 'Put up some sort of excuse for me,' he directed his words to McGrigor. 'But there isn't time... If the Bn's coming out, you know I can't leave A Coy to old Grogram...'

'No, I suppose you couldn't leave A Coy to old Grogram,' McGrigor said. 'He'd be in a fine old mess... I'll put this before the CO if you wish... But we'll have a talk... We'll have to have a talk... We've always been a friendly Bn...'

'A *damn* friendly Bn,' the Major chuckled. 'Have a drink. We've plenty of whisky.'

Gabriel's rage had hardly subsided in the least. He never really knew himself. He had been perfectly calm; he had been even jocose before the Colonel. He supposed he cared nothing really about the Army and its rewards or abasements. Now he was mad.

He was mad. He was out in the battered street, tearing along down the little slope. Under the battered lamp that hung over the street corner; he noticed a little film of vapour. It was coming out through the broken door of an unroofed cottage. He knew dimly, in his hot rage, what it was; but he went straight through it. It wasn't more than ankle high – more or less. A sharp smarting filled his lungs, but he rushed on. He was coughing and swearing. Half an hour later he had forgotten all about the whole morning. He was helping the Coy QMS to check the Mills Bombs as to which a return was needed before they came out. He ought really to have lain down for twelve hours.

And so the affair fizzled out. It seemed to fizzle out into a period of sunshine and comparative rest, during which he felt not at all up to the mark. He was in a tent most of the time, interested, as much as anything, in the sort of contrivances you have to get together to make a tent comfortable.

It appeared that the Adjutant delivered to the CO Morton's

request to go before the Brigadier. And then, when the whole Bn came out into support at RE farm, on the flank of Mount Kemmel amongst tobacco plants and stubble fields, so that all the officers were together and gossip got fully going, Morton heard that five other officers – and all of them attached officers – had asked to go before the Brigadier after the Colonel had strafed them! It gave him a bit of a shock – quite a shock! He was suddenly sorry for old Judas – the nervous, worrying, worried, lean old man with a too difficult job. For it is a terrible job for an aging man – to command a desperately pushing Bn in the line – there are all the papers and papers and papers, and the responsibility – and the considerable danger. It was really too much, Morton knew, for any one man.

And Morton discovered that, as an older, cool and collected man, he was supposed to be leading this assault on the CO. He understood then, the CO's agitated incomprehensibilities. He was supposed to be trying to get the CO kicked out of his job. Probably it *would* get the CO kicked out of his job; a Division doesn't much like keeping a CO when all his attached officers get up against him. Division generally sees that he gets a bar to his DSO dished out to him – and a snug job at home...Turned down!

And Morton suddenly felt that he did not want the CO to be turned down – over him. It would make a stink against the Bn – and one does not want a stink against one's Bn. It was a jolly good Bn – that was to the CO's credit. It shoved in everywhere... So he said some angry things to Williams, the quack dentist, who was one of the five. Williams approached him in the Officers' Club, the little tin hut under Locre Church, and whispering with titters suggested a plan of action when, one after the other, they went before the brigadier. Each and every one of them should hint that the CO was a bit dotty...

Morton let out at Williams, violently and loudly; he said that Williams was every kind of a squit and that he would rather be damned seven times over by the CO than go to Heaven once with Williams and Beveridge and Troup and Connolly and Devine! Morton was not feeling well that afternoon...

Possibly it got round to McGrigor. Williams would certainly inform Beveridge and Troup and the rest of those blighters... At any rate, when, that evening, the CO 'sent for' Morton the anxious, large eyed little man squeezed Morton's arm affectionately above the elbow.

'Keep your beastly temper, old bean,' he said outside the Orderly

Room door, 'Old Judas isn't such a blighted old Judas as you think.'
He sighed, thinking of all the work he had to do that evening when
most of the rest of them would be going in to Bailleul. It was
curious, the way the CO got out of it.

Morton could not remember many of his words. It was rather
his voice, with the rather snuffling, caressing undertones that came
after his second speech. For he began in his usual way:

'I don't understand, Mr Morton, the mysterious rows that you
always seem ....'

He was looking down at a slip of paper that Morton recognised
as the memo he had written in HQ Ante Room at Kemmel
Château. They were then in a barn to which successive Bns had
added matchboard sides, whitewash on the rafters, and a boarded
floor. The Colonel looked upwards at the thatch which lay direct
on the whitewashed rafters.

'What I wanted to see you about ....' He looked at Morton with
eyes that Morton took to be wary. 'You're looking rather ill...
McGrigor says you're rather ill...'

There was suddenly the long, weary whine of a shell – extraordinarily near, just over the thatch. It went wuk, just over the
hedge... Morton thought, with acute displeasure that he hadn't said
to the Adjutant that he was feeling ill. He wondered if there had
been anything queer in his manner lately. He could not remember
the last day or two very clearly at that moment. The CO said:

'Take a seat Mr Morton, if you are feeling unwell!'

Morton drew himself more rigidly to attention.

'I can stand very well, sir,' he said.

The Adjutant walked to the little window that had been inserted
in the side of the barn and looked out.

Several Tommies and a Belgian peasant were looking at
something on the ground beyond the hedge. The evening sunshine
was very bright – a regular St Martin's summer, Flemish effect.

'Seems to have been a jolly old dud,' the Adjutant said. 'Jolly
lucky it was a jolly old dud!'

The Colonel was saying:

'What I wanted to see you about, Mr Morton is... You know
the language of the country... Well then...' He looked up again up
at the thatch and pointed a thin wristed hand upwards: 'Eh, you
see that thatch... It's getting thin... Water will be coming in... You'd
much oblige me if you'd... well...'

Morton helped him out. The Colonel wanted him to buy some

straw cheaply from a Belgian farmer and find a private in the Bn
who could do the thatching. He said he would do it.

'And... And show a little more devotion to the Bn... Don't let
there be ....'

Morton suddenly remembered his labours for A Coy whose
present OC was known as *old forty foot down and keep on digging*
because he spent twenty three hours of the twenty four in his
dugout. The men said as much every time that Grogram showed
his nose. And Morton exclaimed – it was dragged out of him:

'I don't believe, sir, that you'll find an officer more devoted to
the Bn than I am. Not one. Or to yourself!'

The CO suddenly seemed to become extraordinarily agitated.

'No, no!' he said. 'I believe it. I quite believe it... McGrigor has
reported very favourably on you and "A" Company. I know the
returns are very difficult. And the discipline is excellent... I
know...'

Morton wanted to stop that. He wanted extremely to stop it.

'There's a man called Flaherty,' he said, 'Whose wife is very ill
after confinement...'

The Colonel said:

'Ah, Flaherty; I don't know about him. There's a 25947 Pte Ellis,
I wanted to ask you about? What do you think about your Coy
Sergeant Major, now? McGrigor says he has his knife into Cpl Ellis,
don't you McGrigor?'

They were suddenly in the midst of a discussion of the internal
affairs of 'A' Coy – an intimate and confidential discussion. Then
the Colonel said:

'You know most of the junior officers well... Now tell me. What
about Lt Williams – and Beveridge – and Troup? What sort of
fellows are they? Industrious? Keen? What?'

Morton said that Beveridge and Troup were very good officers.
He had known them very well in Blighty – and here. But he
boggled over the others. He did not want to talk about them.
Devine he didn't know at all – a little nervous boy.

'Good officers, those two, are they?' the Colonel said. He was
very friendly.

'Troup's as brave – as a lion,' Morton said, 'No 4 platoon would
follow him – into Hell. And Beveridge is a very valuable officer...'

The Colonel said:

'Ah, I daresay you know... You're a writer or a painter, aren't
you? A judge of character, I mean...'

'I'm a chartered accountant,' Morton said.

The Colonel said:

'Splendid! Splendid!' It was a great relief to him. 'That explains matters. I believe you're the sort of fellow we want. Plenty of experience...'

He looked at Morton cautiously:

'Look here old man,' he said, 'You're certainly not looking well...'

'I can carry on all right,' Morton answered stubbornly.

'Well, you'd better go into the First Line Transport for two or three weeks. You've earned it...'

Morton said:

'If you please I'm not a noncombatant Officer, sir.'

The Colonel said:

'No, no... I've been talking to McGrigor. You want a rest... It's... it's a reward... I mean... if you understand...' He handed the slip of memo-paper with Morton's writing across the table. 'You'll tear that up... Three or four weeks' rest... The Quarter Master will be sick as long as that... You can act for him... I believe things are in a muddle... His books and things... You'll be splendid...'

Morton understood that the soft job in the First Line Transport was the Colonel's bribe to him. He was to suppress his application to go before the Brigadier. He did not want the job much. But he needed a rest. He felt that he could not keep going much longer. Then he heard the Colonel say, very astonishingly:

'It's a great relief to me... I always thought you were a bit of a Bohemian... I suspected it... You see I know the Cohens. Cohen always said ....'

Morton did not know any more. The sides of the barn looked like floating jelly .... Sketchy... McGrigor gave him a drop of brandy... He could still taste that brandy, in bed at No II...

Because there he was again – in bed at No II Red Cross hospital ....

V

These recollections came to him very vividly, in those patches. He could have sworn to his remembrance of the speeches – he could have written them down, the CO's speeches, the Adjutant's and so on. And they must – these patches of life, have taken an extra-ordinarily short time to live. The orchestra down below had only just finished playing the selection which included 'The Old Kentucky Home'; the applause was still going. Quite long applause: the concert must have been a Godsend to the patients!

He returned to thinking how he stood, in the world, in life – how he would put himself before Miss Una Wilson's solicitors. He wasn't, however, so certain that it was Miss Wilson's solicitors he was really reviewing his situation for. At the back of his mind he was pretty certain he was doing it for Hilda Cohen. He was trying to think how he could make himself glorious and desirable in *her* eyes. She seemed to be like a faded, golden spot, somewhere, always in his consciousness. She seemed to be always in all the landscapes that he remembered – Yes, just a faint, golden glow – somewhere, above a church steeple, in No Man's Land; in among the Very lights on a black sky, like, yes, for all the world like the little stamps in the corners of Japanese prints. Like that ....

That was why he still so intensely disliked the idea of the miserable man who had ruined him – the poor, old CO. For it wasn't any more the person of that old, scrawny man, in ill fitting khaki that he any more disliked. It was the *idea* of him. When he saw Littleboy he did not hate him; he just shuddered when he thought of him.

The CO had been affectionate – yes, affectionate – for the rest of the time Morton had been with the Bn – in the First Line Transport, in the rear, always. The CO would pat him on the arm and say: 'Morton old man. Yes, that's right,' or 'What do you think we ought to do about the horse-standings, old boy'.... But still, it was the CO who had sent him mad about his raid, so that, on the 17 9 16 Morton had walked thro' the waft of gas coming under the door. Otherwise he would never have done that. He knew quite well – a gas shell had pitched into the roofless cottage...

. So that in the result he was condemned to the First Line Transport. And he would never, he was now sure, get any nearer the front line. He might get a staff job – the CO had offered to get him one. But that was the last thing he wanted. *He wanted to have a healthy, gay, son by Hilda Cohen...*

And he was done for – for that. He could get staff jobs – but he wanted to do things in the line. That was what would bring her back to him. He knew that her husband and that other fellow – that fat pig that the taxi had taken her to – laughed at him, to her.

He wanted to shew her .... It was four years since he had seen her. He had worked like the devil...

Even with the Transport he had worked like the devil... At first he had luxuriated in the idea that he would wangle a lot of time. He would – he did really – sit for as much as ten minutes in the sunlight in the opening of his tent, in the great field that leads down from Locre Church. He once went up and sat for half an afternoon on Mont Vedaigne watching the shells make little aligned bursts of white in the shadowy furrows that were the Hun trenches;[42] watching the planes going right away to the Hun border; watching the clouds over the sea by Dunkirk – just loafing in the sun.

But the long pull of the war came back – the restlessness, the anxiety to do his duty and a bit more. There was no longer pleasure in the autumn sunlight; in the lines of willows that you could see marching over Flanders. He began to be riding all day over Belgium – getting things for the men. Very soon he was riding all night, too – the muffled, clinking riding, of taking rations down to the Bn in the line. The Bn Transport Officer was extremely overworked; the Divisional Transport Officer was sick and he had to do his work as well as his own. He and Morton would debate for hours about horse standings. Morton just got hold of a huge quantity of bricks, when the Division were [sic] turned into a flying Division. They were perpetually being jerked here and there. They had to leave the precious bricks to make horse standings for some Australians. It was a bitter moment.

Work became unending; unceasing. It became absolutely necessary to get the late QM's returns right. The QM died in hospital. Morton went on and on; there was always a weary feeling at the bases of his short ribs – as if he had been boxing. His absolutely silent servant – a Yorkshireman – used to bring him camomile tea whenever he came in in the dawn. There would also be a hot brick in his flea-bag.

Then the rains began – incessant rains; incessant plashing and dripping on his tin hat whilst he rode beside the agonised mules pulling the heavy ration wagons in the impossible tracks. Wet all day, wet all night. And then his back broke...

They began to send for him to Divisional HQ to interrogate prisoners. He hated the job; he hated the sight of the Huns; pallid

---

42 For other accounts of the Germans shelling Poperinghe see: Preface to *Their Lives*, 'War and the Mind', *No More Parades*, pp. 308–10, *No Enemy*, pp. 82–7.

beasts like rats dislodged from tunnels. And indeed, at that date they
were mostly deserters. He hated the smell of paraffin from the stoves
in the little wooden cubicles where they had to confront him. The
moisture poured out in steam from his clothes and from theirs...

It was a Hun who really finished him, all right... behind
Armentières, in a hospital tent... There had been some muddle.
The Bn ought to have provided a guard over some prisoners in a
CCS[43] somewhere, two miles or so behind the town of Nieppe.
OR had forgotten or something. They had to relieve a RWF guard
and there would be a hell of a strafe. A runner came through with
a memo from McGrigor to Morton. Would Morton mop up any
officer who might be sleeping with the FLT[44] on his way up and
send him with any men they could find to relieve the Fuzzies? The
Adjutant would be very much obliged, and so on...

Morton had to go himself; there wasn't any officer. It was a
perishing night, the roads abominably slippery and the CCS was
hard to find. But he relieved the RWF's just in the nick of time
and got his guard mounted. Then – would you believe it? the
perishing RAMC NCO i/C[45] kept him waiting for nearly three
quarters of an hour in the torrential rain – for some sort of return
or other. They said that British Officers were not allowed inside
the tents – because of the feelings of the German patients. After
three quarters of an hour of it Morton said 'Damn that!' and went
in to the great marquee. There was light there, and warm stoves –
sandbag walls and little white beds. And such peace!

There was a young boy, looking singularly pretty and touching,
with pink skin and bright yellow hair, lying sideways on a white
pillow. Morton asked him where he came from... From
Lohrhaupten, a nest in the Bavarian Spessart... What was he? A
swine herd – he had driven the village pigs out in the morning and
home at night... Was he comfortable... The boy turned his head to
look at Morton: Herr Offizier he lisped sleepily, es ist doch
Himmel... It is just heaven. He turned his head sideways on the
pillow.

That was what had broken Morton's back. It was too much. He
got back to the huts on the Bailleul Steenwerck road, drank half a
pint of whiskey and rode down to the line with the ration party

---

43 Casualty Clearing Station.
44 First Line Transport.
45 Royal Army Medical Corps Non-Commissioned Officer in Charge.

which was naturally two hours late in arriving. Next day he was delirious ....

And there, now, he was in No II – finished for the 'front line and not much good for anything else. From below a woman's voice came up, extraordinarily distinct:

'Ev'ry little while I feel so lonely
Ev'ry little while I feel so sad .....'

And suddenly he found that he was crying – weakly, wearily, the crying of a useless man. And it was the song that had started him crying. It was, he knew, an imbecile song, made only for the appreciation of imbeciles – but it swept over him a sense – yes, a sense of his own uselessness! A large audience down below was now taking up the chorus. They sang softly – a great many – a great many voices singing softly, as if they were religious people singing in reverie. The voices seemed to swirl round the room as if they were slow clouds of mist, warm, and with a sweet odour. It was like that. And he was frightfully weak. And the great pressure of the war was on him; the never ceasing anxiety that came between you and everything at which you looked. And it was over all these people who were singing in that hidden, religious manner... And the dim light, coming from below. It showed the rounded ceiling of the little cell, like the interior of a potlid, near the window – and the Australian major's immense, fantastic hat, on a nail, as if it were glued to the white wall. The voices in chorus finished singing; the clear woman's voice began again. As there was less sound in the cell the pressure of the war seemed to fill it more full. It was a heavy pressure, on his eyebrows, on his chest, on his knees as he lay outstretched on his back. He imagined that if he moved his fingers it would cause a disaster to those out there, in the Line. He did not dare to move...

So it came back to him in after days... It was one of the great, one of the terrible moments in his life, for it was one of the days on which he seemed to see himself very clearly.

In the secret and inmost recesses of his soul he reproved himself for caring so much about the War. What was the war to him? What did it matter to him? Yet he knew he would have screamed out if he had heard that the Hun has broken through a bit of our line. Nay, more. He knew that he would scream out if he imagined it to himself – yes, at the mere thought, carefully imagined, of these people, bunching, lumbering, in field-grey, over one of our parapets; on their stomachs, shuffling in their great, hideous boots round so as to drop feet foremost into our trench. He would scream if he thought about it much. For, at any rate at the moment, it was not the idea of national disaster, national ruin, starvation, and all the remoter issues that hurt him. He had of course those more abstract feelings at times. But no; then it was merely the thought of what would be in the minds of the English Tommies of the regiments that saw the Huns lumbering over the parapet... It was the mental agony of seeing the organisation crack; the will renounce its hold as tired fingers can no more hold onto the edge of a precipice. And curiously enough it was not imaginary officers that he was worried about. It was Tommies, sergeants. And it was their minds, not their bodies... He couldn't at the time think of it in any other way.

And it irritated him that he thought of it in that way. It seemed to show the useless sort of blighter that he was – Useless to himself! For what did the minds of Tommies and sergeants and sections and platoons do for him? Nothing! Absolutely nothing! Could that give him a home? A place in the world? Where he would be welcomed back and where kind and solicitous eyes would look into his face? Never. Nothing would give him that. Not a thousand Tommies; not a hundred platoons! Yet there he was – worrying about their blessed feelings! It was imbecile.

He was useless to himself! That was what it all came to. What was he in the world? A Coy officer who swatted for slackers; who sweated that hooch-soaking blighters might get the credit. Or else he was a chartered accountant – which was a ridiculous and contemptible thing to be. And even at that he did too much for his money. He had always done too much for his money, he remembered. And he had got nothing for it. Not a maravedi![46] The most exiled of Symonds' bravi had more than he had – mistresses who would do murder for them, or for whom they could be murdered. Whom had he to murder for, or work for; to whose embraces could he return after his exile?

For he supposed he would return; he was one of those who would have to endure the ignominy of not dying. It would be something to have lived for, to have stopped a bullet. But he hadn't; and he never would now. That was that.

There was one other thing that would have been an object in life gone West. And what other object had he? None; not any! He

46 An old Spanish coin.

remembered that he had always had the idea that one day he would be distinguished. It had been as it were bred in his bones. His father had been distinguished; his grandfather had been' a bishop of Winchester, one of them. The other had been a very distinguished commentator on Elizabethan Dramas of the more obscure kind. But he himself! He was nothing.

He couldn't imagine what had given him the feeling, that he had undoubtedly had in his past life, that he was distinguished – or at any rate distinctly on the road towards distinction. He couldn't imagine. He was a distinguished tenant of a rather expensive service flat in Whitehall Court. The porter had always treated him with a deference that shewed he was regarded as distinguished. Well, the porter had been killed!

Distinguished! Well, he had once been nearly the runner up in the Sussex County Tennis Championship; he had three times taken the monthly medal of the Hythe Golf Club! What then had he done to earn fame? For the matter of that what had he even done to earn the deference of a hall porter? Nix!

He had always imagined that he ought to have written a book? Why hadn't he ever written a book? Half a dozen books? Why hadn't he? He was well equipped; he was well read; he knew English. When he talked usually he spoke too like a book. Hilda Cohen had told him that. And she had made him read all sorts of modern novels – and Belles Lettres; things in bright clear, green covers with paper labels; things producing dim effects, if that was the way to put it. But he had done nothing. Nix, again.

It was because he was useless to himself; it was because he had never taken a hold on his own life. It was as if he had never taken an interest in himself. The no book stunt shewed that. You wrote books to put yourself down on paper; to express yourself. He had never written a book because he had never taken enough interest in himself to want to give expression to his individuality.

No interest in himself. Was he a sort of Hamlet, then? No, by God he wasn't. If he had been born to set Denmark right, by God, he would have set Denmark right. But not for himself. His life really, had been spent putting Denmarks to rights. All sorts of Denmarks – the Glasgow contractor, the London periodical, the Paris Corset Company. He had put any number of things right, down to drink-sodden officers, and the books of the Battalion Quarter Master. But he hadn't ever put himself to rights. Why?

Was it because he had been too self sufficient, too sure of being the best of the bunch? Was it the result of his public school training? At Westminster, for instance, it had been what you might call a postulate that they were all, all of them, the pick of the bunch. They wouldn't be at Westminster if they weren't. But it wasn't only Westminster. He noticed that sort of note in so many of his fellow men. Of all sorts – costermongers, Manchester mill-owners, bed-makers in the Temple, sergeants in the New Armies, any man or any dilapidated woman – the English nation had that note. It astonished him, sometimes, the extraordinary egotism, the extraordinary hold on life that every human being in the country seemed to possess. No doubt it was an essential necessity for living. Perhaps you couldn't keep on living if you realised that you were just the stuff that filled graveyards and left no memories of your fame, beauty or exploits. How did he go on living, then?

For he hadn't that quality. Or perhaps he had. He remembered that once, when Hilda Cohen had come to his flat to intimate that she was going to chuck him – and 'intimate' was the word, for she did not tell him in so many words – he remembered that there had burst from his lips the phrases: 'Throw *me* over... How *can* you? Why, I'm ....'

As if he were going to say that he was a King or a Poet Laureate. And all that he could have really said was that he was a sort of a partner in a very old established firm of chartered accountants. Too old-established! Oh *damn*! She had stood before him, tall, thin – *too* thin! He didn't believe that her husband could afford her enough to eat! In a frightfully expensive, brown, beautiful, fur coat – a relic of some piece of former financial jugglery of the miserable Cohens. Possibly a present from... Oh *damn*... There she stood with cruel, cold, enigmatic and relentless eyes. He could not remember what pretext she had given for chucking him – just none, probably. He had known it from waves of thought that seemed to come from her to him. He had known it the night before; in the blackness of the night he had awakened and had said: 'She is going to chuck me. God, she is going to give me the giddy chuck!' He had felt her thinking it, a hundred miles away. For she had been at Eastbourne or somewhere. She had come up from Eastbourne to give him, wordlessly, the giddy mitten.

And what were her eyes trying to telegraph to him? They had looked and looked as if they were trying to see in his face the sign that he would take the resolve that should bind her to him, in spite of everything. Cold blue eyes, a little greyish under cruel, straight brows! But perhaps they were appealing. Appealing for what? That he should agree to fake her husband's books? That he should find words that should move her? That his life-force should grow strong enough to sweep her away in spite of himself? His life force hadn't been strong enough for any one of the three.

And he cursed himself for it. Why hadn't he faked Cohen's books, or passed the books that Cohen faked? Automatically he hadn't. That was it. He had an automatic honour. He wouldn't let Cohen be dishonest; he wouldn't even recommend his rich friends of whom Cohen spoke glutinously – 'Your rich friends... your so very rich friends...' he kept on saying – put any money into any of Cohen's schemes, though one or two of them seemed sound enough. But nothing could be sound that had Cohen in it. His automatic honour had rejected that too.

It might have kept Hilda for him. It might. He did not know. Sometimes he thought she was that sort of... Generally he thought that! And then a great wave of passionate pity would sweep over him. She must have starved so, have slaved so... and with that horrible, fawning, mouthing, handwashing creature! For Cohen had been as bad as they made them.

Well, there it was. There *he* was... *Pour tout potage*, he had that memory of Hilda Cohen standing in his drawing room in the rich quiet flat at Whitehall Court – the flat that he supposed he still had. She was standing there, in the beautiful brown furs and the large hat. She was drooping a little over to one side and looking at him with the enigmatic eyes and her gloved hand was stretched downwards and a little outwards in a gesture that might have expressed regret – or any other damned humbug. She was standing so that she had the background of a tall, rich, golden brown cabinet that he had bought in Belgium.

And he had been looking at her precisely as his father had looked at the beautiful lady, twenty years before... Was his father, then, parting from Mrs Minshull? Possibly that too had been, in its perfect tranquillity, just such another hideous moment. Was he just repeating his father – the dreamer who never stretched out his hand to grasp what he wanted. That was it.

For he knew, within himself, that his father was a disillusioned man. He had made a highly successful career – these were just the contemptible words – 'a highly successful career' – but he knew that his father despised his own work, the Renaissance-cushioned and arabesqued billiard rooms and the provincial Town halls for fat

Northern manufacturers – and his knighthood and the letters after his name. All the letters! Gabriel had gathered as much from sly, humorous and rather desolate sentences his father had dropped during their tour in Italy in the early winter and spring of 1892–3. His father had died of influenza in Venice, that March.

It would no doubt have been better for Gabriel if his father had not died then – if it had been put off for a year or two. Gabriel had often thought that. It wasn't so much that his father had had much influence on him; he knew very little of what passed in his father's mind – except regrets. For he knew that this father regretted something that had passed in his youth in a little village called Apperley – in Yorkshire, or possibly in Durham. If something that had passed there had passed differently or turned out differently Morton Senr. might have had a different life. He did not get any further in the way of confidences to his son than that – and the matter had come up very indirectly the day before his father died. He had had a high temperature or very possibly he would not have said as much as he did.

Gabriel remembered his father had had an unusually red flush in his face that evening. He had been asleep and Gabriel had been reading a guide to St Mark's. Suddenly he had sighed so deeply that Gabriel had looked up from his reading. His father's head was lying sideways on the pillow and the eyes, appearing unnaturally blue in the unnaturally red and congested face, had been looking hard at Gabriel. And immediately Morton Senr. had said:

'It's so very difficult, my son'... Gabriel supposed he must have said something like: 'What, sir?' For his father had gone on: 'To think what will become of you.' And he had said a great deal more, rapidly and with deep depression. His words Gabriel never remembered – or only a phrase or so. But he gathered that, in his father's view, his grandparents had behaved wrongly at some crisis of Morton's father's life... 'It isn't that,' Morton Senr. said. 'That's done with... And I don't know that it is the sort of thing that I could talk about to you – to my son...' But what was worrying was how he ought himself to handle the young Gabriel... 'You're sitting there,' he had gone on, 'Reading. What? Forming your character. And what ought I to do... If things had been different at Apperley...' And then he had said, after a long, brooding pause during which his glance seemed to pour over Gabriel like a long caress. 'But then, you wouldn't have been there...' And then: 'And I shouldn't have liked you not to be there, my dear!'

These were the last words Gabriel had heard from his father who became insensible during the night and died next day at noon.

The room in the Venetian hotel had been extraordinarily like a mortuary chamber. Immense maroon curtains had fallen from the gilt cornices above the windows; gilt amorini like the Jesuit decorations in some church or other, sprawled over the frame of the mirror; the maroon-curtained bed had great pillars surmounted by dusky plumes like those on old hearses. And right through the night Gabriel had sat by the dressing table reading in the dim rays of the night light until his eyes grew too tired to see. Then he had sat thinking. Two trains of thought obsessed him – that of the 'little village of Apperley in the North', that his father had mentioned and the phrase from Pico della Mirandola or someone that he had read in the *Renaissance in Italy*, during the week in the Library, the December before.

'The little village of Apperley in the North', and 'Before committing yourself to any action reflect deeply upon the affair in all its aspects and act along the lines of your most generous impulse!' The phrase went round and round in his head. As for the little village of Apperley, he remembered to have read in *Men of the Time*, that his father's first employment had been the restoration of the Early English Church in the village of Apperley – in either Yorkshire or Durham. No doubt the job had been secured for Gabriel's father by his own father who had been dean of several dioceses in succession but had never risen to the episcopal bench. His mother, of course, had been the daughter of a bishop. No doubt, then, the Dean had insisted on his son's marrying the bishop's daughter, so that he should get more and yet more jobs of restoration... And possibly the vicar of Apperley had had a daughter... Or perhaps... He remembered suddenly how his father had said to him, three months before: 'It's a good thing to keep your eyes in your own boat...' Then perhaps...

And all of a sudden, looking deeply into the folds of the heavy maroon window curtains, seated as he was before the great mirror with the gambolling, gilt cupids, Gabriel was going out of the door of a small manor house or a large farm... in Apperley in the North. He did not know if it was he or his father... he was holding in his right hand a fishing rod and in his left a wicker creel. Just beside him was a benevolent old lady; stout in black satin, with white curls on top of which sat a flat lace cap. Her podgy white hands were crossed in front of her and she was half curtseying, half bowing and wholly indulgent. In front of the door was a stretch of garden, then a little stream running level with the turf on each side; what they call in the North a bank, – a low, long hill, rose up against the sky and on it were silver birch trees, their foliage thin and delicate against the sky. And, in among the birches were a grey dress, a large, grey felt hat and two enigmatic, dark eyes. He was standing looking – with hardly any impulse, with hardly any resolution.

PART II

That was how his past life came back to him, in those scenes of strong colours, remembered with strong emotions, though they seemed to be memories of no emotions whatever. And if, when walking through the narrow, imitation mediaeval and squalid street of the ancient city of X——, which for him was much more the HQ of the —— Command than an ancient city – if he had as it were indulged in a stocktaking of his individuality, he would have said that that was all he was and that was all he possessed. He was a record – as it were a Gramophone pot-pourri record – of coloured and connected scenes; and all he possessed were just those memories of scenes, highly enough coloured since he recollected with an extreme vividness alike the gilt amorini of the Venetian hotel and the seven, blue, momentarily immobilised stars of Very lights over Kemmel hill and the stretched, slightly agonised eyebrows of Hilda Cohen and the lady in the olive tree holding rather than picking a shaddock – yes, scenes highly enough coloured and vividly remembered, yet connected so very slightly, – since the only connection between them was his almost unknown self. For indeed he felt that *he* hardly existed....

It was almost as if he were invisible – as if he were just a point, a theoretic spot in space; the centre for the things that he saw all round him. If it hadn't been that he had to return salutes he might just as well not have been in existence at all, and, if he had ceased to exist no-one in the wide world would have missed him. He might have gone out then and there, like an extinguished candle and, it seemed to him no-one would have missed him – except, for a minute or so, the limping officer. And the limping officer would merely have thought that Morton had turned suddenly down a side-street.

He had nothing; he was almost nobody. His only possessions, apart from remembrances, seemed to him to be, in a tent in a camp, a disreputable bed, some dirty army blankets which he would have to return to store, a washstand made of a sugar box that supported someone else's tin basin and that contained an old pot of vaseline, some damp army papers and, possibly, a field pocket book or two and an old razor strap.

Ford wrote short stories throughout his career. His war stories are amongst the most effective. The first two here were written during the war, but before he had seen the Front. 'The Scaremonger' satirises Edward Heron Allen, Violet Hunt's old friend, and neighbour at her holiday cottage on the Sussex coast at Selsey. Hunt said he '*did* go frightening girls about a German invasion'. He had shown 'signs of amorousness' towards her before she got involved with Ford, whom he appeared to resent. He was furious about the story, writing to Hunt: 'I did not believe that even a German Journalist would sit at one's table, make one's house a sort of Inn for the entertainment of his friends and use one's time money & brains in his service for years & then perpetrate an outrage of the kind.' Ford suspected that it was at Allen's suggestion that, on 2 January 1915, he was ordered by the Chief Constable of West Sussex to leave the county. The story was published in the *Bystander*, 44 (25 November 1914), pp. 273–4, 276 (and has since been reprinted in *Women, Men and the Great War: An Anthology of Stories*, ed. Trudi Tate (Manchester, 1995), pp. 268–74). It was perhaps meant as propaganda, confronting real fears of invasion, and showing that hysteria proves suicidal, whereas the stiff upper-lip prevails. The second story, 'Fun! – It's Heaven', also published in the *Bystander*, 48 (24 November 1915), pp. 327–30, is more overtly propagandistic. It offers consolation to the bereaved, and encouragement to the troops, by suggesting that the soldiers are aided by the ghostly regiment of Britain's historic war dead.

'Pink Flannel' and 'The Colonel's Shoes' were both written after Ford had first-hand experience of battle. Like all the stories here, they turn on how the war elicited heightened feelings about religion, superstition or the mysterious and the uncanny. 'Pink Flannel' is a tonally fascinating story about how the mind works under fire. A bombardment begins while an officer is planning an adulterous affair on his next leave. The main focus is on how the conflicting pressures of danger and sexuality have caused him to forget what he did with his lover's letter, but how a bizarre dream enables him to remember. Ford said he wrote the story in a tent on Kemmel Hill. It was published in *Land & Water*, 72 (8 May 1919), pp. 14–15, but the text here also draws on the Cornell typescript.

'The Colonel's Shoes', was published in *Reynolds's Newspaper* (11 January 1920), p. 2; but the typescript at Cornell contains some passages deleted in the published version, which have been restored here. Like most of Ford's post-war fiction, this story gauges the pressures pushing men to the 'edge' of sanity during the war. The climax of the story comes when Hugh Arkwright goes, rationally speaking, over the edge, and begins to have 'illusions' that he is having his uncle's thoughts. All the main characters reflect aspects of Ford: 'Lieut. Hugh' sounds like Lieut. Hueffer; his uncle, the worn out Colonel, sounds like the Ford who wrote to Violet Hunt from Rouen: 'I am tired of fighting'; but it is the enigmatic Captain Gotch who reflects many of Ford's experiences, and concerns about his nature.

The other two stories deal with the after-effects of the war. 'Enigma', published here for the first time, was written between September 1920 and November 1922 while Ford and Bowen were living in Coopers Cottage, Bedham in Sussex. It deals with the mysterious disappearance of a young couple from a cottage not unlike Red Ford or Coopers. It is a detective story left unsolved, but implying that the disappearance was provoked by the arrival of a distinctive stranger. Various motives are hinted at: financial or sexual irregularities; or that the couple have assumed false identities. But there is also the suggestion that the uncanny episode is a product of the war. The main witness to their story is a fellow officer recovering from shell-shock. Like several other works here, 'Enigma' explores how the war's strain, its extraordinary demands on human conduct, make the survivors appear, or feel 'unsound' – with implications of 'unreliable' as well as psychologically disturbed.

The last story, 'The Miracle', first published in the *Yale Review*, 18 (Winter 1928), pp. 320–31, also turns on an intense and apparently inexplicable experience. A biologist recounts to his wife a story about a war-time raid, in which the vital cigarettes he forgot to pack turned up in his kit anyway. His wife, knowing his absent-mindedness, sees that he probably packed them without realising it. But the main interest in the story is in the effect the experience had on the scientist, whose belief in some sort of providence cuts across all his deepest scientific beliefs, and yet has given him a new kind of self-confidence. As his confidence is partly demonstrated by the masterly way he tells this particular story, the whole incident becomes a kind of allegory for the fiction-writer – the person whose confidence in his art, and success in his career, depends upon a paradoxical 'belief' in his own fictions. It's an excellently crafted and entertaining story, but one with much significance for Ford's own life and his writing.

The Scaremonger

A Tale of the War Times

'He ought to be hanged,' the Lieutenant in command of the troops said. 'You think that this collection of bungalows and bathing places is of no importance. And, of course, it isn't. But I tell you, old Blue Funk has done definite mischief. It isn't only that he frightens half the little girls in the village into fits by telling them that the enemy is going to land to-night and cut all their throats. And it isn't only that he spends every night on the beach in a rough-rider's uniform with three revolvers – which is as much as to say that my sentinels go to sleep. But I tell you, General, I have actually traced the rumour about the sinking of three battleships off Chatham to this ridiculous ....'

'Well, we won't hang him this afternoon,' the Inspecting General said, 'more particularly since I am dining with him this evening. But I admit that he ought not to have frightened your little Ina, and I don't see why you should not frighten him out of the place, if you can. Only it must be done officially, as a surprise attack, for my inspection. There must not be any warning your shore unit before the attack. Let's see how quickly the Squire and the scouts and the sentries can get them out. I'll sanction that.'

The Squire of Bleakham – old Blue Funk, as he almost liked to be called – had been a member of an exceedingly opulent city firm, and had retired from business much too early for his soul's health to the marine village of Bleakham, whose lordship of the manor, along with the manor house, he had purchased about fifteen years before. Thus he was an indubitable squire, though few squires could have been less squire-like, since the whole of his time had been devoted to so serious a study of the works of Horace and the mediæval Latinists that he found never a minute, even, to devote to the study of the newspapers. Indeed he was accustomed to boast that, such was the dilettante elegance of his remote existence, not once in the last fifteen years had he perused the day's news. His appointments, his furniture, his electric lighting, his motors, his billiard-room, and his kitchen were, nevertheless, of the most modern and the most sought-after. His port was beyond praise.

Thus the General inspecting the district took pleasure in dining with the Squire when he was in the neighbourhood, and that evening there were at table Lord and Lady Treffries, the General, Sir Thomas Larne, the lung specialist, and a Scholar of Trinity College, Cambridge.

The Squire made no secret of his terror – of his terror, personal, immediate, and frantic. The enemy, he was certain, would land in Bleakham, and in no other place than Bleakham, that night, the next night, or the night after next. They would come in one of the new, great submarines. A hundred cyclists would land, burning, executing, pillaging the neighbourhood during the hours of darkness; then they would disappear again into the black depths of the sea. And the first house that they would visit would be the manor house, because it was the residence of himself, old Blue Funk.

But, as old Lord Treffries amiably put it, 'the White Terror' would have been the more fitting epithet, since sheer terror had rendered the Squire absolutely white. Ever since the first days of the hostilities the Squire's features had fallen away; colour had deserted them till they had the dull opacity of alabaster; his grey hair had, in the four months of war, grown absolutely white – paper-white. His mouth dragged over to one side; only his eyes had any sign of life. These even sparkled when he spread panic in the village. That night he was in a singular state of agitation.

At the opening of the war the papers had struck him with a wave of panic. You have to imagine how a daily paper of the first days of war must appear to a dilettante Latinist who had not looked at such a sheet for fifteen years. In the last fifteen years the papers have, you know, made much progress in the conveying of excitements. And the Squire had had to read them then. They had revenged themselves amply for his neglect of them.

Every bush, every barn, every bridge, concealed for him an armed spy; behind every cloud there was a dirigible bearing two tons of great, explosive, and poisonous projectiles. The words

'national degeneration' were continually on his lips. When an old
cruiser was sunk by a mine he would say: 'There! We used to
believe that we could trust the Navy. But even that faint hope
deserts us!' And his most peculiar personal terror attached itself to
the figure of his once most intimate friend, Professor Eitel-
Scharnhorst, of the University of Berlin. Professor Scharnhorst was
the brother of Heinrich von Scharnhorst-Fosterdingen, the
redoubtable director of submarines of the enemy's navy – and
Professor Eitel-Scharnhorst had been in Bleakham again and again
as the guest of the Squire. Indeed, it would not be untrue to say
that the Squire had learned to believe in the degeneracy of his countrymen from the Professor, whose department had been
Latin-classical philology and whose contempt for British philolo-
gists had been notorious. It had come finally to an almost
ensanguined row, early that summer, between the Professor and
the Squire – over the proper punctuation of the ode 'Planco
Consule.' For incautiously the Professor had let slip the fact that he
had inwardly as great a contempt for the Latinity of the Squire as
for that of the Squire's countrymen. And, since that date, the Squire
had launched an exceedingly venomous pamphlet against the
Professor's edition of the 'Satyrikon' of Petronius. Immediately
afterwards the war had broken out.

In the intervening four months the Squire had received only one
communication from Professor Scharnhorst – and that was not of
a nature to quiet his fears. It was written with all the almost incredible hatred for this country that distinguishes the Prussian
professoriate; it gave fifteen scientific reasons for believing that the
inhabitants of this country are physically, eugenically, and mentally
degenerate; it demolished the Squire's objections to the Professor's
notes upon the 'Satyrikon,' and it stated that the Professor had
begged his brother, Heinrich von Scharnhorst-Fosterdingen, to pay
particular submarine attention to the marine hamlet of Bleakham.

The General, eating his dinner in silence, for the most part
listened more or less attentively to the Squire's description of the
Scharnhorst letter, for the Squire went over it again and again, most
of the time to an accompaniment of laughter. The laughter, indeed,
was uncontrollable, and the Squire accepted it almost as a tribute –
as if he were a Jeremiah, a true prophet of real disaster, preaching
to degenerate fools and Society idiots. It appeared to the General
that there might, after all, be something in the famous letter.
Certainly the Squire knew something about the enemy's

submarines – he had learned several things with accuracy and practical knowledge. No doubt the Professor, who was the brother of the director of submarines, had talked about his brother's activities. He might even have talked a little incautiously; boastful professors sometimes do talk incautiously in the midst of patriotic out-pourings. And suddenly the General asked:

'How often did the Professor stop with you? Every other year or so? Was he – now – interested in, say, fossils?'

But the Professor had not been interested in fossils. He had liked to walk on the sands or sail about the shallows in a small boat, discussing the 'Satyrikon.' It had amused him to go shrimping. But even, the Squire said, if the Professor had been trying to get soundings of the sands off Bleakham they would now be useless. The great storm of September 29 had completely changed the lie of the large sand-banks off the end of Bleakham Bill. What knowledge he had of the position before would be harmful rather than of any use to a landing-party.

That, however, was the only crumb of comfort that the Squire could get into his conversation. Otherwise he was certain that the enemy would land on the Bill that night, or next night, or on the night after next. And he began to talk of the run of the mid-winter tides in the channel, and of the strong motives that the enemy would have for making a dash on Bleakham – it was only about nine miles from Dover. They could destroy an infinite number of telephone wires in half an hour; they could sack half a dozen country seats, including that of Lord Treffries; and, above all, they could hang the Squire, the enemy of Professor Scharnhorst.

It was one of those marvellously still, marvellously warm nights that sometimes visit the neighbourhoods of the Channel waters in mid-December, and, after dinner, most of the Squire's guests sat out on his sheltered verandah, watching the beams of the restless searchlights from Dover as they played upon loose flakes of cloud in a sky brilliant with stars. They had dined uncommonly well, and mostly were sleepily and comfortably silent. Once the General said:

'I should imagine that a lot of chaps landing out of a submarine would be pretty stupid for half an hour or so. I understand the interior air is pretty hellish with stinks, and if there were a hundred it would make it all the worse, wouldn't it?'

The Squire answered that only the most desperate, trained fellows would come.

'Still,' the General said, 'it would make a difference to their shooting, don't you think?' He was the only one of the guests who appeared to pay any deference to the opinion of the host.

'Oh, they'll shoot well enough to get me,' the Squire said; 'right through the forehead, they'll go. It's a consolation to think that they will not hang me.'

There fell on that dark verandah a suspicion of discomfort; the man ought not to talk like that, and for quite two seconds there was a silence.

'Right through the forehead,' the Squire said again. 'I betrayed my country and this place by inviting that fellow here. It's my deserts to get shot, but not to be hanged.'

There was great creaking of chairs; it was getting more than the guests could stand – the sorrowing and the heavy fatalism of the fellow's voice. They all left the verandah except the General and the Scholar of Trinity, who was stopping in the house. The General was waiting for the Squire, who went indoors to arm himself for the vigil that he passed each night on the shore at the end of the Bill. They were quite silent, both of them, until the Scholar said:

'That must be a large liner going down the Channel. Don't you hear the screw? It must be unusually close in.' The thudding of a large vessel's screw was very plainly audible.

★ ★ ★

The Lieutenant in command of the troops billetted in the empty bungalows of Bleakham had called half of them out, and had gone off towards the east. He had previously warned his little daughter Ina that she was not to be afraid if she heard firing. That would only be himself, making a surprise attack on the bungalows in order to demonstrate to the General that his men were prepared. Incidentally, they were going to frighten or to laugh out of the place the unholy blighter who had given his little Ina such a scare the night before by saying that the enemy were going to land and burn the bungalows and cut her throat. He would, he said, get right out on the sands at low tide, fire a volley of blank cartridge, shout commands in German, rouse all the other troops in a hurry, and, if possible, take the Squire prisoner in the midst of ten or twenty of his men who spoke German or something like it – for many of them were chemist's assistants or city clerks with a smattering of language. Ina was not to mind however much firing she heard; it would only be her father having some fun....

The resulting ten minutes – for it did not take more – was a most unholy mix up. The Lieutenant – he is now senior Captain of the Mid-Kent 57th Cyclist Corps – says that, cycling gently along in the dark, at the very edge of the low-tide, about a quarter of a mile from the beach, he actually ran, at right angles, into the cycle of another man, who cursed him vigorously for a clumsy fool, in German. He had impressed on his own men the absolute necessity for silence, so that the men behind him halted themselves with the merest whispers. Then he dimly made out, to seawards, a black and, as it were, a domed blot. From its top rim, in the merest glimmer of light thrown from below, he perceived to emerge against the stars, four bicycles, twisting slowly round, and painted everywhere a dull grey. Then he had a sense that there were other men walking about and whispering, in the sea itself. He had not the least idea what he did after that – or no clear idea. It was, he said, a most fearful jam up of fists, gun-barrels, bicycles getting between your legs, whispers going into shouts. He got landed fearfully hard with something on the side of the jaw. A long light came out of the top of the black dome; there came into existence in the light the absurd thatches and cupolas of the bungalows of Bleakham, the figure of the Squire in a black rough-rider uniform, the figure of a man in khaki beside him. It struck him as being like an absurd cinematograph effect. There was a figure dimly visible behind the searchlight, crouching down.

A voice said in his ear:

'There's a ladder up the side, sir. We could get up and pot into the inside if your revolver's loaded. The men have only got blank cartridge.'

Suddenly, as he ran into the shallow sea, he shot the man behind the searchlight. That was how it presented itself to him in after years. What he saw at the moment was that the long beam travelled swiftly up the sands, lit for the last moment the roofs of the bungalows, and then, as if contentedly, illuminated the road to the North Star. The man he had shot must have fallen on to a lever. The last illuminated object that he saw by its light was an imp-like Boy Scout with a puff of smoke at his feet, high up the beach. And there was a report like that of two fifteen point sevens. The Boy Scout had fired a maroon. A revolver began to crackle from the sands; a bugle called with the hurry of panic from among the bungalows. Then he was being guided up to the foot of an iron ladder by a man with a cool voice. Jenks was the owner of that voice – Staff-Sergeant Jenks, lately of the Coldstreams.

It was obviously Jenks who got the commander of the U174, who was just coming out of the hatch, with the butt of a rifle he had snatched from somebody. But the Lieutenant in command was anxious to impress upon you, when he talked about the matter, that there was not any plan, or any heroism either, though that may have been only his modesty. He and the sergeant sat on the lid, as he called it, of the submarine whilst, in and about the surrounding sea, ninety-eight men of the Mid-Kent Cyclist Corps used fists and rifle-butts on forty-two surprised men from East Prussia who were falling over bicycles. But the cyclists captured that submarine with its crew and the fifty-eight men who had not yet emerged, and the newspapers could comment *ad libitum* on a contest between a whale and foxes, or on the ineffectuality of submarines considered as naval units when directed against bungalows. The casualties of the mid-Kents amounted to three men wounded, and they were wounded by the revolver of the Squire who had advanced alone against the submarine, firing twelve shots from two revolvers. He was found by a Boy Scout at the edge of the tide next morning, with a nasty hole in the middle of his alabaster forehead. He had turned the last shot against himself.

In a letter accompanying his testamentary dispositions, which were complicated and very arbitrary, he expressed the hope that, owing to his having written a pamphlet confuting the views of Professor Eitel-Scharnhorst on the subject of Petronius Arbiter, and by his exertions in the cause of averting national degeneracy, he might be said to have deserved well of his country. No doubt he had, if you think it out.

'Fun! – It's Heaven'

The room was lit by a skylight from above, so that it resembled a tank in which dim fishes swim listlessly. The walls were of varnished grey paint; an immense and lamenting Christ hung upon a cross above the empty grate; a mildewed portrait of the last Pope but one made a grim spot of white near the varnished door. On a deal chair beside the deal table the old doctor sat talking to the very old lay sister who stood before him, twisting her gnarled fingers in her wooden beads.

'Whatever it is,' he said, and he waved his hand round to indicate the grim room. 'This isn't my idea of it. That is what I told the child.'

'There need be no limits to one's idea of it,' the lay sister said. 'What was it you told the poor child? I have not, you must remember, heard anything at all,' she added. 'Dicky Trout, I suppose, is killed. And he was to have married her? He was a dear young boy.'

'He had been just ninety minutes in the trenches. And shot through the head! Ninety minutes! And dead! It's what they call rotten luck. They were both my godchildren.' He said the words with a certain fierceness of resentment.

'I know,' the lay sister said patiently.

The same resentment was in the old doctor's tone.

'What sort of work was it for me?' he asked, 'to console her. What is there to say? How can you console a child of nineteen whose lover of twenty-two has been shot through the head after ninety minutes in the trenches? There is no consolation. It is the most final thing in the world. You cannot make any comments.'

'There are always the consolations of religion,' the lay sister said. 'Believe me, they are very real.'

'But how do they come in when you talk to a child like Joan about the death of a boy like Dicky Trout? What are you to say? "The Lord giveth and the Lord ..."'

He stopped and then began again with his fierce energy.

'Do you know what she said to me? Do you know? She said: "It isn't possible that he won't ever have any fun again; not any fun!

The lights, and the white paint and the young girls; and the tea, and the river, and the little bands playing 'Hitchy Koo.' He wanted it so; oh, he wanted it so." I couldn't stand it. I tell you I had to say that he would have it all again. The lights and the river and the teashops and the little bands playing "Hitchy Koo".'

The lay sister had nothing to say. The doctor went on:

'I'm not a well-read man. Someone once said, "If there had not been any God we should have had to invent one." Who was it?'

'I think it was Voltaire,' the lay sister answered. 'It does not matter. What did you tell the child?'

'I'll tell you,' the doctor answered. 'You know her father was too busy with his regiment; her mother is a permanent invalid. I'm for ever in the house. Professionally. And Joan wanted to see the places in which his last weeks were spent; his billets; the range where he fired .... Well, I went with her, a long way into the Midlands. And we saw them: his billets and the sergeants who had known him and the range where he had fired. I think it was the range that did it.

'You see, what moved me so extraordinarily was her perpetual cry: that she wanted him to have had some fun – because he wanted it so! If she had said she wanted him back for herself – or if she had even cried! But no; she just said, over and over again, that he wanted it so! Fun! It's a curious thing for a young girl to want for her dead sweetheart; but I daresay there was nothing better or truer or more feminine that she could have wanted for him. And, just as God was invented, if He did not indeed exist – so, suddenly, Fun came into existence. On those ranges.

'Try to imagine the Mosslott Range for yourself. In the squalid suburbs of a hideous city, on a dirty, flat expanse of sordid grass, some banks of clay, like long graves. And, in them, beneath the squalid clouds, clay-coloured figures reclining, intent, gazing at the banks before them, at a distance. And flat, black shapes, like the heads and shoulders of devils peep up over the banks in front and lob away. Fun!

'And when you turned your head you saw an immense row of retorts, in silhouette. A long way off, but immense! Eighteen of them, shutting in the horizon, with plumes of dim flames running away down the wind and invisible smoke because the sky was just smoke! Fun! The proper fun for a boy of twenty-two, the sweetheart of a girl of nineteen. Well, I suppose it is all right.

'At any rate, in that *décor,* as the French would call it, Joan caught hold of my arm, and cried out:

"'Oh; do you think God can forgive him .... For practising here to take away lives .... Every time he hit a dummy."

"'My dear," I said, "God has a special pardon for soldiers. If they kill, they don't kill for themselves, but for you and me."

"'Oh, are you sure!" she said. "Can we be sure?"

'I don't know what it was happened then; something cracked in me at the tones of her voice – for there, with the rifles popping away in the middle distance, the first thing was that a band – quite a little band – was playing. Yes, it was playing what undoubtedly was "Hitchy Koo".

'Now you are to understand that I have always taken a desultory interest in the uniforms of the British Army. I know that the infantry, for instance, in the reign of Queen Anne wore scarlet coats with facings, breeches, and long black gaiters. But I had a vague idea that the hat was the Kevenhuller. It was not – as you shall hear.

'For I found myself in a long street, like St James's Street, going into the doorway of a teashop where the band was – the band that was playing "Hitchy Koo". And the ante-room was full of tall young men – fine young men in scarlet coats, with rifles and breeches and black gaiters. And their hats had cockades and were three-cornered. Kevenhuller hats I thought they were.

'Well, as I went in a young blonde fellow was calling out:

"'Ypres! Stap my vitals! A man would be a mole if his blood boiled not at that name."

'Others cried:

"'Have the rout beaten!"

'And:

"'Call out the gentlemen of the firing platoons."

'They laughed and cheered, and their scarlet coat-tails whisked. I think it was "To Wipers!" that they cried, and then there was no one there. The long white inner room was full of young men – quite young men – in that dun colour, with the brass buttons. You have seen khaki, sister? Once, through the grille in the door? And you saw Dicky Trout before he went? Well, then, that room was full of young men in khaki, sitting at little tables, laughing with the young girls, chaffing the waitresses even – and eating éclairs.

'And Dicky Trout got up from a table and came towards me, laughing:

"'They're going to Ypres, those fellows," he said, "won't they make the beggars run! I was fed up with Ypres; but it's all the fun

of the fair here. And Joan will be here! Joan will be here! Fun! I
tell you it's Heaven."

'That was all I saw, just that glimpse ... and then – it was the
range again and the irregular sounds of the rifles. And Joan was
talking to a sergeant who had known Dicky Trout; his eyes were
full of tears.

'Well, sister, I suppose you'll say I was wrong. But that evening,
in the train, I told Joan what I had seen. You'll say it was wrong.
You'll say it was deluding her with false hopes. But put it how you
will I believe I was right. It would not be decent if I was not right
– if Heaven wasn't like that for those poor young things. God must
be good to them. He must. If He were not we should have to make
Him. They die for you and for me. It's our business to invent a fit
heaven for them. Don't say I'm wrong.'

'That,' the old lay sister said,' is a matter for theologians. No
doubt God is rich enough to provide teashops for all who die for
us. We do not know what Heaven will be like.'

'And the strange thing,' the Doctor continued, 'is not the story
– you know the story – that Marlborough's men got out of their
graves and fought for us at Ypres. Though it's a fine story. Damn
it; it's a fine story. They couldn't lie there still and let our men be
beaten back. No; the strange point for me is this:

'This morning, when I went to see Joan she was smiling as I had
never seen her smile. And she said: "You've got to go with me to
the sisters. I must take the veil. I have heard a voice. But it wasn't
the Kevenhuller hat they wore at Ypres. It was a proper cocked hat
with a cockade – the Ramillies hat and the Ramillies tie-wig they
came to be called."

'I asked her how she knew that; I couldn't see how she could.
And she answered:

'"Dicky told me. At the little table, three from the orchestra on
the right. He's having such fun. They were playing, 'Get Out or
get Under,' and he wanted to get under the table, but I wouldn't
let him. Fun! It was Heaven."'

                              *   *   *

The old Doctor paused; the lay sister said nothing.

'For myself,' the Doctor said at last, 'I believe that Heaven will
be like that. I believe that, as you say, God is a very rich man – and
that He has imagination too. And I come back to that: that if there

were no Heaven we should have to invent one. For what is the sense of the world without it? Here is Dicky Trout dead – and Joan taking the veil – I suppose so that she may pray that Dicky has some fun.'

The lay sister sighed:

'I should like to hear the tune of "Get out and Get Under",' she said. 'I never saw a teashop in my life.'

'You shall! You shall!' the Doctor said. 'As for the tune, you must have heard the bands playing it as the drafts go by – to Flanders. It goes...'

And he began to hum the jerky melody whilst the old Religious nodded her head. In a room above the young girl was trying to persuade the Mother Superior that she had the vocation for that cloistral life. Her sweetheart lay dead in Flanders.

Assuredly if there were no Heaven we whom Flanders has not yet claimed must will one into existence with all the volition of united humanity.

Pink Flannel

Mr Ford Madox Hueffer, author of *The Fifth Queen* and many other romances, served on the French front with a Welsh infantry battalion. 'Pink Flannel' is a comedy that might have been a tragedy; and in the story the two strands of life at home and life in the trenches are skilfully interwoven.

W.L. James waved his penny candle round the dark tent and the shadow of the pole moved in queer angles on the canvas sides.

It was a great worry – it was more than a worry! to have lost Mrs Wilkinson's letter. There was very little in the tent – and still less that the letter could be in. When Caradoc Morris had brought him the letter in the front line, W.L. James had had with him, of what the tent now contained, only his trench coat, his tunic, and his shirts, of things that could contain letters. It could not be in the dirty collection of straps and old clothes that were in his valise; it could not be in his wash-basin or in his flea-bag. And he had not even read Mrs Wilkinson's letter! Caradoc Morris had come down from the first Line Transport, and had given it to him at the very beginning of the strafe that had lasted two days. The sentry on the right had called out: 'Rum Jar, left,'[47] and he and Morris had bolted up the communication trench at the very moment when, holding in his hand the longed-for envelope, he had recognised the hand-writing of the address. He knew he had put it somewhere for safety.

But where? Where the devil *could* you put a letter for safety in a beastly trench? In your trench coat – in your tunic – in your breeches pocket. There w*as* not anywhere else.

He was tired: he was dog-tired. He was always dog-tired, anyhow, when he came out of the Front Line. Now he felt relaxed all over: dropping, for next morning he was going on ninety-six hours' leave and, for the moment, that seemed like an eternity of slackness. So that he could let himself go.

He could have let himself go altogether if he had not lost Mrs Wilkinson's letter – or even if he had known what it contained ......

---

47 A 'Rum Jar' was the soldiers' slang for a type of German trench mortar.

He did not suppose, even if he had dropped it in the trench, that anyone would who picked it up would make evil use of it – forward it to Mrs Wilkinson's husband, say? On the other hand, they might?
.....

He took off his tunic, his boots, and his puttees, and let himself, feet forward into his flea-bag. He blew out the candle that he had stuck on to the top of his tin hat. A triangle of stars became important before his eyes. The night was full of the babble of voices. He heard one voice call: 'The major wants: *Mr Britling Sees It Through.*' ...[48] The machine-guns said: 'Wukka! Wukka!' under the pale stars, as if their voices were a part of the stillness. The stars rose swiftly in the triangle of sky; they hung for a long time, then descended or went out. Much noise existed for a moment. He said to himself that the Hun had got the wind up, and, whilst he began to worry once more about the letter, as it were, with nearly all his brain, one spot of it said: 'That insistent "Wukka! Wukka!" to the right is from Wytschaete: the intermittent one is our "G" trenches ..... There's an HE going to the top of Kemmel Hill ......'

So his mind made before his eyes pictures of the Flanders plain; the fact that the Germans were alarmed at the idea of a sudden raid – that our machine-guns were answering theirs – that their gunners were putting over some random shells from 4.2s. Presently our own 99-pounders or naval guns or something would shut them up. Then they would all be quiet ..... A sense of deep and voluptuous security had descended on him. Out there, when you have nothing else to worry you, you calculate the chances: rifle fire 20 to 1 against MGs[49] 30: Rum Jars 40; FA[50] 70 against a shot of flying iron. Now his mind registered the fact that the chances of direct hits was nil, or bits of flying iron, 250 to 1 against – and his mind put the idea to sleep, as it were ... He was in support .....

The noise continued – there were some big thumps away to the right. Our artillery was waking up. But the voices from the tents were audible: tranquil conversations about strafes, about Cardiff, about ship owners' profits, about the Divisional 'Follies' .... The Divisional 'Follies'!

He would be going to the 'Ambassadors' – with Mrs Wilkinson

---

48 H. G. Wells' novel was being serialized in the *Nation* when Ford's essay 'Trois Jours de Permission' appeared in it in September 1916. See pp. 49–51 above and p. 233 below.
49 Machine Guns.
50 Field Artillery.

– within twenty-four hours if he had any luck .... GSO II had promised to run him from Bailleul to Boulogne: he would catch the one-o'clock leave boat; he would be in Town – Town – Town! – by six. Mrs Wilkinson would meet him on the platform. He would keep her waiting twenty minutes in the vestibule of his hotel while he had a quick bath. By 6.45 they would be dining together; she would be looking at him across the table with her exciting eyes that had dark pupils and yellow-brown iris! Her chin would be upon her hands with the fingers interlocked. Then they would be in the dress circle of the theatre – looking down on the nearly darkened stage from which, nevertheless, a warm light would well upwards upon her face .... And she would be warm, beside him, her hand touching his hand amongst her furs .... And her white shoulders .... And they would whisper, her hair just touching his ear .... And be warm .... Warm!

And then .... Damn! Damn! Oh, damnation!.... He had lost her letter .... He did not know if she would meet him .... If she cared .... If she cared still – or had ever cared .... He rolled over and writhed in the long grass in which his flea-bag was laid .... The pounding outside grew furious .... There seemed to be hundreds of stars – and more and more and more shooting up into the triangle of the tent-flap. He could see a pallid light shining down the blanket that covered his legs .... And then, like a piece of madness, the earth moved beneath him as if his bed had been kicked, and a hard sound seemed to hammer his skull .... An immense, familiar sound – august as if a God had spoken benevolently, the echoes going away among the woodlands. And the immense shell whined over his head, as if a railway train or the Yeth hounds were going on a long journey ....

The Very lights died down, the shell whined further and further towards the plains; it seemed as if a dead silence fell. A voice said: 'Somebody's ducking out there!' and the voices began to talk again in the dead silence that fell on the battle-field.

But his thoughts raged blackly. He was certain that Mrs Wilkinson would not meet him .... Then all his leave would be mucked up. He imagined himself – he felt himself – arriving at Victoria, in the half-light of the great barn, in the jostling crowd, with all the black shadows, all sweeping up towards the barrier. And there would be a beastly business with three coppers in a cramped telephone box. And the voice of her maid saying that her mistress was out .... Where, in God's name, had he put the letter?....

He tried to memorise exactly what had happened – but it ended at that .... Caradoc Morris who had come back from a course, had brought the letter down to the trench from the 1st Line Transport. He had just looked at the envelope. Then the sentry had yelled out. And he remembered distinctly that he had done something with the letter. But what? What?

The rum jar had bumped off: then gas had come over: then a Hun raid. They had got into the front line and it had taken hours to bomb and bayonet them out, and to work the beastly sandbags of that God-forsaken line into some semblance of a parapet again – a period of sweating and swearing, and the stink of gas, and shoving corpses out of the way .... His mind considered with horror what he could do if Mrs Wilkinson refused to see him altogether. And it went on and on ....

He couldn't sleep. Then he said a prayer to St Anthony – a thing he had not done since he had been a little boy in the Benedictine School at Ramsgate. The pale stars surveyed him from their triangle. One Very light ascended slowly over the dark plain ....

★   ★   ★   ★

He was standing in Piccadilly, looking into a window from which there welled a blaze of light. Skirts brushed him then receded. An elderly, fat man in a brown cassock, with a bald head, a rope around the waist and a crook from which depended a gourd, was gazing into the window beside him. This saint remarked:

'You perceive? Pink flannel!'

The whole window, the whole shop – which was certainly Swan and Edgar's – was a deluge of pink – a rather odious pink with bluey suggestions. A pink that was unmistakable if ever you had seen anything like it ....

'Pink!' the saint said: 'Bluey pink!'

Yes: there were pink monticules, pink watersheds, cascades of pink flannel, deserts, wild crevasses, perspectives ....

W.L. James looked at St Anthony with deep anxiety: he was excited, he was bewildered. The saint continued to point a plump finger, and the crowd all round tittered.

The saint slowly ascended towards a black heaven that was filled with the beams from searchlights ....

And W.L. James found himself running madly in his stockinged feet, in the long grass beside the ditch to the tent at the head of the line. 'Caradoc!' he was calling out 'Caradoc Morris! Where the hell is my Field Service Pocket-Book?'

He got it out of the tunic pocket of his friend, who was in a dead sleep. He pulled a letter from the pocket that is under the pink flannel intended to hold a supply of pins. Holding the letter towards the candle that was at Caradoc's head, he read – as a man drinks after long hours on a hot road....

And, as he stumbled slowly among tent ropes, he remembered that forgotten moment of his life. He remembered saying to himself – even as the sentry shouted 'Rum jar: left,' in the harsh Welsh accent that is like the croak of a raven – saying to himself: 'I *must* put this letter safely away.' And, before he had run, he had pulled out the FSPB,[51] had undone the rubber bands, and had placed the unopened envelope in the little pocket that is under the pink flannel; 'intended,' as the inscription says, 'to hold a supply of pins' ....

He stood still beside his fleabag for a minute as the full remembrance came back to him. And a queer, as it were clean and professional satisfaction crept over him. Before, he had remembered only the, as it were, panic of running – though it was perfectly correct to run – up the communication trench. Now he saw that, even under that panic, he had been capable of a collected – ordered, and as it were, generous action. For he had tried to shield to the best of his ability the woman he loved at the cost of quite great danger to himself.

For the rum jar had flattened out the wretched sandbags of the trench exactly where he had been standing.

Later, of course, he had lent the pocket-book to Caradoc Morris – who was the sort of chap who never would have a pocket-book – for the purpose of writing a report to BHQ ...... But he had certainly behaved well ......

He said to himself:

'By jove, I may be worthy of her even yet,' and getting back into his fleabag, after he had pulled off his socks, which had been wetted by the dewy grass, he fell into pleasurable fancies of softly lighted restaurants, of small orchestras, of gentle contacts of hands and the soft glances of eyes that had dark pupils and brown iris .....

That is, mostly, the way war goes!

---

51 Field Service Pocket Book.

The Colonel's Shoes[52]

On the 27/9/19 four men were held up at midnight between York and Darlington in a first-class carriage. One was an architect, aged fifty, two were country gentlemen from the neighbourhood of Aysgarth, in the late forties, and the last was the MO of a service battalion returning on demobilisation. He also came from near Aysgarth, where he had a practice. They had been a long time in the train; it seemed longer, and there was a dead silence all down the line. The architect, who had a grey beard, stretched out his legs and yawned.

'Eh, but I'm tired!' he said. 'As tired as the old priest, Peter Monagham.'

One of the country gentlemen asked who was the old priest, Peter Monagham. The architect said he was a good old priest who, on a night when he was dog tired, received a summons to administer extreme unction. But he fell asleep, being so very tired, and only waked in the morning light in great shame and tribulation. So he rode very fast to the house of his penitent and was told the man had died.

'But, father,' said his informant, 'he died easy and in the peace of God. He was very troubled in the early hours, but after you came and administered the blessed sacraments he grew calm, and so he made a good end.' According to the legend, an angel, or it may have been the priest's own soul, had come to confess the dying man whilst the old priest slept. So the old priest was saved from great shame.

'Ah,' one of the country gentlemen said, 'that would be in the old days, and in Ireland.'

'You won't find the like,' the other agreed 'in the North of England today. The more's the pity for us that are getting on in years.' The three of them agreed. But the MO happened to be an Irishman.

---

52 The published version of this story contains additions not on the typescript at Cornell, which suggest Ford's revisions. But the typescript is considerably longer, and as many of the excised passages are of interest, they are included in the footnotes here.

'I'll tell you a story if you like,' he said. And though none of them were very cordial at first, off he went. The story he told was something like this: It was, he said, in the middle days of the war and in France. And if you wanted, he emphasised, to know the heaviest tiredness of all the world you must know the tiredness of the war in France in the winters of '16 and '17, when the Somme push was stopped and the heavy other work began to be felt in Battalion Headquarters and such places. Heavy, hard work, endless papers, endless responsibilities, bitter hard weather – and danger that seldom ceased.[53]

'There were many who went over the edge of unreason – but there were many and many who stayed, by the grace of God, just on this side of the edge. By the grace of God – as in the case of the old priest, Peter Monagham. It was like that with Lieut.-Colonel Leslie Arkwright – and it was very nearly like it with his nephew, Lieut. Hugh, both of my Battalion.[54]

'Well, uncle and nephew were the best of pals; they thought

---

53 The Cornell typescript contains here the following passage omitted from the published version:

> It was hard on the young, but it was bitter, bitter hard on those that were ageing at all. Some knew it less than others – but the MO would know better than any, for he would have a bird's eye view of a whole Battalion and its nerves, and its illnesses, and its tiredness.
>
> 'I didn't know,' the architect said, 'that it was really like that. I thought it was all fine and high spirits, really, and things going with a dash until you – what's the word – stopped one!'
>
> 'Ah, don't ye believe it,' the Irish MO said, 'it wasn't so in the Battalion that I had the honour to be attached to, and it wasn't so in any of the other Battalions that I had the honour to see – and they were many. Did you ever hear of the Colonel of a Regular Battalion who went mad, and walked out of his own lines straight over to the Germans and went walking on and on, stark mad, till the Germans took him, three miles behind their line? Or of the next Colonel of the same Battalion who went home sick and shot himself in his flat in South Audley Street? or of the next who...... Well, there were many!'

54 The Cornell typescript contains here the following passage omitted from the published version:

> And they, mind you, were two of the best men that ever wrote 'Please', at the end of a memorandum about the number of time passes issued to their Battalion.... He was a fine, good, kindly, warm-hearted old fellow – the Colonel commanding; and the boy was a good boy. He had gaiety and sense of responsibility, and youth, and great physical strength. And they say that, never in his life did he sign a memorandum without looking it through to be sure that truth was in it – and commas. Who of us is there of which the like could be said, Heaven help us?

alike, in a way that was strange for the old and the young.[55]

'So their friendship was, till there came the winter of '16–'17, and Captain Gotch (that isn't his name. He is alive still. He would be.) This was one of those men as to whom there is a black mark against their names in the High Books. There are such men and there are such books in the world. (I don't mean the confidential Records of a Battalion Orderly Room – but books kept higher still.) They are men who appear foursquare, able, intelligent, they generally have flashing teeth – and they are unsound. They get on – but they don't get on as well as you expect them to. The inexperienced like them enormously; the experienced hold their tongues about them.

'So Hugh Arkwright liked Captain Gotch immensely.[56] There was a good deal of gossip about him. He came from a Reserve Battalion that wasn't popular in that Regiment. So things were said about him – they were probably untrue.[57] I don't know what was the matter with him. I daresay I am unjust to him; but then I didn't like him.

'But if I didn't there were plenty did. The young fellows in the mess when the Battalion was in support and they could get leave

---

55 The Cornell typescript contains here the following passage omitted from the published version:

> Why, it was queer how, after dinner in the Headquarter's Mess, one would begin a sentence and stop for a word and the other finish it. Of course it was the same blood in them – very old blood and no doubt inbred too. And their voices were alike. Why, if you were at CO's orderly room and had your back to the table you could not tell, supposing the CO said:
> "Six days' field punishment No. II," and the boy repeated it for the purpose of getting it surely correct on the – 252 – you couldn't tell which voice was which.

56 The Cornell typescript contains here the following passage omitted from the published version:

> The fellow had the usual fine teeth – and fine, rather thin legs, and well-kept moustache, and brown eyes that did not always look at you, and fine breeches – but he did not come out till the winter of 1916 – and he came out as a captain of some seniority...... It isn't what you look for – but no doubt he could give some reason for it.

57 The Cornell typescript contains here the following passage omitted from the published version:

> They ranged from nasty – very nasty things about him and women and the Colonel of his Reserve Battalion, to the allegation that a firm, in which he had been a junior partner before the war, had been fined heavily for trading with the enemy. But no doubt they were not true, as I said before.

to go into the big towns and cut a little splash for the night – they'd
swear by Gotch. He was their leader then. And Hugh Arkwright
went with the rest of his age.

'That was how it came to sad disagreement between him and
the old CO. Hugh thought that his uncle was unjust to Gotch.
There would be recommendations going – for jobs at Divisional
headquarters and higher up. Circulars come in, you know, asking
for junior officers who have knowledge of Flemish, Japanese,
Maregasque, Basque, bayonet-fighting as practised in Pushtu: or for
senior officers who have expert knowledge of pig-breeding, the
growing of Jerusalem artichokes, the extraction of solder from old
tins, the unravelling of gold lace – God knows what! And Captain
Gotch would send his name in for all these things, and the CO
would send the name on, but without any recommendation.
Young Hugh would see the memos, and his eyes would be
troubled. He was very intimate with Gotch by March, when the
weather was frightful. I forgot to say that Captain Gotch had a fine
baritone voice. It has an important bearing on the last words of my
story. He would sing popular sentimental songs of the day, and put
in nasty meanings and raise one brown eyebrow when he came to
them. It made him popular with the men of the Battalion who were
not in his Company when he sang to them at smoking concerts
improvised in old barns and tents and pigsties. But his own
Company was nasty.

'One day the Colonel came to me – as MO.

'"Pat," he said. "I don't believe I can stick it. Good God, that I
should have to say I don't believe I can stick it!"

'I asked him what was the matter – but it wasn't necessary to ask
him what was the matter. His mind was overloaded. You see – like
his nephew, he was indefatigable – and he didn't leave as much as
he might have to his subordinates.[58]

'But latterly it was patent that he was feeling the strain. It took
the form of falling asleep. He'd fall asleep at table – in between two

---

58 The Cornell typescript contains here the following passage omitted from the published
version:

> And he knew the name and regimental number of every Tommy in his Battalion –
> and a little bit about each man too. He was a Yorkshireman and they from the West
> Country. But I remember walking with him along the main street in Amiens, in the
> twilight, and there was a Tommy looking into a picture postcard shop.
>
> '"Hullo, 09 Phillips", the Colonel said to him. "Going to buy a bloodstained
> souvenir for the little girl in Cairleon-on-Usk?" – and he knew all his men like that.....

words of a sentence. (That was how we knew that Hugh could complete his sentences for him!) His silver head would drop forward and his eyes close. Or the same midway in dealing at a rubber of bridge. And the officers would wait silent, and worried.

'On the morning he came to me he'd fallen asleep whilst taking his orderly room – for ten seconds. He said he didn't believe they'd noticed it – and I don't believe they had. But he had dozed in his chair, at a table covered with a blanket, with the Assistant Adjutant beside him, and the prisoner, and escort, and Provost Sergeant, and Regimental Sergeant-Major and all in front of him – and Captain Gotch. In the schoolroom of a little town in Flanders, it was. I forget the name. It made it better – or perhaps it made it worse – that the sleeping fits only came on when we were out of the trenches proper.

'"And the devil of it is," he said, "I woke up to hear myself saying, like a bally rifle-shot: 'Case explained!' And the charge was a hell of a serious charge of refusing to obey orders – brought by that fellow Gotch!"

'Apparently on a beastly, cold, wet night, Gotch had stormed down like a madman on his Company who were on some sort of fatigue, carrying stones, or boxes, or cases of dumbells, or something. And two of the men had said they couldn't – or wouldn't – lift something wet and heavy. It was a case that was open to a doubt. Gotch swore the men said they wouldn't. The Company Sergeant-Major, who was a time-serving man with 23 years' service – he was the only witness – was not ready to swear what the word used had been. It might have been "couldn't" or it might have been "wouldn't".

'So that the "case explained" verdict, tendered actually in the CO's sleep, hadn't been outrageous. Whatever the object was that they had been required to lift might, on a dark, wet night, have seemed beyond two men's lifting power. The CO said, with a trick of his old, gentle jauntiness, that he had got out of it all right though Old Forty had not liked it.

'"And I could see that my young cut of a nephew didn't like it either," he said. Young Hugh had been recording the awards on the 252 – the charge sheet.

'"I strafed the two men well," the CO said, "before the Provost Sergeant could march them out. I said that it was for the Company Officer and not for the men to judge what men could do. And so on."

'Then he had cleared the room of the other ranks – the men and NCOs.... "And I said to Mr Forty that I wished that in future all officers giving evidence against other ranks should do it in writing whenever possible as is provided in King's Regulations, though it's apt to drop out of observance here...."

'"And I expect Mr Forty did not like that much, either, sir," I said myself, softly.

'The CO started a little.

'"Did I call Captain Gotch 'Old Forty'," he asked rather guiltily. "It slipped out.... You know the men call him that, too?"

'"Bless you, sir," I said, "I hear it from every one of the sick I get from 'A' Company. And they've been many latterly."

'"I wish to God," the CO said, "the fellow had never.... But that's between you and me and that gate-post." He sighed. And I knew he was thinking of the estrangement that was growing between him and his nephew.[59]

*   *   *

'It was only two nights later, that the nephew came to me – just before driving to some town or other, [Steenwerck], I think, with a brake-load of young fellows, in search of diversion and may be the young ladies. I pray God that one of them was kind to Hugh that night – for he was killed, driving back, by a stray shell that dropped through the bottom of the waggonette the young boys were in, on a clear, still, moonlight night..... But when he came to me was before he started.

'He was terribly depressed about his health – and extraordinarily glad about something else, and he wanted me to give him drugs to keep him from breaking down.[60] He said he'd been having illusions.

---

59 The Cornell typescript contains here the following passage omitted from the published version:

> He knew, you see, what his nephew thought without his nephew having to say what it was – and he knew that this nephew thought he had unjustly insulted Captain Gotch by that verdict. I gave him a nuxvomica tonic and said I'd certify him as fit for six months' at the base. But he wouldn't have it.

60 The Cornell typescript contains here the following passage omitted from the published version:

> He was a fine young fellow, twenty-four, over six feet, with corrugated brows like his uncle, and a normal frown just like his uncle's – only they both used to break into bashful smiles, if you understand what I mean – as if both were ashamed of

And when I asked him what illusions; did he think he saw pink and red or bottle green blackbirds? he said no, it was queerer than that – but he couldn't tell me without telling a long story.' So I told him to take some hooch and fire away.

'He told me a good deal that I knew, about his coolness towards his uncle.... and then he came to that morning. He said that, just before Orderly Room, the CO had said to him that he wanted Captain Wilkins, the Adjutant, to help at Orderly Room, that morning – marking down the cases, instead of Hugh, you know. And that worried him, so that, instead of going to his papers after breakfast, he sat down in an armchair by the fire in the A2 mess dining room. It was a large French house, the Battalion Headquarters at that time, the village school just behind it being the Orderly Room.

'So he sat by the fire, worrying.

'And then Gotch burst into the room and rushed to a writing table at the far end, beside the piano. He snatched at a piece of paper and he cursed, and he began writing with a scratchy pen – and cursing – and scratching out and rewriting and gnawing his beautiful moustache. He said to himself: "A d——d pass it's coming to if officers can't..." Then he roared out for a mess waiter and cursed him for having a cod-fish's face and told him to take the paper to the Adjutant at the double and curse him. And then he got up with his back still to Hugh and sat down at the piano and began to dash off tinkling songs as hard as he could hit the ivories.

'And then, Hugh said, in the midst of his own worries, suddenly, he began to feel another worry – a heavy dreadful worry, as if all the Battalion was going to Hell and as if the war was hopeless.... And as if the officers of the Battalion were not as much to be trusted as they had been six months ago, and as if the men of the Battalion were growing stubborn. Something must be done about "A" Company. But what? And that dreadful bounder, Gotch, with his debts, and the contempt of the men. How was he to get rid of him? "A" Company junior officers would shield Gotch .... They were good boys.... And he was tired. He was dreadfully tired. And all his bones ached. And his nephew Hugh....

---

smiling and the softer emotions, as being effeminate during the war, but they couldn't help liking the queer world and the queer people in it. So there he was, miserable about his health – and happier than you ever saw anybody – about his uncle, the CO......

'And suddenly, Hugh said, he knew that it was his uncle's worries he was feeling. And he wanted to go to his uncle. But he couldn't move. And, of course, he couldn't have gone to the CO in Orderly Room if he could have moved.

'Gotch was banging on the piano; but suddenly Hugh heard his uncle's voice say in his ear, "I can't keep.... Oh, God, I can't keep.... I'm falling.... falling...." And then – he himself – he, Hugh, himself – was sitting on the hard wooden chair at the CO's table. He felt older, older; and wiser, wiser; and surer of himself than he had ever felt sure. But his hand on the blanket table cover was heavy and white and hairy. And he said: "Call in the prisoners." And the Provost Sergeant roared: "Escort and Coy.-Sergt.-Major Wilson."

'And he reached his heavy hand, distastefully, for the buff 252 which was pinned to the Field Conduct Sheet, and had on top of it a piece of scrawled writing paper. And he read a number and the name Wilson and the rank, Company-Sergeant-Major, and the offence: "Highly irregular conduct to the prejudice of good order and military discipline. Using disrespectful language with regard to an officer." And to himself he said: "that swine, Forty, is trying to do in Wilson for not having given false evidence against those two men the day before yesterday." But he said aloud and heavily to the Adjutant at his side: "Ask 'A' company if they can't make out better charges than that!" And he snorted with contempt over his heavy grey moustaches: "Highly irregular conduct to the prejudice."...

'He leant back in his chair and looked composedly at the always worried face of the Company Sergeant-Major.[61]

'And "Old Forty.".... "Forty foot down and still digging," the men called him, because he never left the bottom of the deepest dug-out, was trying to do Wilson in! Well, they would see....

'He said: "Company-Sergeant Major Wilson, you have heard the charge.... The first witness is your Company Commander,

---

61 The Cornell typescript contains here the following passage omitted from the published version:

   And he knew that the Sergt.-Major, with his brown face, black eyes and waved moustaches was the best man in the Battalion. A time-serving man, an old Guardsman with 23 years service and never a mark on his conduct sheet – except that six years before when he had been Regt.-Q.-M.-S. he had gone mad over a woman called Hurlett and broken his leave, and had been reduced to Sergt. – as will happen to the best men. But for that he would surely have been a Guards' Regt.-Sergt.-Major... A good honest man!...

Captain Gotch. He writes: 'On the 17/4/17 "A" Company were
balloting for leave in my orderly room. The Company-
Quartermaster-Sergeant was drawing names from a hat in my
presence and the Company-Sergeant-Major was writing down the
names. There were seven names to be drawn out of twenty-four.
When six had been drawn I said: "Company-Sergeant-Major, put
down the name of Lance-Corporal Howells, 579756." The
Company-Sergeant-Major demurred. I said: "The OC Company
has always the right to nominate a man for special services." The
Company-Sergeant-Major said: "It isn't done in this Battalion, sir."
I said: "Those are my orders." The Company-Sergeant-Major
wrote down the name of Lance-Corporal Howells. As I was leaving
the room I heard the Company-Sergeant-Major say to the
Company-Quartermaster-Sergeant: "Gotch will miss fifty-six
Howells in the next ten days." I ordered him to be put under arrest.'
Next witness!"

'The   Provost-Sergeant   roared: "46721   Company-
Quartermaster-Sergeant Reynolds...."

'Hugh said he could see that originally Captain Gotch had
written: "Company-Sergeant-Major Wilson said: 'Lance-Corporal
Howells has only been a short time with the company. – Since you
came, sir! And all the men whose names are down have been a
minimum of eighteen months without leave. And leave only just
open after three months!'" He had then struck out those words and
substituted: "The Company-Sergeant-Major demurred." He
might have saved himself the trouble, for the Quartermaster-
Sergeant reported the words in full.

"'And what happened then?"

"'As Captain Gotch was going out of the room, sir, the
Company-Sergeant-Major said to me 'Brother Boche will miss
Lance-Corpl. Howells in the next ten days.' Captain Gotch ordered
me to put the Company-Sergeant Major in the clink."

'Hugh said that he reached across – the heavy white hand – and
took the charge sheet from the Adjutant, who had in the meantime
resumed possession of it. He was taking up a pen and writing
heavily, himself, the word 'Case...' whilst he said:–

"'Company Sergeant-Major Wilson...."

'Wilson cleared his throat; he was always husky. A good man,
Hugh said. And it was a pleasure for him to hear Wilson say:–

"'I beg you, sir, for leave to speak" – the time-honoured Guards'
formula. He said that he agreed to the evidence given by Company

Quartermaster Reynolds.

'And Hugh said that, whilst he was heavily writing the word "Dismissed" after the word "Case" on the charge sheet.[62]

'Hugh said that the roaring of the Provost Sergeant getting in the next case, and the men stamping as they marched out suddenly became the voice of Captain Gotch, who had swung round on the piano stool and was saying:–

"'You, Hugh ..." and then: "By God if the CO gives Wilson 'Case explained,' I shall go before the Brigadier."

'Hugh said he answered:–

"'I should, Gotch, I should go before Division. Because if I were in the Colonel shoes, I should make it 'Case dismissed'."

'Gotch said:–

"'By God, what do you mean, Hugh?"

"'I mean," Hugh said, "that Division are asking for a junior officer to look after Divisional Follies."

'Gotch's jaw fell down, and he clenched his right fist. But suddenly he stiffened to attention. The door had opened behind Hugh, but he knew of course that the Colonel had come in. There had been only two cases at Orderly Room.

'The Colonel had a slip of paper in his hand and was looking at it with his brow knitted. It was a 252.

"'Hugh," he said, "I'm getting to write deucedly like you." And then:–

"'Ah, Gotch. The adjutant says that baths are open. See that 'A' Company parades in good time."

'Hugh said he drew himself together and looked at his uncle.

"'I was just recommending Captain Gotch, sir," he uttered slowly and deliberately, "to apply for the job of the Divisional Follies. It's going begging."

'The Colonel nodded at Gotch.

"'I should, Gotch," he said. "I could recommend you cordially." Gotch gathered up his hat, and gloves, and stick, and left the room. The old man fell into the chair by the fire.

---

62 The Cornell typescript contains here the following passage omitted from the published version:

(you must understand that a commanding officer does not usually write these things in ink himself but leaves it to the Adjutant) – he was saying drily:

"'Company Sergeant Major, it is never a good thing for a NCO even to seem to comment on his Company Officer's orders. Captain Gotch is a little hard on hearing." He added: "Case dismissed!"

"'Hugh," he said, "get me a drink... Hugh, were you in the Orderly Room just now?"

"'I don't know," Hugh said. "Yes, yes, I think I was."

'The CO imagined he was confused because he thought he would be strafed for having been there.

"'That accounts for your handwriting on this 252. I suppose the Adjutant was too busy," he said. "I didn't really notice who was there." And then he lifted his tired eyes and looked at Hugh with an awful apprehension.

"'Was I... was it... all right?" he asked.

"'You were splendid, sir," Hugh answered. "You looked tired ... ill. But you were splendid."

'He was mixing a whisky, and as he handed it to his uncle he said:–

"'I hope to God that swine Gotch goes the Division."

'The Colonel drank down his whisky.

"'Thank God, Hugh, my dear," he said. "I thought I was asleep in my own Orderly Room.'"

Enigma

In 'Literary Causeries: XII: On Causeries as Such', *Chicago Tribune Sunday Magazine* (Paries, 4 May 1924), 3, Ford tells a story he calls 'the *Hotel Sublime*', with a plot very similar to 'Enigma', saying: 'There then is the story which was told me as being true. I present it to the reader, for as far as I can see I shall never make use of it myself'. He then proposes – in the manner Hemingway was to parody with such gusto in *The Torrents of Spring* – a competition for 'the best "full-dress" arrangement of the story called the Hotel Sublime and told either as an after dinner anecdote or as a short story'. The typescript of 'Enigma' predates these comments, however, by at least eighteen months.

'What should one do,' the young man who had been in my battalion asked, 'in such circumstances?'

'It doesn't,' I answered, 'seem to me to be a difficult question to answer.' I had been the sort of Dutch uncle to so many of these nicish boys for five years or so; it was natural that he should come to me for advice. Besides I had given him the reference that, along with his agreement, he still held in his hand. 'I should just sit tight – if your nerves will stand it. You've tried the police; you've tried the solicitor; you've tried the telephone; you've got the agreement.'

'It's rather... ghostly! That's what it is,' he answered uncertainly. 'But I think my nerves will stand it.' He added that every time that he came up from the bottom of the rough meadow and entered the low parlour he expected to see Mrs Rockingham-Denman sitting in a chintz cane arm-chair; and he expected to jump. And he couldn't afford to be made to jump. 'But of course,' he finished, 'she'd probably be in the kitchen making the tea!'

'She might even write before she came!' I said. But he did not seem to think there would be much chance of that. he thought that Mr and Mrs Rockingham-Denman would return with the startling suddenness of their disappearance. But they haven't yet. They had been gone a month before he consulted me; and that is now a twelve-month since. His nerves too are standing it all right.

I suppose it is possible, even in the twentieth century, to vanish. I mean, to go out completely, in a minute, leaving as you say of hares, the form still hot after you. Without any debts left behind you. Just walking out of the house. That was what the quite pleasant young couple, Mr and Mrs Rockingham-Denman had done. One's evil mind suggests the worst to one: but there was no worst discoverable. Nothing. Not even any good foot-prints. A complete blank!

As the police inspector put it: If there had been foot-prints his detectives would have been able to fit them to Mrs Rockingham-Denman's elegant boots of which in her bed-room there remained half a dozen pairs. But there was no sense in fitting boots to foot-prints when you could not lay your hand on the owner of the boots. It was a hiatus beyond the experience of criminal-hunting .... He was quite polite – but indifferent. Nothing was known against the Rockingham-Denmans in the neighbourhood. He had had a good look at them because, just before buying the cottage, they had called to ask him a question that took a long time in answering – about regulations in the district against importing plants from various foreign countries. In various districts certain plants cannot be introduced even under licence for fear of disease. It had taken the police-inspector two hours to look the matter up and they had been in and out of the office, getting their lunches in the small county town. Polwarth, it was. Mr Denman was noticeable because he had a slight defect in the pupil of his right eye: it was not perfectly circular – or rather there was a little, as if chipped, irregularity, projecting into the blue of the iris. Not a deformity – but something you could not counterfeit. No habitual or new criminal was 'wanted' in the whole country with that ocular peculiarity – nor yet was it mentioned in the circulars from the police of various European countries .... Naturally, said that rustic inspector, he had asked the question of the Central Authorities of our efficiently policed land. And polite but bored he remained; he seemed to think it was my young friend Price's trouble, and no very serious trouble at that!

The solicitor had taken the same tone. Of the Rockingham-Denman's he knew nothing at all. They had just walked into his office from the street; had instructed him to make arrangements with the solicitors for the people who were selling the cottage as to the purchase of the place with its furniture, lock, stock and barrel. The old owner's young wife had died abroad and he could not bear the sight of the rooms they had inhabited for no more than a few days. So that it was as new as a new pin, really.

The man of law had looked at young Price's agreement; he had suggested that Price had better get it stamped or registered or something. Then it would be perfectly valid and would absolutely warrant Mr Price's remaining in charge of the cottage – in possession of it till the crack of doom if, before then, no representative of the Rockingham-Denman's turned up. Young Price said that when he had told that not unamiable gentleman that he, Price, was only then recovering from shell-shock of a complicated kind, he had seemed to lose what little, rather chuckling, interest he had hitherto had in the affair. He patted Price on the back, said: 'I'll see to getting your agreement stamped for you. You can depend on it that Mr Denman knows what he's about. I can tell you one thing about him. He has been in, or studied the law – at one of the London Inns of Court. I could tell that from his accent: if I hadn't I could tell it from the language of the very generous – the extremely generous! – agreement he has made with you!' And he pushed Price amiably out of his inner office ....

Naturally Price had consulted – but rather warily – a great many local authorities before that. – And it had taken time! The local authorities were very slow to part with information; some being rustically suspicious; some thinking that Price was merely having a game with them; some merely uncouth and disagreeable. The village doctor had never seen the Rockingham-Denmans; neither had the parson. Why should they have? The Denmans had not been in the place for a complete day. They had come at dusk in a hired automobile with a good deal of luggage; they had walked out with nothing just after tea of the next day.

The woman who had been trusted with the key and had handed it to them might have been trusted to provide information; she had acted for one morning as their charwoman. But, apparently, she had been told that she would not suit and that sealed her lips except for occasional and defined sniffs. She was a London Cockney of a lean, small, mean, disagreeable type wearing a dilapidated bonnet with strings and a continuing drop at the end of a sharp, reddish nose. Price found in the dust-bin a great – a very great! – quantity of broken glass, the debris of certainly half a dozen rather good, antique tumblers. With them the sudden departure of that housekeeper was certainly connected ....

And then there was the 'Cock-eyed' man of criminal type.

He, my young friend was certain, was the maggot in the heart of that enigma. It was immediately after he had mentioned to them that cock-eyed fellow with the soft, dishonest voice, fiftyish, with a startlingly bald head arising out of extravagantly thick, blue-black, grizzled side fringes of hair, that the Rockingham-Denmans had so incomprehensibly disappeared. 'Incomprehensibly otherwise!' the young man said rather ruefully to me.

Young Price was one of a hundred thousand – a little better off than some, he had come out of the army with his undistinguished university career that should have fitted him to be a schoolmaster or something like that, completely stopped. Real, bad – and I assure you quite genuine – shell-shock had made it absolutely impossible that he should continue his studies. It hadn't made it impossible for him to let the greatest part of his small capital get into the hands of ingenious swindlers with a sham automobile agency. So he had an incredibly small sum a week, interest from a few railway shares which he was determined not to sell and had been tramping about the country with a ruck-sack in search of agricultural work. For two months or more before he had come to the Rockingham-Denmans' cottage. He had been born and brought up on a farm and knew something of pigs, dairy-cows, vegetables, poultry, patent-manures and fruit.

He had been walking along a friendly, level road in the extremely ordered countryside on a perfect Indian summer day. On one side of the cottage was a green-wired-in field with poultry houses; on the other a staked-in field dotted with oak-trees that said: 'Acorns! Pigs!'; behind the cottage a row of admirably tidy, stone and slated steadings and a great meadow like a park, running up a gentle hill-side that, like the cottage itself lay open to the south sun. To a country-bred young man the breezes that came from over that admirable lawnland whispered: 'Glorious dairying!'

The cottage was white, low, longish, not very new, not very old – and friendly. There are cottages that look at you with eyes neither scowling nor browbeaten: just contemplative, so that if you are a good fellow at all they seem to like you. The road was straight for a quarter of a mile so that, for a quarter of a mile, young Price had seen the man with the cock-eyes as he afterwards came to know him – staring, like a disreputable tramp with a scare-crow's, black morning coat and a square topped, green-with-age, billycock hat, over the trimmed holly-hedge, at the white cottage. Lugubrious rags of silk lining hung from the skirts of his coat.

Young Price asked him suddenly if there was any chance of a job here. He spun round, like a panic-stricken hedgehog, with his gapped teeth, his one chalk-white eye, and his white-streaked beard. He shuffled hastily up the road.

Young Price strode up twenty yards or so of garden path, between chrysanthemums and Michaelmas daisies to the cottage porch. He knocked firmly. Looking back up the path, he could see the square-topped hat, persistent as it were, in a slight irregularity of the trim, not quite six-foot hedge.

Young Price, when he talked to me, speculated that this was not improbably the Husband, disguised, who had tracked the guilty – but absolutely lovable – couple to their lair. Or a Detective set on by a – properly! – wronged husband. For young Prince made no secret of the immoral fact that – if *that* were Mrs Rockingham-Denman's husband then the young couple, he considered, being absolutely made for each other, had done the right thing in eloping to that rural dove-cote...

I pointed out that, even husbands disguising themselves, do not adopt clothes of an extravagant filthiness and rags; and knock out half their teeth!

'But,' young Price objected, 'Rockingham-Denman might have got him falsely accused of forgery. So he might have been in gaol for years!'

I said that Life is seldom so obliging to the moving-pictures; but he assured me gravely that Truth – as he himself had experienced – was often stranger than fiction. And he fell back on the Detective theory from which I could not shake him by pointing out that a criminal-investigator with one chalk eye could hardly be expected to make such of a success of life. Price said that Cock-eye, as he called him, evidently hadn't made a success of life!

He stuck to his theory; though nothing has since occurred to disprove or to confirm it. Or to re-place it with another. For what is one to think?

That cottage-porch-door opened on the friendliest, most charming and absolutely straight young couple that, Price said, he had ever imagined. Let alone seen! The man thirty-ish; tall; be-legginged and with a trustworthy, sandy moustache; the young woman twenty-three-ish; apparently fascinating to young Price who was not good at description; but certainly fair too, small, and singularly light on her feet. Price had noticed that when she had slipped out of the porch after her husband...

The porch-door, then, had opened on that man, with behind him a chintzish, grandfather's-clockish glimpse. A blue bowl of pink chrysanthemums from the bed along the path...

Young Price in a firm, mechanical voice had begun the question that, three or four times a day, Sundays not excepted, for the last two and a half months he had asked at farm and villa doorways. Had they a job for him? He knew about pigs, dairy-cattle, poultry, patent-manures, vegetable-growing and fruit; he could drive many makes of car; he had had such and such service and had been invalided out of the army, such and such a corps, with such and such a rank. He spoke his words like a gramophone; the man in front of him tried to interrupt from time to time; but he kept on. Then the man said:

'My boy! You're a fairy godmother!'

He stepped back into the parlour and called:

'Nell! Nell, darling! Here's our fairy god-mother... A fellow from the old crowd, too. We're settled!'

Her voice called from above-stairs:

'No! Oh.... You *can't* say so! What delightful luck!'

And that it was. They knew the same people; talked the same language; had been over the same territory. They walked in the sunlight over the green, cowless, pig-less, poultry-less fields, Mr Rockingham-Denman explaining that he had pedigree-short horns and pedigree all the rest of it, galore, coming down in the course of the week. He shewed young Price a drawer where there reposed bank-notes in envelopes – to pay for all this live-stock on arrival, and to pay wages for dairy assistants. He took Price over the steadings whilst Mrs Rockingham-Denman was making tea for them. Price proposed me as a reference and Mr Rockingham-Denman said that that would be all right.

And, as Price said, that did not seem really strange: there are for every soul of us in this world some people whom you can trust and who are bound to trust you absolutely, like a thing that can't be helped! And then, you see, they had been in the same crowd; they had not met because one had been in a fourth and the other in a twenty-third battalion... But they both knew, say, Fatty Saunders and his wife. The odd thing was that Fatty Saunders and his wife did not know the Rockingham-Denmans by name when Price wrote to them – and Price's description of them would have described two thousand other couples. Friendly, lovable, absolutely straight: as if they had known you, and you them, for a life-time and a half ....

So young Price was to live with them; to take all the animal-responsibility and two thirds of the profits. Price remonstrated; but Rockingham-Denman at a small bureau drew out and signed the agreement while Price drank tea at a little table beside the lady. Then Rockingham-Denman said:

'We shall be out a good deal, Mrs Denman and I. We're gad-abouts with a new two-seater.' The two-seater still remains in the little garage. 'So there in the drawer is the money to pay for anything that comes ....'

It was then that young Price brought in the cock-eyed man. He said:

'Isn't it risky to have so much money in a house. On a main-road. Thick with hoboes!' And he had described the cock-eyed man, bald head and all, whom he had seen looking over the hedge. The cock-eyed man had taken off his square billy-cock to wipe his bald head with a scarlet, white-spotted handkerchief, just before my young friend had come up to him at the hedge-side. 'The very worst type of hobo!' the young man had finished his speech.

Mr Rockingham-Denman was standing with his back to the bureau at which he had been writing; he stooped a little. He said:

'Oh-Ah!' as if he had not been very interested and strode slowly across the room and out at the open door. Two breaths, as it were, later, his wife edged herself out of her deep, bright armchair and went out after him, with a tripping, light, unhurried step.

Price finished his tea and sat waiting. They never returned.

I have no answer to offer to this enigma. It is just possible that .... But I had better not confuse the issues by suggesting solutions to which I myself can advance a hundred valid objections! It seems best to leave the matter to an intelligent Public.

The Miracle[63]

The former Miss Sinclair, lying in her great four-post bed, the sheets to her firm chin, was aware that her husband, coming from his bath, was walking briskly and humming. She was still in the stage of studying him. She was aware – though he wasn't – that he was a man of deep and suddenly aroused moodinesses, and these she watched with attention because his career was very precious to her – though she herself had abandoned none of her own hopes of scientific honours. This was a new mood! He pushed the door open sharply, and, with long strides – for he was a tall man – in his elegantly cut trousers and admirable white shirt, crossed the floor to the foot of the bed where he faced her.

'I maintain,' he exclaimed good-humouredly, stretching out his hand in a parody of himself when lecturing, 'that A Man of Intellect cannot be an efficient Man of Action. I have solved in my bath a considerable problem. Yet I have again lost my collar-stud!'

'For myself,' his wife asserted in imitation of his tone, 'I maintain that the age of miracles *cannot* return and never existed. Yet you are addressing remarks to me before breakfast. Here are four irreconcilable phenomena!'

He was a very young, tall, brilliant Professor, and they had been married not quite a year though they had been engaged for four years. In those four he had naturally had a good deal of leeway to make up; she, on the other hand, having remained at the rather, but not very, old university of which her father was the distinguished Principal, had, as it seemed to her, always been remarkable for looks, vivacity, and learning, her 'subject' being scientific eugenics. And having intensely disliked the period of waiting for her lover to make up his leeway, she was determined that now he should do nothing to retard his future progress. With a good brain, she thought, he had touches of the poet about him. Not a bad thing for a scientist, but dangerous in a keenly competitive university society. They had the world, now, as a ball before their feet. She

---

63 Published in the *Yale Review*, 18 (Winter 1928), 320–31; and the *English Review*, 51 (August 1930), 243–52.

was determined that nothing should delay its swift rolling.

He, for his part, had made up his leeway on his return to that place with a tenacity, a force, and a rapid grasping of opportunity that had astonished such of the dons as had known him before. He had gone away a boy, heavy and, above all, shy; possibly gifted but nervously unable to do himself justice. He came back seeming to know the ropes of that university with unaccountable address; over-hauling his arrears of work as a liner overhauls a fishing smack; overwhelming as a wave overwhelms a sea anemone the brilliant Miss Sinclair, whom before to speak to would have paralysed him. His department was some branch of biology so abstruse that one hesitates over the spelling of the name, but their minds were reputed to fit as acorn fits cup. They were humorous, good-humoured, and comely, and it was agreed between them not to converse before breakfast, when the Professor, pottering over his careful toilette, which desultorily occupied him for a full hour, was accustomed to think over the subject of his coming day's labours.

The former Miss Sinclair lay motionless, her eyes like coals above the white sheet of a great state bed – high pillared. Mirrors shone deeply; the curtains were pink-flowered, calendered cretonne. There was a great deal of light in the tall, white room. Miss Sinclair's long black plaits, from each side of her head, ran parallel and pointed at the tall professor. She was not so certain of his truce.

She pointed with her chin: 'There's a collar-stud there,' she said, and the Professor lumbered pensively towards the old white mantelpiece searching under its flowers for his stud.

'I am thinking,' he said, 'but not about Portfolio B 14. I thought *that* problem out in my bath. Where *is* that collar-stud? ... An hour's scribbling and B 14 can go to the university printers!'

His wife ecstatically adopted a sitting posture, her black plaits hanging now parallel over blue and white, faintly figured silk.

'*Douglas!*' she exclaimed. 'Then the age of miracles *isn't* past. After all these months, you've thought it out! But why today of all days? I can't believe it!'

'That *blasted* stud,' the Professor mumbled between his teeth and continued to sway from side to side in front of the mantelpiece.

'It's *behind* the antirrhinums,' his wife said; 'I put it there last night – for safety. I know what you are.'

The Professor straightened his back, turned with meaning right about, and regarded her under serious brows. He was rather an ugly fellow, she thought, with his large mouth, high cheek bones, and overhung eyes. But his long line of trousers, his strong neck arising from his white, still uncollared shirt – rather a gargoyle – but a fine figure of a man. Passionate, humorous, and abstracted. He considered that he had the Scientific Mind! He! ...

It was as well, however, not to shake him in *that* belief. Their living sumptuously depended on that.

He said: 'You think you know me? H'm! H'm! ... We're agreed, aren't we, to regard phenomena set beside phenomena *as* phenomena set beside each other? Dried fir cones side by side. Without connection or purpose!'

'That,' she said, 'was our premarital agreement. I suppose that we stick to it. We *have* the Scientific Mind .... You want to tell me something? About Portfolio B 14?'

'No!' he said. 'This is an anniversary!'

'It can't be *ours!*' she said sharply, 'because we haven't been married a year. Then it's Miss... '

'No!' he said with decision. He swung half round again to glance along the mantelshelf for the collar-stud. 'Oh, you said it was *behind* the antirrhinums,' he muttered, and then adopting an easy attitude of his long trousers, and slightly extending one hand, he cleared his throat. His wife lay down, drew the bedclothes to her chin, arranged her plaits on the sheet.

'It's a question of a miracle,' he said. 'You have twice used the phrase "an age of miracles". There is a proverbial saying, "The age of miracles is past!" I question whether it is. I am about to lay before you for your *scientific* consideration a single circumstance. Within my own experience. Exactly observed! One that I have since considered profoundly and that has influenced my whole life. And I cannot see that it is anything but a miracle! It concerns the creation of something that formerly was not: in a given place and in answer to prayer. My own personal prayer. Whilst, obviously, that in no way affects my biological position, it must affect my attitude towards a Special Providence and all that that entails.'

His wife, speaking on purpose very slowly, said:

'You have considered that the expression of such a belief might lose you your job. Or, at least, it might make it extremely difficult for you to get another here – not to say a better one, when this one runs out. The Big Ones of this place are not distinguished by tolerance. Father himself... '

'They will hardly,' the Professor said, 'eject me because I make to you in private a communication of a quasi-religious nature.'

'You had better let me hear.'

'I must,' he answered, 'think a moment more on the exact terms. I naturally wish to spare you disagreeable emotions and must choose my words with care.'

His brows drawn together, he turned to the mantelpiece, thinking deeply. His wife, motionless, watched him with an anxious intensity. She was aware that of whatever he did in such moments of painfully abstracted thought he would be absolutely unconscious. And it occurred to her that, possibly, such an abstractedness made him not absolutely fitted for personal scientific observation – personal! For abstract thought he was magnificent. Unrivalled.

But she had known him, whilst thinking deeply, to move the slide in a microscope and to be perfectly unconscious of having done so. Naturally, that had altered the whole aspect of the section he had been observing. Yet when she had mentioned the fact to him, he had been so painfully affected, so absolutely certain that he had committed no such action, that, at last, after a distressing scene – the only one they had ever had – she had thought it wiser to withdraw her absolutely true allegation. There were, she knew, times when it was wiser to submit, the whole being greater than the part. Indeed, he had gone almost out of his mind, and she had never again mentioned or – as she naturally might have – made fun of his unconscious actions.

She watched him then. His brows still drawn tightly together he moved the old silver vase of scarlet, sulphur, and blazing magenta snapdragons on the mantelpiece. He took the collar-stud thus uncovered and, as again he turned to his wife, fitted the small metal object into the stud-hole of his white linen shirt. His eyes gazed at nothing.

He brought his mind to earth with a jerk. 'This is naturally painful to me,' he said. 'You must excuse me if I have kept you waiting.' He cleared his throat.

'We have never,' he continued, 'discussed religion. Why should we have? You, as a don's daughter here, have naturally hardly considered or heard of the subject. I myself have naturally wished to spare you the contemplation of the disagreeable and the unimportant. But this being the seventh anniversary... '

'The seventh!' his wife said bitterly. 'I knew it would have something to do with that hateful period.'

'I repent,' the Professor said, 'almost as bitterly as you can, my share in those proceedings. At the time I conceived it to be my duty. I was then young and easily out-argued and convinced. You have since convinced me that my duty should have led me into far other paths. I have acknowledged my fault, and re-acknowledge it now. I will be as short as I can .... Seven years ago today, then, I was in charge of a large bombing raid .... Can you stand this? I will spare you all the details that I can.'

His wife said, 'Go on!'

'In those days,' the Professor continued, 'bombs were very primitive affairs; they had time fuses instead of detonators. You had to light the fuse and then hurl the bomb; the bombs themselves were mere jam tins filled with an explosive surrounded by fragments of metal. The important point was that you had to light the fuse. For that purpose cigarettes were supplied to the troops – Oriental cigarettes because, being mostly adulterated with saltpetre, they burn longer than the Virginian sort. I hope I make myself clear. The officer in charge of the bombing party was responsible for the cigarettes. I was the officer in charge of the bombing party. It was a very large one – a raid, in the technical language. I was then in charge of it. And it happened on the day after my arrival actually in the line of that distant and precipitous country. I had been for some time with what is called the First Line Transport, waiting for an opportunity to be sent up; but movement over that terrain had not been easy, and opportunity had not occurred. My morale, in the military sense, was not good. *You,* hating as you do all military manifestations, will not despise me when I say that my morale was distinctly bad. We were shelled, from time to time, from a distance; we had to sit still under the shelling. I feared it dreadfully: I do not conceal from you that I was an arrant coward.'

His wife said: 'Oh, *Douglas!* ... But you've got decorations and things, haven't you?'

'We won't go into that,' her husband said. 'We never have; there is no occasion to do so now. It is sufficient to say that then – seven years ago today – I was an arrant coward, from having to sit all day in a bright sunshine doing nothing, with a few shells falling near us from time to time.'

He swung half round, looked at the mantelpiece absently and minutely, returned his gaze to her, and went on: 'I am being as vague as I can as to place and details .... I got up then into the line towards ten of a black night. I was caught hold of immediately by a superior officer, thrust into a hut with maps that I was to study, and told that at two that morning I was to take charge of that bombing raid. Its purpose was to go a long way up into the hills, in enemy country, and there, before daylight, to establish ourselves in a certain circle of stones, or hollow, overhanging a road. When, all unsuspecting, a certain strong body of the enemy, as to which we had information, was to march beneath us we were to bomb them to pieces; at the same time, by the noise and by other signals we should make, our artillery would know that the enemy force was actually firmly engaged on that disadvantageous and narrow road. The slaughter was expected to be − and it was − dreadful! I re-apologize, my dear, for my share in this transaction. But so it was!'

The Professor broke off, and then, with tenderness in his voice, said: 'But perhaps you cannot bear this narration? It would be sufficient if I assured you that circumstances warranting a belief in a Special Protection occurred during that night.'

His wife, the sheet right up to her dark eyes and her voice in consequence muffled and altered, said, 'Go on. I must hear it' − or something similar.

'In that hut, then,' the Professor continued, 'I remained for three hours or so. Officers came in and out: shadows, but not many. An engagement was proceeding all the while; musketry and Maxim guns mostly; quite close at hand. There was not a man to spare: we were dreadfully short of our establishment. I had not even a batman allotted to me. I had myself to unpack my knapsack; make what alterations I had to make in my clothes − with fingers that shook so, I assure you, that I could hardly do it. And panting. Breathless, with pure dread. In a very dim light, and with the terrific detonations of rifles close at hand in rocky defiles − I am now breathless at the thought of it.' And indeed he was.

'There is a detail that I wish to impress upon you,' he went on. 'That was the cigarettes. I had to fill my knapsack, my pockets, and everything that would hold them with the jam pot bombs; all my party had to do this; but on the top of the bombs in the knapsack were to repose two tin boxes of the indispensable fire-makers.

'Someone had brought them into the hut: tin boxes with a green and gilded label. They stood on a rough wooden shelf under a shuttered window, blinking in the dim light from a paraffin lamp. The bombs stood on a deal table; it seemed to take me hours to pack them into the knapsack ....

'Hours and hours .... And then it went extraordinarily quickly.

These things do. A man rushed in: the assistant adjutant, I think ....
But that means nothing to you. He shouted, "Now then O/i/C
Bombers!" helped me to buckle on my accoutrements, exclaimed
something like, "Rough luck, old chap, to have to go so soon. I
wish to God we had someone else to send!" – and conducted me
out into the dark. He said that he had got me a first-class guide and
that the men and NCOs were all first-class men. They were not
even allowed to carry pipes or matches – for fear of showing a gleam
of light. You see, everything depended on *my* matches and *my* cigarettes ....

'With them, that is to say, we could at least put up a fight; without
them .... I forget the detail of a bombing party in those days; it was
changed so often. Four men with bombs to two with rifles and
bayonets; but the bayonet men were so cluttered up with bombs
themselves that I fancy they carried only a dozen rounds apiece of
small-arm ammunition. So you see the enormous importance of
those cigarettes to us – a party crawling miles, at night, into enemy
mountains. Without them, every one of my men was dead. After
tortures, very likely. Think of it! *My* men! Mine! You can't imagine
what the feeling would have been like!'

His wife sat up slowly. 'You didn't have to feel it?' she asked.
'But of course you didn't. You forgot the cigarettes. But something
saved you.'

The Professor started a little away from the foot of the bed, 'How
did you know? I never told a living soul.' He exclaimed irritably,
'Where the hell *is* that collar-stud?'

'You put it into your shirt,' his wife answered. 'Of course I knew
you had forgotten the cigarettes. I know you. Besides, you said so.
You said it took hours to pack up the bombs; you never mentioned
the cigarettes.'

He felt the band of his shirt and fingered the stud. But in the
engrossment of the other subject he forgot to express amazement
or irritation, and his wife felt that one corner at least had been
turned.

'That,' he said, 'was the *miracle*. I had forgotten them!... I spare
you the details of the landscape at night; the crawling; the hanging
on to tufts of rosemary. And my emotions.'

'You need not,' his wife said. 'If I am judge, I want some details.
Besides,' she added more softly, 'you do not think that your
narration is unsympathetic to me!'

He looked at her rather gratefully; but, as is the habit with those used to speaking in public, he had already composed his next sentences, and he went on: 'I remembered only when we were within a hundred yards of our objective – the hollow of the rocks overhanging the road that the enemy column must pass along. It was beginning to dawn when I remembered, and in those latitudes day comes quickly. There was no chance to go, or to send a man, back. No chance at all.

'And I remembered with absolute precision – that I had forgotten. It was no hallucination. I remembered not only that I had forgotten, but *how!* I had said to myself once or twice in the hut where I had waited, "By Jove! I must not forget those cigarettes," and had looked at the green boxes with the gilt stripes winking in the dim light .... And then that assistant adjutant had come in, a blustering, breezy fellow with an overpowering personality, and had slapped the knapsack on to my back, and had forced me out of the hut into the darkness where the men were falling in.

'You *see!* I *remembered!* I remembered the *action* of forgetting. As I went out of the hut, I had had the sensation that something was unsatisfactory. Omitted! You know what I mean about that sensation: it is like a little thirst .... And there I was with that sudden remembrance. You see! It is scientific. Nothing in this world would ever shake me as to that conviction.

'The other material detail is that I prayed. As no man before me has ever prayed. I am sufficiently aware that you will object: I was praying for the deaths of unsuspecting men – what sort of Deity can it be that will allow the deaths of one set of men merely because of the prayers of an individual of another set? ... I can't help that! I was praying for men lost by my fault. My own men ....

'And an amazing calm fell upon me. We were in that hollow, on a high place; the dawn was coming over that ancient sea; the tufts of herbs were absolutely still on the bare stone mountains. It was the stillest – the supreme – moment of my life. I knew then! I tell you I *knew*. There *is* a Special Providence; there *is* answer to prayer. I had my men lying in their places, overhanging the road. I said, 'Cigarette detail! On the hands down. Fall in to draw cigarettes!' You may call it the calm of desperation: going through the motions of fire-arm drill with empty rifles .... I slung my knapsack round in front of me; picked open the brass gadgets with absolutely firm fingers; threw up the stiff canvas lid of the knapsack .... The sun was just coming over the sea; its reflected rays shone on the green and gold labels and the bright tin ends of the two boxes. I noticed that the manufacturer was purveyor to the German Emperor.

'But from that day, I assure you, I have never looked back. And what am I to think of it but that it was a miracle? They were not there. I prayed. They were there .... You will perhaps despise me.'

His wife lay for a long time looking at the silver vase from which rose stiffly, in stripes, the scarlet, sulphur yellow, and magenta flowers. She said at last, 'It was for that that you got your ... '

He said, rather sharply, 'It was agreed that we should never talk about my decorations. What I got from it was ... confidence! I am the man you see because ... '

'You mean,' she interrupted him, 'that if anything shook that faith in you' – she became a little breathless – 'you would ... you would ... lose the lucky touch you have had ever since ... ever since that miraculous event? You have been since then, haven't you, rather a fortunate man?'

He corroborated her gravely. 'I did, as you seem to have heard, rather well out there. Afterwards, I do not mean that I was insensible to fear. Of course I never was. But I was ... I will call it buoyed up! I never prayed again, of course. One isn't the man to trouble Providence with *my* trivial vicissitudes. But just the remembrance *transfused* me. It has ever since. Why, only this morning in my bath .... You know how I have worried over Portfolio B 14. Well! Suddenly, remembering the anniversary, I became calm. In that serenity the solution was absolutely clear to me. There it was. In a definite pattern. And let me tell you – but you know it as well as I do – that means almost – oh, it means *certain* – fame in the scientific world!'

He fetched his collar from the dressing table and looked at her with almost apprehensive eyes whilst inadroitly he fumbled with the front stud. It was that at which she looked when at last she answered.

'That,' she said with her clear scientific intonation, 'seems to settle it. I at least am determined never to question the ... the miraculous interpretation you attach to that specific event!' She swallowed rather painfully, but went on: 'I should suggest that on this anniversary we should ... you might like to ... go to a service at the Cathedral. And, side by side ... oh, offer thanks, and whatever it is you do to confirm yourself in ... Faith!'

With an ecstatic face he had tiptoed to the head of the bed and now, bending down, he folded her in his arms.

Prefaces

Preface to *Their Lives,*
by Violet Hunt

Violet Hunt sent Ford the proofs of her novel *Their Lives* (London: Stanley Paul, 1916), while he was in the Ypres Salient. He drafted the preface there; it not only moves between descriptions of watching a gas attack and reading the book, but seeks to connect the two experiences, making the startling claim that the Victorian family animosities recorded in Hunt's novel contributed to the war's cruelty. See the 'Introduction', p. 7 for further discussion.

SOMEWHERE IN BELGIUM,

September, 1916.

I took the proofs of this book up the hill to read. From there I could see the gas shells bursting in Poperinghe; it was a very great view, but I am prohibited from descanting on it. But the gas shells that the Bosches were sending into Poperinghe set me thinking. You see, there was not much sense in gassing Poperinghe; it killed a great many Belgian civilians and that is all. It was in fact, just casual cruelty, quite systematic. And as I write now, I can hear them shelling another little town a mile away – and giving us a shell too now and then, for the love of God, I suppose?

And while I was looking at that great view, perceiving the little white mushrooms of our own shells suddenly existing in the dark line under [Wytschaete] – miles and miles away – and then turning down my eyes and reading the last interview between Christina and her sister, that numbed and broken attempt at an outbreak of sentiment – suddenly it occurred to me that Violet Hunt's characters, these remorselessly rendered people who were without remorse or pity – these people were Prussians. Their cold materialism, their absence of any shading, their direct methods of wanting a thing, and 'going for' it without shame, or the anticipation of reproach – these are characteristic of the people whom Gambetta styled – and Destiny has proved to be – *l'Ennemi*.

This attempt to apply the method of Jane Austen told of the Eighties, gives to 'Their Lives', the character of a work of history. It *is* history – and it makes it plain. For that horrible family of this author's recording explains to me why today, millions of us, as it were, on a raft of far-reaching land, are enduring torture it is not fit that human beings should endure, in order that – outside that raft – other eloquent human beings should proclaim that they will go on fighting to the last drop of *our* blood.

This may sound a little obscure: but if the somnolescent reader will awaken to the fact that selfishness does create misery he may make a further effort of the imagination, and see that the selfishness of the Eighties – of the Victorian and Albert era – is the direct Ancestor of ... Armageddon. Those fathers, and particularly those mothers, ate of the vines of Carlyle, Ruskin, and Self-help Smiles; our mouths are filled – are burned – by *minenwerfer*. And just as Orinthia and Virgilia and Christina set little devil-kites adrift into each other's skies, or let off little devil-ships into the ponds of each other's loves, so ... But the parallel jumps to the eye.

Most of the great books of the world are unpleasant books. And whilst I write, the Boches are shelling out of existence the rather ugly little church close at hand. 'C .... r .... r .... ump!' go the 4.[2] shells into the mediocre but sacred edifice. (It never contained anything more inspiring than some hideous 'Stations of the Cross'. ... It contains nothing now and has ceased to exist.) Then, in the silence after the shell has burst, whilst you are saying 'Thank God!' because it has not hit you, you hear the thin, sifting sound of the stained glass dropping down into the aisles. There is no reason why the Boche should object to our having a church in our village. They are just destroying it for the love of God – as Christina Radmall manœuvred to prevent Virgilia 'having her hair up.' Truly, Our Lord and Saviour Christ dies every day – as he does on every page of this book, and in every second of this 7-9-16.

MILES IGNOTUS.

The Trail of the Barbarians

When Ford was back in England in 1917 he resumed his propaganda work, translating Pierre Loti's pamphlet, *L'Outrage des barbares* (Paris, 1917). His 'Translator's Note' to *The Trail of the Barbarians* (London, [1918]) is printed here. Like Henry James, Ford was a great admirer of Loti's style, so the work represents an act of literary as well as political propaganda. It can also be seen expressing his belief in the regenerative power of the countryside, and influencing his later praise of French landscape and culture.

It has been my ambition, for more years than I can remember, to devote the closing stage of my life to rendering into English some masterpiece of a French stylist. Well, here is the rendering of the masterpiece of a French stylist; and Fate wills it that it has been performed between parades, orderly rooms, *strafes*, and the rest of the preoccupations that re-fit us for France ... so it is not a good rendering. You need from 11.45 pip emma of 8/8/17 to 11.57 pip emma of 9/8/17 for the rendering of almost any French sentence!...

But, in spite of lack of leisure, I will quarrel with the Master as to his employment of one word: the word 'irreparable'. I have seen ruined France – such of it as is ruined – and have seen on the Somme the mole-work that is demanded of the foot-slogger, and, probably because the mole can see what is going on below ground better than he who passes beneath the rose and grey skies of a French spring, I am more sure than Mr Loti that the grass is already moving that shall cover the graveyards and the rusty heaps of recovered provinces.

It is not only that the horizon-blue soldiers – and the mudcoloured ones! – are billeted amongst the ruins: it is that the inhabitants – all those upholders of the matchless 'little industries' of France – are astonishingly hidden amongst the gaping rafters and the brick heaps, and the husbandmen are astonishingly and tenaciously hidden in the fields, *Agricolam expellas furca: tamen usque recurret!*[1] I have bought a melon in the ruins of Mametz...

And last year, whilst we were eating bully beef and biscuits in a field that we had recovered only three days before from the Germans, a dour, tall man in corduroys, carrying a brass-bound whip, approached us and peremptorily desired to know who was going to pay him for the damage that we were doing to his corn-field! The 4.2's were ploughing it for him at that moment ....

Well, today the tall wheat rises over that field behind Bécourt Wood; for in France nothing is irreparable, since France possesses the secret of eternal life.

> FORD MADOX HUEFFER,
> Lieut. 3rd/attd. 9th Battalion,
> The Welch Regiment

9th August 1917.

---

1   A play on Horace, *Epist.* 1. 10. 24: *naturem expellas furca, tamen usque recurret* – 'you may drive out nature (in Ford's version, the farmer) with a fork, but s/he keeps coming back'.

from 'A Note by way of Preface' to *All Else is Folly* by Peregrine Acland

The third preface, to Peregrine Acland's *All Else is Folly* (London, 1929), is a more substantial discussion of the issues confronting a war-novelist – a discussion which has important implications for the understanding of *Parade's End*, and its unusual hero.

I do hope that, quite apart from the aesthetico-literary considerations that are my usual *tic* and that as a rule prevent the British reader from paying any attention to books that I urge on his attention, so that I practically never, whatever may be the case with the United States, write any prefaces for the English editions of books – I do hope, then, that a very large public may be found for Major Acland's book on both sides of the Atlantic.

For it is the convincing, mournful and un-relieved account of a simple soul's sufferings in the late war.

And I believe that those sufferings have never been sufficiently brought home to the public as a whole, and that that is why the late war has not aroused half the horror of war as a whole that it should have aroused. For the defect of all novel-writing is that, as a rule, the novelist – Heaven help him – must needs select unusual, hyper-sensitized souls to endure the vicissitudes that he is pleased to make them endure, and that makes him lose half the game with the normal reader. I remember very well – for I am not pleading Not guilty! – thinking to myself when about half-way through a novel about the late war, 'Well, my central character is altogether such a queer, unusual fellow that I do not see how anyone is going much to sympathise with him in his misfortunes.' Thoughts to that effect. And pretty nearly as much can be said of the books of most of my Anglo-Saxon or Latin colleagues, whilst, on the whole, writers from the Central or Slavic Empires emphasize the note by dwelling on the sufferings of mournful but unusual peasants. The result is that the normal man says, 'These are not normal people!' and continues to comfort himself either by imagining that the late struggle was for those engaged a perpetual picnic varied with sexual jamborees, or by ignoring the matter altogether.[2]

That is a misfortune. But it is a misfortune that Major Acland's book may do a great deal to mitigate. For his central character is about as normal in temperament and circumstances as it is possible to be. He is neither high nor low in station; neither hyper-sensitized nor callous; neither Adonis nor Caliban; neither illiterate nor of the intelligentsia; neither a brute nor a poet, though, like so many of us, he writes an occasional very mediocre sonnet which fails to cause the lady of his devotion to fall for him. And he is no coward and no hero – though he endures without much squealing sufferings out of which he, like the rest of us, would very gladly have got – wangled, used to be the technical word! .... 'If one could only,' one used to say and hear said innumerable times, 'wangle a Staff job.' Or a home job. Or a week-end's leave in Paris .... Or even a Blighty!

So Major Acland's Falcon would eventually very gladly – but, like all of us, how vainly! – have accepted a staff job; have been sent home to Canada to train details – with young woman for the use of officers, one, complete .... And when he is worn and wearied out he is put into the most hellish scrap of all. And gets his Blighty .... But with his bashed-in face and mangled limbs his young woman, who also is wearied out, turns him down, and back he goes to Canada – and presumably carries on.

Nevertheless, at the skirl of the pipes, 'war-lust again surged through him'. As it does for us all. And that really is the lesson of the book – the lesson that our publics and law-makers would do well to ponder. 'Yet now,' Major Acland concludes, 'with the skirling of the pipes in his ears, he would have signed away his liberty, his life, for another war. It wouldn't have mattered much what the war was about .... Not when this vast hall rocked with the tread of two thousand feet and his hot blood leaped to the pipes ....'

I have, myself, by coincidence, felt much the same in Montreal when Major Acland's kilted regiment went by on the street. For the matter of that, I felt much the same on the yesterday of this writing when the 165th Regiment of United States Infantry went past the Public Library on Fifth Avenue with the equivalent for the

---

1   Compare Sylvia Tietjens' thoughts in *No More Parades*, p. 167: 'This whole war was an agapemone. . . . You went to war when you desired to rape innumerable women. . . . It was what war was for. . . . '.

King's Colours and the other colours flying and the band playing
for St Patrick's Day in the morning .... Of course not *quite* the same
feeling... '

[...] And how admirably it is all done! ... When I read of the
marching and fighting towards the end of the book, I feel on my
skin the keen air of the early mornings standing-to, I have in my
mouth the dusky tastes, in my eyes the dusky landscapes, in my ears
the sounds that were silences interrupted by clickings of metal on
metal, that at any moment might rise to the infernal clamour of all
Armageddon .... Yes, indeed, one lives it all again, with the fear,
and the nausea ... and the surprised relief to find oneself still alive.
I wish I could have done it as well myself: envy, you see, will come
creeping in. But since I couldn't, the next best thing seems to me
to be to say that it will be little less than a scandal if the book is not
read enormously widely. And that is the truth.

The Three Dedicatory Letters to *Parade's End*

These Prefaces to the individual volumes were, strangely, not included in either of the two collected reissues of the sequence. But they give important insights into the genesis of the novels, their degrees of fictionality, their psychological emphases, and their conception as a sequence. As Samuel Hynes argues, these letters make it clear that Ford thought of the fourth volume as an integral part of the project, and not the afterthought that its detractors have claimed. The dedicatory letter to *A Man Could Stand Up –* calls that book the 'third and penultimate' volume.[3]

Dedicatory Letter to *No More Parades*

TO WILLIAM BIRD

My dear Bird, –

I have always held – and I hold as strongly now as ever – that a novel should have no preface. It should have no preface for aesthetico-moral reasons, and because prefatory matter takes away from the reality of, and therefore damages, a book. A dedicatory letter is a subterfuge. That subterfuge I feel forced to adopt, and must take the consequences.

The reason is this: All novels are historical, but all novels do not deal with such events as get on to the pages of history. This *No More Parades* does. It becomes, therefore, necessary to delimit what, in it, is offered as, on the author's responsibility, observed event.

State, underline and emphasize the fact how you will it is impossible to get into the heads of even intelligent public critics the fact that the opinions of a novelist's characters as stated in any novel are not of necessity the opinions of the novelist. It cannot be done.

3 Hynes, 'Ford Madox Ford: "Three Dedicatory Letters to *Parade's End*"' with Commentary and Notes', *Modern Fiction Studies*, 16 (1970), pp. 515–28.

How it may be with one's public one has no means of knowing. Perhaps they read one with more generosity and care. Presumably they do, for they have either spent money on, or taken some trouble to obtain, the volume.

In this novel the events, such as it treats of, are vouched for by myself. There was in France, at the time covered by this novel, an immense base camp, unbelievably crowded with men whom we were engaged in getting up the line, working sometimes day and night in the effort. That immense army was also extremely depressed by the idea that those who controlled it overseas would – I will not use the word betray, since that implies volition – but 'let us down'. We were oppressed, ordered, counter-ordered, commanded, countermanded, harassed, strafed, denounced – and, above all, dreadfully worried. The never-ending sense of worry, in fact, far surpassed any of the 'exigencies of troops actually in contact with enemy forces', and that applied not merely to the bases, but to the whole field of military operations. Unceasing worry!

We took it out in what may or may not have been unjust suspicions of the all-powerful ones who had our lives in their hands and seemed indifferent enough to the fact. So this novel recounts what those opinions were: it does not profess to dictate whether those opinions were or were not justified. There is, I think, not one word in it which records any opinions or words of mine as being my words or opinions. I believe I may say that, as to the greater part of such public matters as are here discussed, I have no opinions at all. After seven or eight years I have been unable to form any. I present therefore only what I observed or heard.

Few writers can have engaged themselves as combatants in what, please God, will yet prove to be the war that ended war, without the intention of aiding with their writings, if they survived, in bringing about such a state of mind as should end wars as possibilities.

This obviously is a delicate task. If you over-state horrors you induce in your reader a state of mind such as, by reaction, causes the horrors to become matters of indifference. If you overstate heroisms you induce indifference to heroisms – of which the late war produced, Heaven knows, plenty enough, so that to be indifferent to them is villainy. Casting about, then, for a medium through which to view this spectacle, I thought of a man – by then dead – with whom I had been very intimate and with whom – as with yourself – I had at one time discussed most things under the sun. He was the English Tory.

Even then – it must have been in September, 1916, when I was in a region called the Salient, and I remember the very spot where the idea came to me – I said to myself: How would all this look in the eyes of X ... – already dead, along with all English Tories? For, as a medium through which to view struggles that are after all in the end mostly emotional struggles – since as a rule for every twenty minutes of actual fighting you were alone with your emotions, which, being English, you did not express, for at least a month! – as a medium, what could be better than the sceptical, not ungenerous, not cold, not unconvincible eyes of an extinct frame of mind. For by the time of my relative youth when I knew X ... so intimately, Toryism had gone beyond the region of any practising political party. It said for a year or two: A plague on all your Houses, and so expired.

To this determination – to use my friend's eyes as a medium – I am adhering in this series of books. *Some Do Not* – of which this one is not so much a continuation as a reinforcement – showed you the Tory at home during war-time; this shows you the Tory going up the line. If I am vouchsafed health and intelligence for long enough I propose to show you the same man in the line and in process of being re-constructed.

There is nothing more to it: I no more back the political opinions of General Campion than those of Sylvia Tietjens, who considered that the World War was just an excuse for male agapemones; I no more accept responsibility for the inaccuracies of Tietjens quoting King's Regulations than for the inaccuracies of the general in quoting *Henry V*. I was roundly taken to task by the only English critic whose review of my last book I read[4] – after he had *horribly* misrepresented the plot of the work at a crucial point – for my inaccuracy in stating that poor Roger Casement was shot. As a matter of fact, I had been struck by the fact that a lady with whom I had been discussing Casement twice deliberately referred to the shooting of Casement, and stated that she did so because she could not bear to think that we had hanged him. In making therefore a lady – who had loved Casement – refer to his execution in the book in question, I let her say that Casement was shot .... Indeed, I should prefer to think that he had been shot, myself .... Or still more to think that we had allowed him to escape, or commit suicide, or be

---

4   See Gerald Gould, 'New Fiction', *Saturday Review*, 137 (17 May 1924), p. 512.

imprisoned during His Majesty's pleasure .... The critic preferred to rub in the hanging. It is a matter of relative patriotism.

Whilst we are chipping, I may as well say that I have been informed that a lively controversy has raged over the same work in the United States, a New York critic having stated that I was a disappointed man intent on giving a lurid picture of present-day matrimonial conditions in England.[5] I hope 1 am no rabid patriot, but I pray to be preserved from the aspiration of painting any nation's lurid matrimonial conditions. The peculiar ones adumbrated in *Some Do Not* were suggested by the fate of a poor fellow living in a place in the South of France in which I happened to be stopping when I began the book. His misfortunes were much those of my central character, but he drank himself to death, it was said deliberately, after he had taken his wife back. He came from Philadelphia.

So, in remembrance of our joint labours and conspiracies, and in token of my admiration for your beautiful achievements in another art,

I subscribe myself, my dear Bird,

Your humble, obedient and obliged

F.M.F.

PARIS, 31 October, '24 –
GUERMANTES 25 May, '25.

'Author's Note' to *A Man Could Stand Up* –

TO GERALD DUCKWORTH

My dear Duckworth,

Permit me to address to you this Epistle Dedicatory, for without you the series of books of which this is the third and penultimate, could not have existed. We have been working together for a great number of years now and always without a cloud on our relationships. At any rate there has never been a cloud on my half of the landscape.

I fancy that you at least know how much I dislike not letting a

---

5   Probably Joseph W. Krutch's review in the *Saturday Review of Literature*, 1 (18 October 1924), p. 197.

book go merely as a book; but it appears that if one has the misfortune to be impelled to treat of public matters that is impossible. So
let me here repeat : As far as I am privately concerned these books,
like all my others, constitute an attempt simply to reflect – not in
the least to reflect on – our own times.

Nevertheless as far as this particular book is concerned I find
myself ready to admit to certain public aims. That is to say that, in
it, I have been trying to say to as much of humanity as I can reach,
and, in particular to such members of the public as, because of age
or for other reasons did not experience the shocks and anxieties of
the late struggle:

> This is what the late war was like : this is how modern fighting
> of the organised, scientific type affects the mind. If, for reasons
> of gain or, as is still more likely out of dislike for collective types
> other than your own, you choose to permit your rulers to
> embark on another war, this – or something very accentuated
> along similar lines – is what you will have to put up with!

I hope, in fact, that this series of books, for what it is worth, may
make war seem undesirable. But in spite of that hope I have not
exaggerated either the physical horrors or the mental distresses of
that period. On the contrary I have selected for treatment less
horrible episodes than I might well have rendered and I have
rendered them with more equanimity than might well have been
displayed. You see here the end of the war of attrition through the
eyes of a fairly stolid, fairly well-instructed man. I should like to
add that, like all of us, he is neither unprejudiced nor infallible. And
you have here his mental re-actions and his reflections – which are
not, *not*, NOT presented as those of the author.

The hostilities in which he takes part are those of a period of
relative calm. For it should be remembered that great battles, taking
months and months to prepare and to recover from, were of relatively rare occurrence. The heavy strain of the trenches came from
the waiting for long periods of inaction, in great – in mortal –
danger every minute of the day and night.

The fighting here projected is just fighting, as you might say at
any old time: it is not specifically, say, the battle of the 21st of
March, 1918, or any particular one of the series of combats after
the 9th of April, of that year.

Finally I have to repeat that, with the exception of the central
figure – as to whose Toryism I had my say in the preface to the

last-published book of this series! – I have most carefully avoided so much as adumbrating the characteristics – and certainly the vicissitudes – of any human being known to myself.

And, in the meantime, my dear Duckworth, let me say that I shall always describe and subscribe, myself as

Yours very gratefully,

Ford Madox Ford.

Paris, May 18th, 1926.

Dedicatory Letter to *Last Post*

To ISABEL PATERSON

Madame et Cher Confrère,

I have for some years now had to consider you as being my fairy godmother in the United States – though how one can have a godmother junior to oneself I have yet to figure out. Perhaps godmothers of the kind that can turn pumpkins into glass coaches can achieve miracles in seniority. Or, when I come to think of it, I seem to remember that, for a whole tribe of Incas converted who knows how and simultaneously, in the days of the Conquistadores, an Infanta of Spain went to the font, she being, whatever her age, of necessity junior to the elders at least of the tribe. That, however, is all a trifle – except for my gratitude! – compared with your present responsibility.

For, but for you, this book would only nebularly have existed – in space, in my brain, where you will, so it be not on paper and between boards. Save, that is to say, for your stern, contemptuous and almost virulent insistence on knowing 'what became of Tietjens' I never should have conducted this chronicle to the stage it has now reached. The soldier, tired of war's alarms, it has always seemed to me, might be allowed to rest beneath bowery vines. But you would not have it so.

You – and for once you align yourself with the Great Public – demand an ending: if possible a happy ending.

Alas, I cannot provide you with the end of Tietjens for a reason upon which I will later dwell – but I here provide you with a slice of one of Christopher's later days so that you may know how more or less he at present stands. For in this world of ours though lives may end Affairs do not. Even though Valentine and Tietjens were dead the Affair that they set going would go rolling on down the generations – Mark junior and Mrs Lowther, the unborn child and the rest will go on beneath the nut-boughs or over the seas – or in the best Clubs. It is not your day nor mine that shall see the end of them.

And think: How many people have we not known intimately and seen daily for years! Then they move into another township, and, bad correspondents as we all are and sit-at-homes as Fate makes most of us, they drop out of our sights. They may – those friends of yours – go and settle in Paris. You may see them for fortnights at decennial intervals, or you may not.

So I would have preferred to let it be with Tietjens, but you would not have it. I have always jeered at authors who sentimentalised over their characters, and after finishing a book exclaim like, say, Thackeray: 'Roll up the curtains; put the puppets in their boxes; quench the tallow footlights' ... something like that. But I am bound to say that in certain moods in Avignon this year it would less have surprised me to go up to the upper chamber of the mill where I wrote and there to find that friend of mine than to find you. For you are to remember that for me Tietjens is the re-creation of a friend I had – a friend so vivid to me that though he died many years ago I cannot feel that he is yet dead. In the dedicatory letter of an earlier instalment of this series of books I said that in these volumes I was trying to project how this world would have appeared to that friend today and how, in it, he would have acted – or you, I believe, would say re-acted. And that is the exact truth of the matter.

Do you not find – you yourself, too – that, however it may be with the mass of humanity, in the case of certain dead people you cannot feel that they are indeed gone from this world? You can only know it, you can only believe it. That is, at any rate, the case with me – and in my case the world daily becomes more and more peopled with such *revenants* and less and less with those who still walk this earth. It is only yesterday that I read of the death of another human being who will for the rest of time have for me that effect. That person died thousands of miles away, and yesterday it would have astonished me if she had walked into my room here in New York. Today it would no longer. It would have the aspect of the simplest thing in the world.

So then, for me, it is with Tietjens. With his prototype I set out

on several enterprises – one of them being a considerable periodical publication of a Tory kind´ – and for many years I was
accustomed as it were to 'set' my mind by his comments on public
or other affairs. He was, as I have elsewhere said, the English Tory
– the last English Tory, omniscient, slightly contemptuous – and
sentimental in his human contacts. And for many years before I
contemplated the writing of these books – before the War even –
I was accustomed to ask myself not merely what he would have
said of certain public or private affairs, but how he would have acted
in certain positions. And I do so still. I have only to say to my mind,
as the child on the knees of an adult says to its senior: 'Tell us a fairy
tale!' – I have only to say: 'Tell us what he would here have done!'
and at once he is there.

So, you see, I cannot tell you the end of Tietjens, for he will end
only when I am beyond pens and paper. For me at this moment he
is, oddly enough, in Avignon, rather disappointed in the quality of
the Louis Seize furniture that he has found there, and seated in front
of the Taverne Riche under the planes he is finding his Harris
tweeds oppressive. Perhaps he is even mopping the whitish brow
under his silver-streaked hair. And I have a strong itch to write to
him that if he wants to find Louis Treize stuff of the most admirable
– perfectly fabulous armoires and chests – for almost nothing, he
should go westward into the Limousin to ... But nothing shall make
me here write that name ....

And so he will go jogging along with ups and downs and plenty
of worries and some satisfaction, the Tory Englishman, running his
head perhaps against fewer walls, perhaps against more, until I
myself cease from those pursuits .... Perhaps he will go on even
longer if you, as Marraine, succeed in conferring upon these works
that longevity ....

But out and alas, now you can never write about me again: for
it would, wouldn't it? look too much like: You scratch my back
and I'll scratch yours!

So don't write about Tietjens: write your own projections of the
lives around you in terms of your delicate and fierce art. Then you
will find me still more

>Your grateful and obedient

F. M. F.

New York,
October 13th, 1927.

Miscellany

Early Responses to the War[1]

From 'Literary Portraits – XLVIII. M. Charles-Louis Philippe and "Le Père Perdrix"', *Outlook*, 34 (8 August 1914), pp. 174–5.

I am sitting up here in Scotland and the rain pours and pours and drips from the window-sills, and when the windows rattle I think I am hearing the thunder of German artillery in the North Sea, which is a few miles distant. And what is the good of writing about literature – the 'edler Beruf', the noble calling? There will not be a soul that will want to read about literature for years and years. We go out. We writers go out. And, when the world again has leisure to think about letters the whole world will have changed. It will have changed in morality, in manners, in all human relationships, in all views of life, possibly even in language, certainly in its estimates of literature. What then is the good of it all? I don't know.

It is extraordinary to think of the usually good and kindly Germans, the sinister Russians, the detestable Servians, those queer people the French, the highly civilised Austrians, and ourselves, all at each other's throat. And about what? God knows. But perhaps God does not know... I am not in the least a pacifist. I do not mind who cuts whose throat. Pictures of the horrors of war in no way appal me. The greater part of humanity is merely the stuff with which to fill graveyards; and if the preliminary for the grave be a shambles, with the rain falling and the clay sticky with oozing blood, I do not mind. It is as good – it is possibly better – to expire of wounds in the rain than gradually to peter out in a hospital ward amidst the smell of anaesthetics, or to dribble away from life in one's bed, with the nurses shaking their heads over you. [...] We have, at any rate, all got to go through with death, and it does not much matter how it comes. It is bound to be a disagreeable business. No, death does not much matter. But what is senseless, what is imbecile, are the ideas for which people are dying – the ideas for which the

---

1   See Nora Tomlinson and Robert Green, 'Ford's Wartime Journalism', *Agenda*, 27:4/28:1 (Winter 1989–Spring 1990), pp. 139–47.

'noble callings' are to be strangled for a decade. I like the French so much; I like so much the South Germans and the Austrians. Whichever side wins in the end – my own heart is certain to be mangled in either case. I should feel no triumph in a German victory over France; I think I would cut my throat if the German Fleet destroyed the British Fleet; I should mildly like France to get back the Reichsland. I should feel intensely any mortification to Germany; almost more intensely any mortification to France; and any blow to this country would cause in me emotions more horrible than any others of a life not wanting in horrible emotions [....] it is none of my business to lecture people about these matters. At the same time, because for my sins I am a cosmopolitan, and also, I suppose, a poet so apt to identify myself with anyone's sufferings as to be unable to take sides very violently, I have probably thought more about these things, and certainly suffer more over them, than most people.

From 'Literary Portraits – XLIX. A Causerie', *Outlook*, 34 (15 August 1914), pp. 206–7.

With the disappearance of the sempiternal topic of conversation in literary circles one only subject now holds the conversational field: What will be the future of literature? What then will be the future of the arts when we have a little quiet again? – after the reaction from the war strain. I do not mind prophesying that there will be a Neo-Romantic movement, but I would not like to forecast the day of its arrival. I fancy that we are in for eight years of war – or rather of wars between one set of allied nations or the other, or between one isolated unit and several.

From 'Literary Portraits – LI. The Face of Janus', *Outlook*, 34 (29 August 1914), pp. 70–1.

I do wish that, as far as this country is concerned, this war could be fought in terms of 'the gallant enemy'. For I confess that when, as I have to do many many times a day, I read or hear that the chief sovereign of the confederacy opposed to us is a mad dog, I am rendered more miserable than I can well express. I am rendered miserable by the thought that there are millions of humanity – a whole infinite sea of human beings – in this country, in France, in Germany, in Russia – possibly not in Austria, where civilisation is an older, sadder, semi-Oriental, and fatalistic affair – at any rate there is a whole sea of humanity, many many of whom will shortly be facing their Maker with words like 'mad dog', 'mercenary', 'brute', 'tyrant', upon their lips. It is a horrible thought [....]

For I think that our job in life – the job of us intellectuals at this moment – is to extract, for the sake of humanity and of the humaner letters, all the poetry that is to be got out of war. I, at any rate, have no other mission at this moment. [...]

It is not for me to condemn my fellow-poets of this country; but I must confess to a deep depression, to a deep misery, when I read their poems about this war. It is all about mad dogs, and throttling fists, and trampling heels.

From 'Literary Portraits – LIII. The Muse Of War', *Outlook*, 34 (12 September 1914), pp. 334–5.

I have been asked by at least two editors and by several common people to write a poem about the present war, and I always like to do what I am asked. It is part of my theory of the proper man that he should be able to do anything [....] So that if I say that I am unable – absolutely and helplessly unable – to write a poem about the present war, I say it with shame. It is a confession of sheer impotence.

I simply cannot do it. I should like to; but the words do not come. There is the blank sheet – and then... nothing. It is, I think, because of the hazy remoteness of the war-grounds; the impossibility of visualising anything, because of a total incapacity to believe any single thing that I read in the daily papers. Yes, I cannot believe any single thing that I have read about this war. And I do not want to believe so much of it. Anyhow, the roots of poetry draw their nourishment from seeing and from beliefs. Here I see nothing... As to former wars I can see them much more clearly [....] this present war is just a cloud – a hideous and unrelieved pall of doom. I do not even see the country over which this cloud hangs, though by accident I know most of the country over which fighting is taking

place. (My God, that one should come to write such a phrase!)
[....]
As it is, I will tell you what I could write a poem about... It is the
story of the British Tommy who, when his regiment had repulsed
one attack, painted over a biscuit-tin the inscription 'Business as
usual,' and stuck it up on the trench in front of him. That is full of
terrestrial yet heavenly, of sardonic yet kindly, humour. It is only
an English Tommy who could have thought of that, and it is only
a very fine real man who could have done it. I hope that man is
not dead. I should like to make him a present of my collected
poems. He has done me so much good...

And, for the rest of it, that is how I see poetry about war or about
anything else. I want something to stir my emotions and something
sharply visual to symbolise them. I want a gesture, a tone of the
voice, a turn of the eye. I don't think I could make a poem out of
fine words like avenging slaughtered saints or unsheathing
freedom's sword. I cannot see things in that way – it is my misfortune.

**From 'Literary Portraits – LXIX. Annus Mirabilis', *Outlook*,
35 (2 January 1915), pp. 14–15.**

The other night I was in a cinematograph theatre. I read in huge
letters on the screen that I was to see pictures of the fall of Antwerp,
the burning of the Cloth Hall at Ypres, of German troops in occupation of Longwy, German aeroplanes over Paris, and British
submarines in the Dardanelles [....]

And suddenly I heard myself say to my companion: 'Do you
realise that, if we went out this moment and read on the placards,
"A Million Germans Killed", we should say "Thank God"? – and
we should really mean that we were thanking God!'

I wonder what it really all means? Three months ago, I remember
– and it seems as if it were a dream of another age on this planet –
I wrote that I wished the war could be conducted in terms of 'the
gallant enemy'. Now I should thank God to know that a million
Germans were killed; and my gentle companion would have
thanked God, and every soul in that building would have uttered
words of gratitude to that Most High, Who presumably made the
Germans as well as ourselves. It is certainly queer. I do not think

that I would hurt so much as the feelings of a single soul of the earth, and almost every soul in that audience would feel a little queer at seeing a cat die of the mange. Yet we desire – and are ready to pray for – the deaths of millions of our fellow-beings.

And in this last, still, windless spell of this declining year – of this year that seems to be cut in half – I sit and ask myself innumerable questions. I have nothing but questions left in the world, though in the beginning of the year 1914 I would have dogmatised cheerfully in the columns of *The Outlook* 🏃 to any topic beneath the sun except the integral calculus or the sailing of schooners. And so I ask myself: Is it wrong to thank God for the deaths of a million of one's fellow-beings? I should do so myself, automatically and instinctively, as I breathe deeply after having been under water after a dive. It would be a feeling just like that. Can, then, any feeling so instinctive, so automatic, so self-preservative be wrong? And I go on asking myself innumerable questions [....]

Is it then right? is it then wrong? I don't know. I know nothing any more; nobody knows anything. We are down in the mud of the trenches of right and wrong, grappling at each other's throats, gouging out each other's eyes – and amazed, still, to think that we can be doing such things. [...]

And to think that there was once a time when there was beneath my window a kitchen garden with apple-trees that bore; that there was once a time when we talked about Limehouse; that there was once a time when I occupied these columns with praise of writers of *vers libre* and disquisitions upon Futurism. Futurism! – I ask myself sometimes whether it was the ebullient and aggressive spirit of Futurism that caused this war, or whether the ground-swell that came before this war had for one of its symptoms just Futurism? Or whether it was just larks that we shall never have again? Or whether Cubism, with its turning from the representation of material phenomena, heralded a new religious age in which truly we shall not make to ourselves the graven images of houses in Park Lane, motor-cars, and all the outward signs of the works of Mammon?

From 'Literary Portraits – LXXI. Enemies', *Outlook*, 35 (16 January 1915), pp. 79–80.

[...] I find myself as it were, awakening from a long sleep. For certainly since August 4, 1914, I have been in a sort of trance of attack – of attack upon Prussia. I have read hundreds of books; I have written a hundred thousand words of engrossed, deliberate, and breathless attack upon that Prussia who is 'L'ennemi'. [...] But all that seems to have come of it, as far as I am concerned, is some speculations as to the nature of hatred. I ask myself [...] how does one get oneself hated, since obviously any man at all active in any field of life gets himself an amount of enmity disproportionate altogether to any hostilities of his own? And I ask myself: How should one act when one discovers that one is hated? How should one act when one discovers that some one person – or some large body of persons – is actively desiring one's humiliation, death, imprisonment, or silencing? I am not a combative person. I like a scrap, of course, but I get tired of it after ten minutes or two days or a week, according to the scale of the combat. Then I begin to hope that there are no bones broken, and generally I discover that I have broken some thighs and heads. I suppose that that is an experience of most people, particularly in the writing world.

[...] I think – and do you not, oh gentle reader, think the same of yourself – that a more inoffensive person never existed than the author of these words. I seem all my life to have been helping over stiles lame dogs who, having recovered the use of their legs, used them for kicking me in the eye. I seem to remember tens and scores... Yes, certainly, I remember twenty-seven such persons. No doubt it is the twenty-five per cent. of them that have denounced me to the police or the military – as a German spy.

Well, well. I try to be like the East, and let the legions thunder past and go to sleep again. I suppose one irritates people by one's very insouciance which is meant to be tolerance.

[...] I have always wondered why I had 'enemies' – shoals and shoals of enemies. I guess I must have trodden on their poor dear toes, all unknowingly. I don't know. I am a mild, inoffensive creature – like yourself, oh gentle reader, and the chucker-out at the Dash Music Hall and William II and, let us say for the sake of inclusiveness, the Chancellor of the Exchequer. Neither you nor I nor they would hurt a fly if the insect called our attentions to its existence. But I suppose I write about books and people, and, if I come to think of it, I have impatiences. I get impatient at the thought of the Yellow Press, of the average reviewer, of the novelist who comments upon his characters, of the critic who does not understand the character of *vers libre*, or of poets who try to reconstitute golden ages in obsolescent dialects. And when I am impatient with them I try to take quite gentle dabs at their eyes. I suppose one is stronger than one thinks. I know that I always take a great deal of trouble to please the writers about whom I write. And I remember taking particular trouble to please one writer of works of the imagination – I was writing about him in these columns. I even took trouble enough to ask four friends to read the article and search for any possible cause of offence. I cut out quite a lot – upon their advice. And then that writer told a friend that I had said about him the one unbearable thing [....]

Anyhow the *Golden Ass* of Apuleius is jolly good stuff – and so is the *War in the Air* of Mr Wells. And the point, as far as I am for the moment concerned, is that both books are *contes de fées*; that both give you a sense of light and air; and that each gives you a rendering of a sort of celestial hatred. In the *Golden Ass* there are the two sorts of hatred – that of the hero Lucius for his mistress, the maid Fotis, a hatred, to which I am growing mildly accustomed, for a person who has made one ridiculous. It was inconsiderate of Fotis to let the hero slay three old goats in mistake for robbers, and Lucius felt himself filled with a hatred almost murderous but transitory – the sort of hatred that must be felt for me by the person who writes me hideously abusive letters because something I have written has, quite gratuitously, hurt his or her feelings. At least I hope that feeling is transitory. And then there is the real, temperamental hatred of Venus for poor Psyche. In and about the temples, the shores of tranquil, cerulean, and rocky seas, through the defiles and over the meadow and down to Tartarus and up again, this pitiless, unchanging hatred pursues the poor thing – that hatred of woman that no man can ever understand though he may feel it or its effects.

And in the *War in the Air* you have, in what strikes me as a marvellous piece of prophesying, the picture of the hatred of the immense gas-bags for the immense city that they are destroying. It is an extraordinarily good picture, that of the vast things of silk and rubber, pondering over the towers of New York and letting down the fruits of modern-divine hatred. And that group-hatred, of a democracy deified, is the most mysterious or the most understand-

able of all. That ten thousand men should come over the seas to
smash tables, pictures, teapots, card-trays, and looking-glasses for
people who have never done them any harm – that is very queer.
Does it arise, then, from comprehension or from non-compre-
hension? Upon my word it is very hard to say. Why, for instance,
should Germany be bubbling over with Songs of Hate?[2] We have
never hurt the Germans that I know of. I suppose we have been
just insouciant – happy, tranquil, prosperous, rather negligent of
the feelings or the very existence of other people. Yes, I suppose
that must be very exasperating – that quiet ignoring of the existence
of a nation, as of a person. It is as if we had been walking tranquilly
along a country road in the warm sunshine, entirely ignoring abuse
that was being shouted at us from over a hedge.

For I fancy that the feeling that finds issue in the Songs of Hate
– the organised collective desire to cause intolerable pain – is not
a growth of just yesterday. It is a product of many, many years.

---

2   Ernst Lissauer composed a popular anti-British 'Hymn of Hate' at the start of the war.

Joining Up

From Ford's reply to *L'Intransigeant*'s question, 'Que Pensez Vous de la France?' (5 January 1934), p. 1.

Between the 4th August 1914 and the 4th August 1915 I wrote at least three hundred articles and two whole books of propaganda for France. And then, as M. Herriot was kind enough to write once: 'This English poet, still young – but, alas!, advanced enough in years (it's me he's describing) – threw down the pen to take up the sword'. And that was with the sole purpose, I beg you to believe, of helping to preserve France and civilisation.[3]

From *Zeppelin Nights* (London, [1915]), pp. 303–7.
Though published as a collaboration with Violet Hunt, most of this book of historical sketches was written by Ford. 'Serapion Hunter' is the Fordian writer; Hunt appears as 'Mrs Candour Viola'. The 'contemplative politician' who teases Serapion sounds like Masterman. The 'friend and writer' who asked them where they all stood is presumably based on Henry James, whom Ford parodied elaborating on the expression 'So that here we all are' (see *Mightier Than the Sword*, p. 35), and who became a naturalised British subject on 26 July 1915. Ford got his own British nationality certified on 23 August 1915.

Serapion finished and looked at us all, sitting quietly in the white drawing-room.
'That's the last thing I shall ever read to you,' he said.
Candour suddenly exclaimed:
'Oh, *don't!*'

---

3 Translated by Max Saunders. Ford was certainly a ferociously productive propagandist at the time, though the number of articles was smaller than he remembered it twenty years later. David Harvey's *Ford Madox Ford: 1873-1939: A Bibliography of Works and Criticism* (Princeton, 1962), cites less than fifty between those dates. Ford refers to Edouard Herriot (1872–1957), the Radical–Socialist premier and man of letters.

'It's pretty rotten,' the defender of Arkwright said. 'Serapion, old man, you can be as yellow as the yellowest. It is really rather astonishing. You can write all that pretty fairish stuff about history, and then all that stuff, without perspective ...'

'I don't know,' the gentleman who had originally asked where we all stood, said. 'I sometimes think that, if one has too much power to resist great waves of popular emotion, one cannot be much of a poet – much of a writer at all. It's probably a question ...'

He was interrupted by Serapion's getting up to fetch a glass of water for Candour, and by his asking her if she would not like a little brandy in it. We perceived that she was very pale, and asked, in undertones, if she was not ill. The speaker continued:

'It's probably a question of degree. It is necessary to stand out against popular emotion if one is to be an artist – true! But, if it goes on and on .... A poet you know must have human feelings or – I at least am certain for what my certainty is worth – he cannot be a poet. Poetry, in the end, is the voicing of emotions of humanity, and, if the emotion embraces enough of us, it has got to be voiced or the art is wronged. So it is with one. The emotion goes on. It is cried in the streets; it calls to you from the walls; it bends down all features as if there were fingers pulling them down; it gets hold of your heart; it writes itself for you with those moving fingers' – and the speaker pointed to the searchlights – 'with those. And then – when you're sure; when you can't but be sure – you, if you're any sort of a poet, do something. You get naturalised on the side you adhere to; you write to the press you call yellow, in golden – my dear Serapion – not merely sulphur hues; you ... you ... you enlist ... you ...'

'No... no... no!' Candour called out. 'It isn't right. It can't be right. Serapion is too good. The country needs his writings. Isn't he a great artist? Do you want to extinguish that power of words by using it to stop a bullet? ...'

Serapion looked at her with that superior air, that air of masterfulness that made us all wonder how she could do anything but detest the fellow ....

'My dear,' he said heavily, 'no man ever knows whether he is an artist or no – no artist who is ever worth his salt. What is there to show me that I'm an artist? Popular support? I don't get it. My inner convictions? I have not got them; or I haven't got them half as much as the worst writer in the halfpenny press or the last literary knight. And our amiable friends here? If you asked them they'd say that I was a very valuable person, too good for cannon fodder. But they would not believe it, because every one of them thinks that he alone is good enough to be the exception. Then here I stand. If I had the conviction, I might stand out. Or no, I could not. For that would be an argument for every man to stand out. There is no man – no shoeblack, no baker who does not feel the conviction that he has an intimate and precious gift that should exempt him from the embraces of death. And the pressure of which our friend and master has spoken is too strong. It has spoken to me from the streets; it has delivered its messages from the walls. Do you think I can look into the dark shadows of those trees and not feel it? Damn it all, haven't I been for forty years or so in the ruling classes of this country; haven't I enjoyed their fat privileges, and shan't I, then, pay the price?'

'Oh, but tell him he's too valuable,' Candour appealed to all of us. 'Art alone is too valuable ....'

'My dear,' Serapion said, speaking a good deal more tenderly than we had ever heard him speak to her, 'our friend here asked us in the beginning, what it all led to – the burnings of the martyrs, the printing of the Golden Legend, the discovery of leaden pipes, the stricken waves of sea combats ... well, they led up to the shadowy London that we know, to these Zeppelin nights; to this immense strain; to all the tears; to ...'

'I say, Serapion,' the contemplative politician said, 'you aren't telling us all this because you're going to spend six months in room 2981 at the War Office? As a principle of popular oratory, you should key your peroration down to some proportion with the subject. Of course on occasion you can get into a fine fury over the parish pump. But not when you have the house with you. Damn it all, we all of us wish that we could enlist ....'

'Oh, don't you understand?' Candour cried out. 'Serapion enlisted this morning. He put his age down at thirty-three and they jumped at him.' And she went out of the room crying.

Letter to his mother, Catherine Hueffer [August–September 1915]: House of Lords Record Office.

Dear Mrs H:
Of course I sh^d. not have gone off to the bloody wars without

telling you: but I wanted to get a commission without talking about it, & a commission in the regular army, not in any of the fancy services which are only a form of shirking. I think this is my perfectly plain duty. If the war goes on another six months every man will just have to fight & I may as well be in it sooner rather than later. If it is over within six months, I shall be out of it of wh. I shall be heartily glad for I don't *relish* the idea of fighting, tho' I hope to behave all right if it comes to that. [...]

Letter to Catherine Hueffer, 18 September 1915: House of Lords Record Office.

3ᵈ· Bn. The Welch Regt.
Tenby
18 Sep. 1915.

Dear Mrs H:

You ask me why I have gone into the army: simply because I cannot imagine taking any other course. If one has enjoyed the privileges of the ruling classes of a country all one's life, there seems to be no alternative to fighting for that country if necessary. And indeed I have never felt such an entire peace of mind as I have felt since I wore the King's uniform. It is just a matter of plainsailingly doing one's duty, without any responsibilities except to one's superiors & one's men. Of course it is a pretty hard life, but I really enjoy every minute of it. I am bang in the middle of examinations wh. are very tiring & exciting too, but I hope to get through all right.

I hope your bothers with O.[4] & Russian ladies & the like are subsiding; they seem to be rather complicated.

O. cᵈ· certainly have had a commⁿ· had he wanted it. Perhaps he has 1.

Yʳ· affte son
<u>Ford M. H.</u>

---

4 Ford's brother, Oliver Madox Hueffer, who got his commission in the 10th Battalion of the East Surrey Regiment in October 1915.

From 'Dedicatory Letter to Stella Ford', prefaced to the 1927 edition of *The Good Soldier*.

This book was originally called by me *The Saddest Story*, but since it did not appear till the darkest days of the war were upon us, Mr Lane importuned me with letters and telegrams – I was by that time engaged in other pursuits! – to change the title which he said would at that date render the book unsaleable. One day, when I was on parade, I received a final wire of appeal from Mr Lane, and the telegraph being reply-paid I seized the reply-form and wrote in hasty irony: 'Dear Lane, Why not *The Good Soldier*?' ... To my horror six months later the book appeared under that title.

I have never ceased to regret it but, since the War, I have received so much evidence that the book has been read under that name that I hesitate to make a change for fear of causing confusion. Had the chance occurred during the War I should not have hesitated to make the change, for I had only two evidences that anyone had ever heard of it. On one occasion I met the adjutant of my regiment just come off leave and looking extremely sick. I said: 'Great Heavens, man, what is the matter with you?' He replied: 'Well, the day before yesterday I got engaged to be married and today I have been reading *The Good Soldier*.'

On the other occasion I was on parade again, being examined in drill, on the Guards' Square at Chelsea. And, since I was petrified with nervousness, having to do it before a half-dozen elderly gentlemen with red hatbands, I got my men about as hopelessly boxed as it is possible to do with the gentlemen privates of H. M. Coldstream Guards. Whilst I stood stiffly at attention one of the elderly red hatbands walked close behind my back and said distinctly in my ear, 'Did you say *The* Good *Soldier*?' So no doubt Mr Lane was avenged. At any rate I have learned that irony may be a two-edged sword.

From 'From a Paris Quay (II)', *New York Evening Post Literary Review* (3 January 1925), pp. 1–2.

Mr Hemingway [...] writes like an Angel; like an Archangel: but his talk – his matter – is that of a Bayonet Instructor. He never gets very far away from the Spirit of Berlud! (In the Welsh Regiment

we had a Bayonet Instructor from whose lips those syllables were
never absent. He stuck imaginary Germans with the cold inches of
steel. He rolled his eyes and appealed to his classes to remember the
murders, rapes, and all the rest of it, of Louvain and, with exaggerated grunts, he pictured us pushing the bayonet home into the
chest of a p[oo]r b[lood]y Hun, whilst mechanically this admirable
and kind father of a family exclaimed: 'That's what yeh've gotter
have .... The spirit of Ber*lud* .... The Spirit of Ber*lud*! ...') So Mr
Hemingway, beginning one story with: 'They shot the six Cabinet
Ministers at half-past six.' ... Another with: 'Everybody was drunk.
The whole battery was drunk going along the road in the dark ....
It was funny going along that road. That was when I was a kitchen
corporal.'... Or to quote a whole episode:

> The first matador got the horn through his sword hand and
> the crowd hooted him out. The second matador slipped and the
> bull caught him through the belly and he hung onto the horn
> with one hand and held the other tight against the place and the
> bull rammed him *wham* against the wall and the horn came out
> and he lay in the sand and then got up like crazy drunk and tried
> to slug the men carrying him away and yelled for his sword but
> he fainted. The kid came out and had to kill five bulls because
> you can't have more than three matadors, and the last bull he
> was so tired he could not get the sword in. He could hardly lift
> his arm. He tried five times and the crowd was quiet because it
> was a good bull and it looked like him or the bull and then he
> finally made it. He sat down in the sand and puked and they held
> a cape over him while the crowd hollered and threw things down
> into the bull-ring....

That is very marvelous writing. If the American Father and
Mother will just for a moment withhold their protests against the
blood on the sand, they will realise that they now possess an incom-
parable picture and that that picture has been presented with almost
fewer words than is believable.

And the great need of our modern world is just knowledge. Any
one who has read the paragraph just quoted has been at a bull fight
just as any one who has read the *Iliad* has seen the face that launched
a thousand ships. So the great need of our time being the saving of
time, any soul that can give us very quick, irrefutable and consum-
mate pictures confers a great boon on humanity.

Joseph Conrad gave you Malaysia, South American republics;

the Secret Service, the pre-Soviet efforts of Russian revolution-
aries, the Congo, the Sea – and above all the English public school
frame of mind. Hudson gave you La Plata, London through its birds
the Sussex Downs by way of thistle-down. Doughty has given you
Arabia of the Desert; Clarendon the Great Rebellion; Defoe, the
Plague of London; Cervantes, the death of altruism – of Christianity
itself. It is up to the writer of today to give us today.

Letter to his daughters, Christina and Katharine Hueffer, 18 July 1916[5]

My dear Kids:
I am just going up to the firing line – so that seems a proper moment
to write to you both – though I do not seem to have much to say
– Or rather, I have so much that it w^d be no use beginning. So take
it all as said. I was looking thro' the dedication of the book called
Ancient Lights that I wrote for you, the other day. I don't think I
want to change it or add to it. Read it again yourselves if anything
happens to me. You know I have always loved you both very, very
dearly – but I c^d not wrangle for you. I took the Commun[ion]
this morning & prayed for you both. Pray for me.
Yr. old

y.

---

5   Transcribed in Katharine Lamb's letter to Arthur Mizener, 1 December 1969: Cornell.

Shell Shock

From *Mightier Than the Sword*, pp. 264–6.

At any rate, after I was blown up at Bécourt-Bécordel in '16 and, having lost my memory, lay in the Casualty Clearing Station in Corbie, with the enemy planes dropping bombs all over it and the dead Red Cross nurses being carried past my bed, I used to worry agonizedly about what my name could be – and have a day-nightmare. The night-nightmare was worse, but the day one was as bad as was necessary. I thought I had been taken prisoner by the enemy forces and was lying on the ground, manacled hand and foot ... and with the enemy, ignoring me for the time, doing dreadful stunts – God knows what – all around me .... Immense shapes in grey-white *cagoules* and shrouds, miching and mowing and whispering horrible plans to one another! It is true they all wore giant, misty gas-masks – but wasn't that the logical corollary of the bitter-hating age that produced the mid-Victorian Great Figure? Wouldn't, I mean, poison gas be just the sort of thing that, could they have invented it, the Ruskins and Carlyles and Wilberforces and Holman Hunts would have employed on their enemies or their blood-brothers become rivals? So their Germanic disciples used it when their Day came. Inevitably! Because the dreadful thing about nineteenth-century Anglo-Saxondom was that it corrupted with its bitter comfort-plus-opulence mania not merely itself but the entire, earnest, listening world. What effect could a serious and continued reading of those fellows have had but 1914?... And 193 ...

It has only just occurred to me that that Corbie-phobia of my middle years must have taken at least its shape from my childhood's dreads. I might well, I mean, have had as my chief dread in those white huts surmounted with the Red Cross, the fear of being taken prisoner by the Germans – but I doubt if my imagined Germans would have taken just that gigantic miching and mowing shape if it hadn't been for the nature of my childhood's ambience. I was then horribly imbued by those people with a sense of my Original Sin so that I used to have innumerable fears when the candle was put out .... But that was the worst of all ... the dread that Mr Ruskin or Mr Carlyle or Mr Holman Hunt – or even Herr Richard Wagner! – should with their dreadful eyes come into a room where I was alone and where there was no other exit ... and, fixing me with their dreadful, shining eyes ... God knows what then ....

Western Front

Letter to his mother, Catherine Hueffer [n. d. but *c.* late August 1916]: House of Lords Record Office.

attᵈ 9/Welch
19ᵗʰ Div.
B.E.F.

Dear Mrs H:

Yes: I have been very remiss in not writing to you & I am very sorry: I will try to do better in future. But somehow I do not find very much to write about except matters of shot & shell wʰ I thought might worry you.

I got pretty well after my shaking up & got back to the Bⁿ on this front in about a week. Here, tho' of course the war goes on it is rather like the peace of Heaven after the Somme; the Boche seems to be wanting in ammⁿ; we hardly ever see one of their planes &, although there is a good deal of rain & much mud, when we are out of the trenches, there is very little to trouble one except an occasional shell overhead. I am pretty well – indeed quite well & view life with considerable composure; I don't know how I am going to stand being continuously wet – but hitherto it seems to have done me little harm. I am sorry you are still queer, I had hoped the fine weather would have done you good. Thank Juliet[6] for her letter, will you. I will write to her almost immediately.

Yr affte son
<u>F. M. H.</u>

From *The Marsden Case*, p. 12.

One day, afterwards, I heard a man, half of whose chest had just been blown away, say: "Ere's another bloomin' casualty!'

---

6   Ford's sister, Juliet Soskice.

From *No More Parades*, p. 35.

A man, brown, stiff, with a haughty parade step, burst into the light. He said with a high wooden voice:

"'Ere's another bloomin' casualty.' In the shadow he appeared to have draped half his face and the right side of his breast with crape. He gave a high, rattling laugh. He bent, as if in a stiff bow, woodenly at his thighs. He pitched, still bent, on to the iron sheet that covered the brazier, rolled off that and lay on his back across the legs of the other runner, who had been crouched beside the brazier. In the bright light it was as if a whole pail of scarlet paint had been dashed across the man's face on the left and his chest. It glistened in the firelight – just like fresh paint, moving!

Letter to Catherine Hueffer, 6 September 1916: House of Lords Record Office.

Dear Ma!

Thank you very much for y^r letter – wh. I still don't deserve. But it is very hot here & things are enormously exciting & the firing all day keeps me a little too much on the jump to write composedly. However it is jolly to have been in the two greatest strafes of history – & I am perfectly well & in good spirits, except for money worries wh. are breaking me up a good deal – & for the time, perfectly safe. [...] / God bless you.

F. M. H.

From 'O Hymen': unpublished typescript, Cornell, pp. 7–8.

[A] State can only afford to legalise polygamy or frequent divorce when its finances are perfectly satisfactory since polygamy and divorce so easy as to amount to prostitution are both expensive affairs, the last perhaps the most expensive of all. The most convenient image universally to express all kinds of marriage is a 'digging-in'. In the late war we made holes in the ground which we protected with mounds of earth against immediate missiles; we then furnished them rudimentarily; improved the protective mounds; acquired more furnishings; dug more mounds and so on according to the length of our stay or our intended stay. The most elaborate specimen of a digging-in that I ever saw was the temporary home of a German general of division. His dug-out was panelled with wood-work taken from a château, tiled with admirable old tiles, contained a piano and was adorned with a remarkable brass fire-place in the Nouvel Art style. Upon the mantel stood the statue of a recumbent German lion on a canon, on the four sides of [the] plinth of the statue were inscribed the words *La Boisselle* and the dates 1915, 1916, 1917 which shewed that he intended that union to be permanent or at least durable. But alas, it was then still 1916 and there we were in his home .... And I do not know how many temporary homes I did not dig into during that period. We would be allotted a hole or a hut or a tent or an empty room and, at once, some sort of bed made, we would stand a bully-beef case on end, decorate it with a sheet of newspaper for a cloth, an empty bottle for a candle-stick, a strip of sacking for a bedside rug, a hook on which to hang the water-bottle .... Well, we dug-in .....

That, the world over, and back through the illimitable corridor of the ages, man has always done when he married or went to war – and that, grow the habit of promiscuity as it may, throughout the world he will have the tendency to do. Marriage re-places war at times, but for the one as for the other, the ambition, the aim and the ideal are the acquiring of permanent property.

With that stated we arrive at one of the current explanations for the loosening of the marriage-tie that is said to characterise the present world-situation. The late war, certainly for European populations and no doubt, if in a lesser degree, for Occidental republics markedly shook not only the ideal, but even the belief in the possibility of .... permanent property descending in the hands of families down the generations. Even for those who, after the war, still had great possessions the spectacle of the innumerable dispossessed was enough to make them think on impermanence whilst those who with the coming of peace were beginning the painful task of amassing were almost universally convinced of the futilities of economy. The result was a very wide-spread determination not to dig-in, embracing indeed nearly all European and European-descended nations.

From 'Last Words about Edward VIII': unpublished type-script, Cornell, pp. 4–6. Broadcast on NBC on 7 December 1936 – four days before the Abdication. There is à recording of the broadcast in the Museum of Broadcasting, New York.

In the Autumn of 1916 my regiment was in support behind Kemmel Hill that looks down the Ypres Salient. About the middle of September – I should think on the day before the one on which we first used tanks – I was sent for to Army HQ at Dranoutre to be given instructions for letting an inspecting General from Home see as little of operations as possible. You took those fellows up onto a high place where they could see the landscape and then somewhere where it was being heavily shelled. Then as a rule they left hurriedly.

Well, headquarters was very overworked those days so I was told to wait in the mess and the second chief of staff would give me my instructions at lunch... So, in a long hut decorated by more copies of the *Vie Parisienne* than I had imagined to exist, I sat down and played at a defective piano. There was no one else there.

I was getting away with a brilliant execution of the finale of *Tristan und Isolde*.

A motor bicycle chugged and made violent noises outside in the sunlight; then stopped. A little, shining, staff-captain stepped across the door-sill; gawdy, but not too gawdy, sporting several ribbons I did not know. I was rather shy at being heard to play the piano but he said:

'Don't get up ... Go on playing,' and stalked across the mess and out at an inner door.

I did not know who he was, but from his set quite unsmiling face and his heavy step for such a small man I imagined he must be quite a somebody who had done something distinguished.

So at lunch, the second chief of staff gave me my directions and then I asked who the little officer was who was set on the right hand of the general. He answered:

'The Prince of Wales of course. Running around without even an orderly. One day he'll be killed and no one will know about it. Then there'll be hell for us.'

I saw the Prince next day from a little distance, going through our lines, but with several attendants, that time. He stopped talking to a P[riva]te Evans of B company, for a few seconds, his face still perfectly sphinxlike, as if all the miseries of the world rested on his shoulder ... until he acknowledged the salute of Pte Evans. Then his face splintered into a perfectly mechanical, kindly smile, that in a second was gone as he stalked towards the camp kitchens. He wore his red hat band – which the rest of his escort didn't, so near the Enemy lines ... I suppose to spare him the danger from Enemy planes that a lot of red hatbands shining in a group might have caused him.

I remember saying to myself:

'Why the hell should he look so? Couldn't he have all the damn larks he wanted in all the land between here and the sea[?] ...'

And I devoutly hoped that he might have all he wanted... poor kid!

In half an hour after that it was all through the battalion in the words of 09 Evans:

''E sez ter me: "The Welch ain't you? ... You motto's 'Stick it the Welch' ain't it? ... Anything I can do for the Welch? ... Can you stick it?"

'I sez ter im: "Surely to cootness we can stick it, sir, surely to cootness," and if his speaking timid like hadn't made me feel timidlike I'd have said "Till the cows come home." ... Surely to cootness I would have.'

From _Return to Yesterday_, pp. 118-19.

I have already told – I think in one of my novels which was not otherwise autobiographical[7] – how, having a guard to mount over a hospital tent of German prisoners, in France in 191[6], I went into the tent and there, washed, in a white bed was a young boy like an angel. I asked him where he came from and he said: 'From Framersdach near Lohrhaupten in the Bavarian Spessart.' I asked him what he did at home and he said he was the swineherd. I asked him if he had ever been in a bed with sheets before and he answered: '_Niemals, Herr Offizier._' I asked him if he felt himself well there and he said: '_Es ist doch Himmel, Herr Offizier._'

---

7   The novel is 'True Love and a G.C.M.'. See p. 130 above, and also the Introduction, note 17.

From *Great Trade Route*, pp. 339–40; p. 266.[8]

I wish I could manage to tell two anecdotes at once. For if that one narrates my first and strongest emotion in Memphis of the Mississippi, my strongest emotion, after my childhood, in connection with the State itself came to me in France during the first Battle of the Somme. My battalion was marching into the line; the goat – not the magnificent white one with the silver shield between its horns that had been given to the Regiment by Edward VII – but a little, thin, Picardy nanny that had adopted the battalion and ran always in front of us of its own accord – the goat, then, preceded the scratch band we had got together, jumping now and then into the hedges on either side of the road when it saw a particularly attractive rag or tin can. And suddenly the band dropped giving the drum and fife effect and, just before it was timed to fall out and let us go on, that ragtime collection – and every man sang too ... heavens, didn't they sing! And what voices the Welsh have! – that ragtime collection of musicians burst out with:

'Way *down* in Tennessee, that's where I'd like to be,
On my old Mammie's knee; she thinks the world of me.
And when they meet me, when they meet me, just imagine
    how they'll greet me
When I get back, when I get back ...'

Only we sang 'if' instead of 'when.' ... And I assure you the State of Tennessee would have felt complimented if it had known how sincerely we 678 men – who were soon to be not more than 215 – desired to find ourselves within her border ....

She was sitting by her nearly red-hot stove, her head bent over my dripping tunic whose sleeve she was sewing up. On the corrugated iron roof of the kitchen the rain fell in such merciless torrents that the crepitating noises completely drowned out the sound of the shells that the Germans were throwing from Lille into the church not fifty yards away. You could not hear them, but every half-minute the pots boiling on the red stove solemnly jumped up and sat down again. And that Flemish peasant woman never moved, only her hand with the needle went backwards and forwards.[8]

---

8   Compare 'Epilogue'.

Reading Behind the Lines

From 'Stevie', *New York Evening Post Literary Review* (12 July 1924), pp. 881–2.[9]

In the early autumn of 191[6], when the haws, as I remember, were beginning to turn scarlet, I came in at two o'clock in the morning after a job of trench digging behind Kemmel Hill. And, as I was unable to sleep, I took up *The Red Badge of Courage* and read it till dawn. Toward five I got up and looked out through my tent flap. The mother-of-pearl light from the east threw a mother-of-pearl wash of color over the innumerable tents of a sleeping division. The stillness was absolute. But what worried me was the men bending over the red brands of some small wood fires. They were dressed in greenish dust color; it seemed to me they should have been in blue. And it gave my mind an extraordinary wrench to come back to the realisation that I was where and when I was, instead of being upon the Potomac half a century ago, so great was the illusion set up by this marvelous book, which, with its matchless projection in the very opening pages, created a sleeping and be-tented host having a reality possessed by no mortal division and an immortality that shall outlast the memories of innumerable wars! And indeed, if the public service of literature be to provide vicarious experience, and so to instruct mankind, *The Red Badge of Courage* does this to the fullest. For myself, the real memory of that night's warfare, with the candle stuck on a bully beef case beside my head – the unforgettable memory, which is part of my intimate being, is just that created by Crane's words. The reality is a part of oblivion.

---

9   Besides the versions printed here, Ford recalled re-reading *The Red Badge of Courage* in: 'Stevie & Co', *New York Essays*, p. 30; *The English Novel*, pp. 55–6; and *Return to Yesterday*, p. 49.

From *Mightier Than the Sword*, **pp. 163–4.**

[...] I had been reading, actually, *The Red Badge of Courage* by the light of a candle stuck on to a bully-beef case at my camp-bed head. And so great had been the influence of that work on me that, when at dawn I got out of bed and looked out of my tent flap to see if a detail for which I was responsible was preparing carts to go to the Schiffenberg and draw our Mills bombs ... against and below hills and dark woods I saw sleepy men bending over fires of twigs, getting tea for that detail, it did not seem real to me. Because they were dressed in khaki. The hallucination of Crane's book had been so strong on me that I had expected to see them dressed in Federal blue.

From *Thus to Revisit*, **p. 108.**

And, for the life of me, I can hardly tell which is to me the more real – the dawn appearing over a host just standing to in Crane's book, or the dawns that we used to see, between the dusty thistle stalks, glimmering over those hammered, violently chiselled and blasted downs. That was the sheer instinct of the Poet who searches the hearts of man – that writing.

From 'Literary Causeries: IV: Escape...', *Chicago Tribune Sunday Magazine* **(Paris) (9 March 1924), pp. 3, 11.**

During some late troubles – but you all shared them! – I said to myself one day very definitely: 'Here I am who was once and during a longish life a man of letters – as who shall say, even a Critic. It is as like as not I shall die in this other occupation and before long. Let me then see whether the books that during all that other life I praised and championed with my pen can here still hold me.'

I imagine, these things passing in July and August 1916 in a 'France' whose name had other echoes – I imagine that few vicissitudes of humanity can have been more engrossing than those from which we then suffered. It was not merely the dangers, the fears or the fatigues; it was the endless responsibilities, the perpetually

having to rely on not immensely reliable human material for the
carrying out of life and death jobs. So that, the other nightmares
recurrent from those days having in the order above given gradually
faded away still at nights I awake with a start and find myself
groaning: 'Good God! It cannot be done!' – the 'it' being the
sending of Mills Bombs up to a detachment of the 6th Wiltshires
on the Scherpenberg behind the Ypres Salient, that having been
once my occupation.

Well then, having taken my resolve I wrote to London for the
books that I had always championed. I present you here with that
Bedside List: The *Education Sentimentale* and the *Trois Contes* of
Flaubert; *Fathers and Children, The House of Gentlefolk* and *A
Sportsman's Sketches* of Turgenev; the *Red Badge of Courage* and the
Open Boat of Stephen Crane; *Nature in Downland, Green Mansions*
and the *Purple Land* of W.H. Hudson; *Fort Comme la Mort* and the
original *Yvette* volume of Maupassant; *Histoire Comique, Sur la Pierre
Blanche* and the *Crainquebille* volume of Anatole France; *Lord Jim,
The Nigger of the 'Narcissus'* and the original *Youth* volume of Joseph
Conrad and *What Maisie Knew, The Spoils of Poynton* and *The Portrait
of a Lady* by Henry James.

Let me say at once that with the exception of three books to
which I will come later all these stood the extreme vital, if not
literary, test to which I put them, so that the valley of the Somme
and the highlands behind the Salient even now remain for me
singularly tapestried over with other landscapes and, at times, if I
let my memory alone, I could not say whether at a given date I was
not seeing Kensington Gardens, the scented East or the Potomac
instead of Albert, the wood of Bécourt-Bécordel or the landscape
that stretched below Kemmel Hill.

The most vivid of these superimposed landscapes came to me
from Stephen Crane, who was of course a landscape painter and,
curiously enough, from *What Maisie Knew*, Henry James having
been less of a hand at description than most of us; and *Nature in
Downland* it was almost unbearable, *Nature in Downland* being still
for me I think the most beautiful book in the world. But there on
those scarred and raddled chalk downs it was too harrowing to read
these intensely vivid projections of our own south country hills.[...]

This is perhaps not Literary Criticism... Or perhaps it is! But I
will give an instance or two. I re-read *Youth* and *Heart of Darkness*
in a regimental ammunition dump that had been dug out in the
side of a hill in Bécourt wood – on 15 July it was; *What Maisie Knew*

in and around the town of Albert during the 2 and 5 August and the *Red Badge of Courage* whilst we were in tents, in support, somewhere between Kemmel Hill and the small town of Locre. I remember these dates in 1916 because of other circumstances – the regiment coming out on such a day and moving up North on such another.

As for the *Red Badge of Courage*, having come in late from a trench-digging fatigue I started to read this in my tent with a single candle on a bully-beef case beside my bed-head towards three o'clock in the morning. Just after dawn I heard a voice call from one tent to another: 'Evans! The major says have you done with *Mr Britling?*' this, the only sound I had heard bringing me back to a world in which there were other armies than Lee's and Sherman's – and other readers for other books. I got up then to stretch myself and to take a look at the dawn. There were then endless grey tents beneath a dying moon, the tents, bleached-grey going down hill to the quietest looking of level grounds; here and there a man in khaki, standing in a tent-opening or bent over a fire. I assert solemnly that I could not believe that those men could be in khaki, so convinced had I been that I was amongst men in the blue or grey uniforms of the Federal or Confederate Armies of poor Steevie's book. This opens, you will remember – or you ought to if you do not – with a projection of the dawn coming down upon the Federal Army in tents, beside the Potomac I think, and it is the most vivid scene of anything that I remember in literature – unless it be the description at the end of *Youth*, of the Eastern faces looking down upon the sleepers in the boat that has come in and caught up to the jetty.

But the most queer of my pictures of those days connects itself with *Maisie*. (I hope I have not written this somewhere before; if I have and the Reader has to read or skip it twice, I can't help it.)[10] I had been detailed to march some men to the baths in Albert and, as this was a duty that took time I had taken *What Maisie Knew* with me in my pocket. The doubling of vision that resulted is one of the most bewildering of my memories.

The baths for troops in Albert were situated in a nearly ruined water-mill in which the sappers had set up some boilers so that the buildings, leaking badly from room to room, were always full of

---

10 Ford had written about this episode but not yet published the book: see *No Enemy*, pp. 160–4.

steam. The officer in charge had reserved for him a tall room that must have been the miller's counting house; it contained at any rate a glass fronted book-case, the books being masked by very faded green blinds. And there I sat for hours reading *Maisie*. And I was sitting on a chair beneath the high skies of Kensington Gardens with a lady with whom I presume I should not have been sitting – at any rate with Maisie's mother; and Beale Farrange with his egregious beard was bearing down upon us over the slope. I was asked for orders once or twice by a sergeant called Motte. There was also an infinitely pathetic old private of the Lincolns who, aged over sixty, had come back from Canada – to 'elp the Old Lady sez I to mother – and being much too aged to lug about me bloomin' ipe, I beg pardon, I mean rifle, Sir, had been put in charge of that officer's room in the Baths. But I could not see him or the Sergeant because I was walking round dark London squares with Mrs Wi[x] and Maisie, Mrs Wi[x] constantly expressing her fear of being 'spoken to'. And I went on doing that though the Germans started trying, as they did every afternoon, to knock down the near-by factory chimney; but afternoon after afternoon about five they started to put a heavy shell every quarter of an hour for an hour and a half as near to it as they could get. I had to get my men out of it as quickly as I could; but I know I had to get the sergeant to march them. I could not. I was on the parade at Brighton with Maisie.

[...]

I wish I could put it more fuzzily than that; more with blurred edges because the memory does not come back very clearly, but more than anything with the memory of being in an awkward and embarrassing affair – the affair of Maisie's parents. (*What Maisie Knew* is the story of a child who lives in an atmosphere of the singu-larly intricate and vindictively if genteely conducted divorce suits of her parents.) And, by an extraordinary coincidence, whilst I was still reading the book – I finished it indeed in the train – I was ordered to Paris to perform an unusually exhausting duty, and, quartered in a tremendous, marble and white enamel hotel in the Avenue de l'Opéra, I fell right bang, bewildered weariness and all, into the midst of an Affair that must almost exactly have duplicated the affair of Maisie and her parents.

... No, not the most delicate minded of readers need here feel alarm. What happened was that whilst I lay extended in a lounge in the hotel hall in a state of utter exhaustion I at some point found upon my knee a small, fluffily clothed, dark, preternaturally intelligent child who said very clearly with a strong French-American accent: 'They *say* Mummie's gone to Heaven. But I can't find any tram-car that takes you *au ciel*', whilst at the same time a man that I didn't in the least know, with an accent of the most extreme nervousness, was muttering in my ear: 'What else could I do? I had to knock the fellow down. And take the child! So I got a barouche and pair whilst she was walking with the nurse beside the lake-side and bundled the child in ...'

In that singular way Life came over into the mood of the book read; so that it remains extraordinarily difficult to me, in that queer doubling of effects, to recover which the more harassed me.

From *Provence*, pp. 298–9.

It was one of those *erreurs grossières* that awaken you in cold sweats at night; that remain with one to the end of one's life; that are one's ruin here in earth, and that no doubt in the end the Recording Angel will tally against you far more heavily than your weightiest sins of commission .... As when in 1916 I asked the French Foreign Minister for ferrets for my battalion instead of a decoration for myself .... That is really a champion instance of the *bévue* [howler] ....For if I had asked for a decoration M. Delcassé would have been pleased, and I could have proceeded to ask for ferrets and got them. As it was I offended His Excellency, who thought I was drunk – or perhaps even in the clutches of delirium tremens.

For what could he know about ferrets? The French soldier is ratproof. Whereas my poor comrades in arms having lost all their ferrets by influenza missed their most congenial form of sport and passed sleepless nights with the rats trying to pull out from under their heads the knapsacks containing stolen ducks or mutton bones .... I have already told that story somewhere.[11] But it continues to grow and grow on me and recurs whenever I eat beef at night ....

---

11 See the introductory note to 'Trois Jours de Permission', p. 49.

From *A Mirror to France*, pp. 276–9.[12]

In another landscape, then, with an outfield of thistles and a ground
of dust, we were playing cricket, with axe-handles for bats, beef-
boxes for wickets, and a tennis-ball. We were jumping about and
making a good deal of noise: the ball ran in among the feet of
picketed mules. The battalion had just come out from a nasty place.

I perceived, standing twenty yards off, a Frenchman that I knew
– a man of very good, serious, high-bourgeois family, very tall,
unbending, and unexhilarated. A pillar of blue-grey, with a blue-
grey helmet, he was very lightly bending back so as almost to sit on
his walking-stick, and, quite motionless, he thus resembled a metal
tripod. Through his monocle he was regarding my men, and he bit
his moustache, which was cropped to resemble exactly that of the
late Lord Kitchener. As I approached, he said, in English:

'I find that very shocking! To jump about and cry out amongst
the dust where have fallen so many men!'

I said:

'Mais, M. le Capitaine! nous venons de sortir des tranchées et
cela remonte le moral des hommes!'

He repeated expressionlessly:

'All the same, I find that very shocking. When one comes out
of the trenches one should think. Perhaps one should even pray a
little: but certainly one should think.' [...] From time to time he
would look up in the course of a monstrous shell going overhead
to fall far behind us, then he would repeat that in the intervals of
desperate days perhaps one should pray a little. Certainly one should
think. And that is the real lesson of France to the world of abstract
thought and of the Arts.

As for me, I was furious – properly enough, considering the time
and the place and the natures and vicissitudes of my comrades. I
never looked up at any shell: I was too heated. And when – as was
inevitable – he made his speech to the effect that no doubt I should
look at things differently had we a devastating foe astride our islands
from Manchester to York I fair let him have it, as we used to say.

But I think he was right – if, for the occasion, grudging. The
truth is that the French cannot afford to be thought-free – not ever!

---

12 Fuller reminiscences of this episode appear in *No Enemy* (New York, 1929): in English,
as Chapter 7, entitled 'A Cricket Match' (pp. 131–43); and in Ford's original French as
the 'Envoi' (pp. 293–302).

They never could, and, make what military dispositions they may, they never will be able to. As long as they possess Provence or one inch of the shores of the Mediterranean they will always have, stretched from Manchester to York, as it were, potentially devastating foes.

Illness and Regeneration

Letter to his mother, Catherine Hueffer, 15 December 1916: House of Lords Record Office.

IX Welch, No 6 I. B. D., Rouen
15. 12. 16.

Dear Mrs H:

I don't know whether you'll be glad or sorry to hear that my health – or rather my lungs – have gone altogether to pieces – the Dr. says, owing to the touch of gas I got at Nieppe. Anyhow there is no hope – or fear – of my going up the line as a regimental off[ice]r., any more. The M[edical] B[oard] wanted to send me home – but I protested that I didn't in the least want to see Blighty ever again, so I am marked R[eserve] B[attalion] & left to do staff jobs here.

However, I am not doing much, as my cough keeps me awake all night & sitting up: then I sleep till two in the aft[ernoo]n: crawl about a bit & then tumble back into bed, wheezing all the time like a machine gun. It wd. be really very preferable to be dead – but one isn't dead – so that is all there is to it.

Love to Juliet.

> Yr. aff[ectiona]te son
> Ford M H

Letter to Catherine Hueffer, 5 January 1917: House of Lords Record Office.

IX Welch, No II Red + Hospital, Rouen
5. 1. 17.

Dear Ma!

Many thanks for your letters: I haven't been really gay enough to write to people for some time past – as it's not much good writing depressingly. I was getting much better till Xtmas & then had a relapse with a temperature looking on the chart like a section of

the Alps – with most of the concomitants of temperatures that look
like

However the doctors & nurses have now got it under & I expect
to be sent off to the South on Monday or thereabouts & shall be
there about three weeks, I suppose. After that I hope to get into
one of our Bns in the East – though I am not by any means certain.

It is very quiet here: I don't hear anything either of or from
anybody nowadays wh. makes one feel rather like a ghost.
However, the war seems to be drawing to its close – at least, people
out here are all very cheerful.

I hope you keep well – they say the weather is better in Blighty
than it is here – it could easily be, for Rouen is more dismal in that
way than I c^d have imagined possible – it pours & pours & pours
& that is all there is to it.

I hope the young men prosper like green bay trees – tho' I
suppose not too quickly.

Yr. affte son

FMH

**From _The Marsden Case_ (London, 1923). pp. 301–2;[13]
pp. 304–5.**

What dreadful things railway stations were in those days!

I remember that of Hazebrouck: I suppose it was in February,
1917, I found myself in the station of Hazebrouck. There was not
much light there. Or there were great shafts of light, running up
into the cylindrical barrel roof. I was going up the line; I had no
idea how long I should have to wait for a train. No one had. A
tired creature with a Prussian blue tunic and red flannel trousers,
with a grotesquely disproportionate rifle and an immense zigzag
bayonet, lounged beside an exit. It was as if he made me a prisoner,

---

13 Compare _It Was the Nightingale_, pp. 173–4, and the excerpt from 'Supper Reminiscences'
   below on seeing his own book on station bookstall: perhaps the French translation of
   one of his propaganda books, _Entre Saint Denis et Saint Georges_ (Paris, 1916), which was
   published around September. Also _Joseph Conrad_, pp. 90–1, 102.

though I don't suppose he really did.

I stood at a bookstall for a long time; the light of a dim candle threw out the closely packed yellow backs of novels. There were many trains in the darkness; and market women with geese they had not succeeded in selling in Hazebrouck market. It had all the effect of being shrouded in gloom, in depression, and of being commonplace beyond belief.

Naturally I stood at the bookstall. I was an author. I had been. There were the usual books of the bookstall at a French – or was it a Belgian? – provincial railway station. A gentleman with a forked red beard in a black cloak and top hat was conducting a red-haired *décolletée* nymph, on some cover or other, to a just outlined bed room. And then, pressed and constricted, nearly beyond the rim of light, I saw the back of someone's translation of one of my own books. Dusty! No human soul would ever assimilate it. And no human soul, I thought, would ever think of me again ....

A stalwart fellow touched my elbow. A sergeant, an invalid I suppose, attached to the Railway Transport Officer. He said:

'The train for Steenwerck is in, sir!'

I have no doubt that it was really just a kindly attention; but it enhanced my sense of being in prison. They were watching me; they did not mean that I should miss my train up into the Line. Once I had been a free man: I had sat and written!

I was not well, of course. I had just come out of hospital, I think.

At some time in the black hours there had been a great crash. A *great* crash. Someone in the outside blackness said that the Germans had dropped a highly successful bomb on our engine and our first six carriages. Ours was about the eighth. I daresay that was what it was: we could hear their planes overhead, but no one from our compartment got out to see. I have nothing personal to record, and indeed I was not, after that, much good until, in 1921, I saw on a sort of dais of the splendid Hotel Geneva, Lord Marsden holding a large white ten pound note over the head of a kneeling waiter.

But I hear – indeed I know – that some of our splendid *Intelligentsia* are doing what they can to trepan this country into another war. I pray that God will force them to gain their glories and fortunes in other ways. Wars are very terrible things. It is not merely that people die and suffer: people must die and people must suffer, if not here, then there. But what is dreadful is that the world goes on and people go on being stupidly cruel – in the old ways and all the time. I used to think that, once out there, we should be surrounded by a magic and invisible tent that would keep from us all temporal cares. But we are not so surrounded, and it is not like that. The one nail does not knock out the other. There is that never ceasing waiting about; and the cold; and the long depressions. Now and then there is terrible noise – wearing, lasting for days. And some pain. All that is bearable. But what is desolating, what is beyond everything hateful, is that, round your transparent tent, the old evils, the old heartbreaks and the old cruelties are unceasingly at work.

From 'Supper Reminiscences', *New York Herald Tribune Magazine* **(18 August 1929), pp. 20–1, 23.**

It was in January, 1917, outside what remained of the town of Hazebrouck in Flanders, and I was in a first-class railway carriage that had neither doors nor windows. The enemy planes had destroyed the railway track with bombs and we waited and waited whilst the queerly effeminate looking Annamites[14] in their blue-furred silk hoods and high furred boots laid some more rails. Effeminate they can't have been, for the country was deep in snow and the northeast wind that blows over the Flanders levels has more edge to it than any other wind in the world.

The train had moved out of the station at dusk and had not gone a quarter of a mile before the Germans dropped their bombs in front of it and most of us who were in the train went back to the town to get a modest dinner at one of the remaining inns. But we were not half way through that before the nervous R[ailway] T[ransport] O[fficer] who was responsible for our arrival with our units routed us out with the information that the train was about to restart. It didn't – and toward 4 in the morning we were not only sleepless and frozen, but ravenous, for in face of the RTO's injunctions only the boldest among us dared again leave the train – and I was not among the boldest. Then I thought of my batman.

My batman was not among the miraculously faithful and devoted heroes with which fiction has supplied you. His name was Peters – Peters, 764209, Private E. T. 3d. attd. 9th Welch Regt. – and he

---

14 Annam is a region of what is now Vietnam.

comes back to me as a little, squat, fair man whose voice was a grunted bark, who had next to no English and who sat whenever there was nothing else to do – and he had little enough to do for me! – forever on his heels against a wall. That is the perpetual leisure pose of the Welsh miner. I remember that when I was carried on a stretcher into the casualty clearing station at Corbie just behind the line during the first battle of the Somme he planted himself on his heels against the wall of the Red Cross huts with his pack and rifle and trenching tools beside him, and there he was, impedimenta and all complete, when ten days or so later I came out again. By rights he ought to have been returned to duty, but I suppose he had wangled out of that distasteful vicissitude by rendering himself useful to the Red Cross people. Anyhow he was on the train with me and when I had rooted him out of a third class carriage where he and his mates contrary to all rules had got a stove burning, he set about warming supper.

That supper I shall never forget – not the luxurious fat of it, or the turnips, the haricot beans and the Australian mutton in chunks. For he had simply taken one of our ration tins of Machonochie and tying five candles together had held the tin, tied round with wire, at the end of his bayonet over the flame – all on a biscuit lid on the torn and bespattered cushions of the poor carriage. Why he had not warmed the Machonochie over the stove that he had in his own carriage I could not exactly discover, my knowledge of Welsh being limited to military instructional terms. I think it had a vague relation to the idea that his orfcer-mahn ought to be spotless, even to the extent of the heating of his supper. Yet showing a light in any of the carriages was just as forbidden and there he had five candles.

Anyhow that supper, as I remember, marked rather a turning point of my career. For it is not just a subway ride going back to the line after a period in a particularly luxurious hospital in the Riviera – going back from that Midi that is always like Heaven, or near it, to me – to that frozen Gehenna, and having to wait for hours, as it were, on the very brink of it. And I was rendered particularly moody by the fact that on the dim bookstall of the dimmed station I had seen a dim copy of one of my own books. It seemed to me amazing that I had ever written books at all.

But it was astonishing what, in that world where all the physical aspects were so marked and all the psychological ones so, as it were, nearly rubbed out – what a merely physical sensation like that of a simple bellyful of tepid, neutral-tasting food could do for you. I don't suppose I shall ever taste a Machonochie ration again. Indeed I know I shall not: I shall avoid doing so for fear of destroying an illusion. For not only did it seem to me that an army that could supply its men with a cuisine so admirable must in the end be victorious here on earth and not only did it seem to me that a world where such inward comfort could at 4 of a January morning descend from black and snow-filled heavens – that such a world must be a tolerable world .... But it seemed to me that one day I might even once again take pen in hand and ... well, here I am doing it.

And indeed, when I come to think of it, I remember another supper of that period. I had been put for my sins as second in command of divisional transport and enjoined, in addition, to write French verse for recital to the French Tommies – and I hated the responsibilities of the job and could not get a minute in which to write even English prose, let alone French verse. And I had been out – it was in September, 191[6], near Locre at the very entrance to the Salient – I had been out after nightfall, riding beside the G[eneral] S[ervice] wagons that were taking Mills bombs up to a detachment that was on the Scherpenberg – though what a unit on the Scherpenberg could want with Mills bombs, which are things that you throw by hand, I don't know, for the hill must have been two miles from the nearest German trenches.

At any rate, I had been being strafed all day by Division because those bombs and some other rations had not reached that detachment. And as in the dark I rode with another officer on the top of a bank with below it a sunken road which the wagons took, the Germans, who must have had that road marked with extraordinary accuracy, dropped a shell right onto the horses of the last of my four wagons, and then another right on top of that. It was a more disagreeable affair than most, for the noise made by horses struck by large projectiles – the noise between coughing and screaming, is very tearing to the nerves, at any rate of infantry – and the shells had been pretty close and, though the other three wagons got away all right, I had to bother a bit about the responsibility for the loss of the one. I had, that is to say, done all that I could to see that the wheels and metal work on the wagons were muffled, though on those shell-holed roads a bit will click now and then or a wheel give out a hollow, wooden sound ....

Anyhow, I got back to my transport lines toward 11:30 in a pretty nervous and irritable condition. And there some sort of quartermaster – he was killed immediately afterward; but I remember that, for all the world like the father of Shakespeare, he had once kept a butcher's shop in Stratford-on-Avon – the Quarter was eating a welsh rarebit which had been made for him by a Welch transport man (Welsh rarebits, leeks, anthracite and poems are spelt with an 's', but my regiment and its men have to their credit an army order authorizing them to use the older and quite nonsensical 'c'.) So the Welch transport man had made for the Warwickshire transport officer a welsh rarebit [...]

Now Welsh and Welch alike do not call Welsh rarebit that which we call by that name – that preparation of melted cheese seasoned with ale, cream, Worcestershire sauce, french mustard or what you will. That they call toasted cheese – hissing the sibillants. And what they call Welsh rarebit, or they really call it 'rabbit' – is to toasted cheese as an *omelette au lait*, or *aux champignons,* or *chasseur* is to an *omelette nature*. That is to say that it contains, folded into it, such other ingredients as the funds of the cook or the traditions of his native valley dictate. And that transport man had made his rarebit of cheese, I should think stewed in milk with innumerable onion rings and fresh mackerel, and the result was something extraordinary, though that sensation also I have never again attempted to recapture. It was so stimulating and awakening that I sat up all night in my Connaught hut with the Quarter snoring beside me and wrote this poem:

Je voudrais pouvoir me figurer
Une nuit ou les mitrailleuses se tairaient.

Or in English:

I should like to imagine
A night in which there would be no machine guns!
For it is possible
To come out of a trench or a hut or a tent or a church all [in
    ruins,]
To see the black perspective of long avenues [...]
All silent,
The white strips of sky
At the sides, cut by the poplar trunks,
The white strips of sky
Above, diminishing –
The silence and blackness of the avenue

Enclosed in immensities of space
Spreading away
Over No Man's Land ....
Then, far away to the right thro' the moonbeams
'Wukka Wukka' will go the machine guns ....[15]

It was recited, I was told, by the actors of the Odéon with great success to the French poilus of the trenches.

---

15 The poem is a variant of the opening of 'Clair de Lune', published in *On Heaven*, pp. 42–3. Compare 'Epilogue', pp. 54–5 above.

Wartime England

From *Return to Yesterday*, p. 329.

A little later it was me whom the sight of [Ford's friend, the American publisher] Mr [Ferris] Greenslett covered with confusion. It was in 1917 and I was returning from Belgium with a report of a confidential nature but not of earthquaking importance. It was to be enshrined in a ministerial pronouncement in the House of Commons that evening and to form part of a reply to the German Government as to the treatment of German prisoners in the lines of communication. German Zeppelins searching for an ammunition dump many miles behind the front had succeeded in killing a number of prisoners over whom I commanded the escort.[16] They had also killed several of my men. No one had bothered much about them, but I had had to be tried by a court of enquiry for being short in the roll-call of my wards. And I may say that at that time the prisoners were being a great deal better treated than my unfortunate men. So I was not in a very good temper. I had not yet had time to write my portion of the report – which was addressed to the Ministry of Information. I was irritated by the whole affair and I had private worries unconnected with the war. A special compartment had been reserved for me and I was writing away in a corner long before the train started. I was suddenly aware that there was a stranger in the carriage and, without looking at him, I said to the guard who was outside:

'Guard, remove this civilian. You know you have no right to allow civilians in a messenger's compartment.' I had not indeed the right to allow civilians in it myself.

I heard a faint protesting noise. It was made by Mr Greenslett.

---

16 At the end of February 1917, after returning from Menton, Ford was put in charge of a hospital tent of German prisoners at Abbeville.

From *It Was the Nightingale*, pp. 76–82.

One evening of a great air-raid I had been on leave and in pitch-black silence had wandered out of the jetty darkness of Glasshouse Street into the dimness of London's Great White Way beneath the stars ....[17] The white, Greek houses loomed against the celestial pin-points, like temples, like forums. And it was as if, awfully, they listened, awaiting doom ....

The minute was majestic; it had been as if I were alone in a vast cave, the heart of a city that had paused in its beat.... And the houses all listening [....]

As Charles Masterman had predicted in 1913, London had indeed once more, after 250 years, heard the roar of foreign guns. Nay, more, she had undergone her baptism of fire.

And it had been no trifling visit. At that moment the German plane squadron had disappeared to the south-west and those houses were listening for its return. It had already smashed many houses and killed a great many people in their cellars. It would smash and kill yet more that night ....

In the line we were used to consider that air-raids over London must be trifling enough. But I know I found that one sufficiently frightful and disagreeable, and hilarious and a nuisance and an occasion for prayer. With all the range of emotions of the line enhanced .... It provided even Blighties – the thing we all prayed for .... I met next day a colonel of my own regiment who had come home to receive the Victoria Cross, and who was so badly shell-shocked by a bomb falling on his house in Belgravia that he was rendered unfit for further service. I met also a young man who had insisted, to the distraction of his female friends, on emerging from the sofas and champagne of a bomb-proof cellar under a Piccadilly Club, in order to walk around the parapet of the fountain-basin, whilst all sorts of things fell from the sky, and the deserted ladies accompanied him.

It was the raid when the *John Bull* office was destroyed, with God knows how many poor people in what was supposed to be a bomb-proof shelter beneath the building. For myself, I had been dining the wife of another of my colonels at Kettner's, which had been quite close enough to the *John Bull* affair. I had got her safely home

---

17 *The Times* noted on 4 January 1915 that the blackout in London made the stars appear brighter. See Gerard DeGroot, *Blighty* (London, 1996), p. 200.

to the Berkeley – these names of a former London come savorously off a foreign pen! – and though the All Clear had not sounded I had gone for a stroll in the soft black air. So I had come into Regent Street. I was seeing it for the last time in that state! And even then I had a sense of it in my bones.

I was home and nearly in bed by the time they came back. But when the noise began again I thought I had better go and see how my mother was. She lived on Brook Green, and I can assure you that walking along High Street, Kensington, was a sufficiently frightful experience, so that I prayed I might be back in places where you would be hit by a nice clean piece of shell-casing. In there the air seemed to be filled with bits of flying chimney pots and coping stones and our own shrapnel, whilst the guns in Holland Park, past whose wall I had to go, made a noise which seemed to render memories of the first battle of the Somme very pale affairs.

I found my mother sitting in her bedroom window – which she should not have been! – reading *Lorna Doone* in between the shrapnel flashes in the sky. She was a lady of romantic temperament and complete absence of physical fear – except when it was a matter of cows .... For her everything with horns was a mad bull ... a portent of malignant destiny's. But shrapnel, shells, air-bombs, and the rest were merely the toys of the silly children that her menfolk were and, wrapped in a good shawl, she ignored them.

She held her book to her candle flame and said:

'Fordie, isn't this a beautiful poem:

"Love and if there be one, come my love to be,
My love is for the one, loving unto me
Not for me the show, love, of a gilded bliss
Only thou shalt know, love, what my value is!"'

I agreed that it was a beautiful poem – Lorna's song. And indeed I am proud still to be able to write it – as, as a boy, I could have written the whole of *Lorna Doone* – by heart .... So we had a little pre-Raphaelite conversation – about Rossetti and Lizzie Rossetti, and the pictures of my aunt Lucy Rossetti and all their tantrums and alarums. Then, the All Clear having gone, I borrowed the tin hat of my brother, who had lately been wounded and in hospital, and precious glad I was to have it. I had started out that day in a top-hat and morning suit, and was still in them, because when one was home on leave one did not waste much time changing one's clothes .... So I left the top-hat with my mother. And that was the

last time I saw it or wore one. And in tin hat and morning coat –
which would have got me sent back to my unit if there had been
a provost marshal in High Street – I started back home up the
completely empty street in the dead silence.

Then I met a friend and we walked up and down for a long time
in the quiet, talking of old times. When we were just in front of
Holland House it all began all over again – the whole jamboree. I
suppose the Germans must have got as far as Windsor, say, and that
they had been chased back again. We continued to walk up and
down and to talk of old times .... I just hated it .... But we were
Londoners of the old school, and Londoners of the old school do
not acknowledge that anything can happen to their city, because
the London police, the County Council, the Home Secretary, and
the other incorruptibles will see to it that she does not put on
corruption. The skies must first fall [....]

I tell this tale of a London air-raid not for what it is worth in
itself, but in order to emphasise my point that London really had
undergone a baptism of fire. To me – and I daresay to others – it
takes fire, pestilence, sieges and sackings to put the final seal on a
city's dignity. Until then London had lacked that. It had had its
Fire, its Plague, and it had heard the roar of foreign guns, all within
a decade, in the reign of Charles II. But it had to wait a quarter of
a thousand years for final consecration. It had found it ....

Lecturing to the Army

Ford's notes for three military lectures, unpublished manuscripts, Cornell.

[a] With the S[cottish]. W[omen's]. H[ospitals] in France[18]

1.
[Descrip[tio]n of <u>progress of wounded from lines to us</u>]
Man wounded – dressed – ambulance – train.
Train – hanging stretcher – [padded?] sheets – doctors & attendants.
In train [night?] men – stat[io]n in the camp.

2.
Hospital – a long path, dust in summer & thick with mud in winter
– on either side rows of huts & barracks. These were wards, kitchen,
office, sleeping place for staff – store – everything.
Wards two rows of beds, bathroom, wash up place.

3.
<u>[Recep[tio]n of wounded]</u>
Everyone ready & waiting – men arrive taken to receiving ward –
looked at by C[hief]. M[edical]. O[fficer]. who decides on ward to
go to – carried there
Business of washing & putting to bed & feeding. Difficult. Clean
up.

---

18 Possibly the talk he told Stella Bowen about: 'I am going to lecture to 3000 WAC's and
VAD's [the Women's Army [Auxiliary] Corps and the Voluntary Aid Detachment] this
week. Imagine it! It is a job for Yeats or Ezra [Pound] rather than for poor old me'. Ford
to Bowen, 26 June 1918. Sondra Stang and Karen Cochran, editors, *The Correspondence
of Ford Madox Ford and Stella Bowen* (Bloomington and Indianapolis: Indiana University
Press, 1994), p. 4. This volume prints notes for other lecture on Censorship, Cyphers,
and Musketry; pp. 13–15.
   These are very rough and scarcely decipherable notes for the lectures, though the
first gives a vivid impression of an experience Ford didn't otherwise describe, and the
others indicate the cultural topics his lectures would cover. Editorial square brackets have
been used for expansions, conjectures, and (in the case of topic headings) phrases inter-
polated from Ford's abstract of the first lecture.

4.
[Operat[io]n & after.]
Serious cases straight to operating theatre – Clean room sweep the dust[?] – doctors, cupboard & floor. After that may go to sisters[?] ward or base town.

5.
[Normal ward life.]
Own ward. [illegible insertion] Names of latrines. own bed, table, box, bag
[illegible passage] – Doctors visit
lunch sit up at middle table, or on own little table

6.
[Amusement. Cinema, gramophone, concerts.]
Cigarettes, gramophone, cinema events – tables put together – decorated
Men [selves?] sing, read[?], play fiddle etc. choruses. fruit – coffee. Games.

7.
Xmas. Preparat[io]n. – days before start prep[aratio]ns. coloured
            paper ...
            / work – all morning – Hosp. doesn't st[op?]
Day itself – / Decorat[io]n of wards –
Got dark – Carol singers – cloaks & lantern
            big & festive dinner – turkey – fruit
            Entertainment – Present – songs & jokes
            beds & chairs   Father Xmas. & presents.

8.
Spring retreat: dark days – guns day & night
men depressed & in bad heart – raids – retreating civilians
Ordered to pack up to go – [The awful night –]
Night before we were to go – lot of men coming in – very badly wounded, came by ambulance – raid. lights out. Stretcher[s?] on floor – some in bed.
Leaving [illegible: shaded?] candles allowed – & carried on.
huts rattling – & whine of mortars.
    Stat[io]n hit.
    Next day we had to leave – too danger[ous] – men can't

stand it. But no train – mention the line. Had some ambulances –
these to carry the ,men while staff walked – [hot sun?] dust road –
had to join rest of refugees – got lifts – Some stayed to end. every
man away before we left – men anxious not to be left.
Hated to go – our own gardens – growing well, but kitchen hit
later ∴ best.

We [illegible] to another hopital & began straight away work
there – [illegible] – sleep.

For the fallen   B[inyon] ?

[b] Geography & Strategy.

	{Rivers
Main Features of Strategy =	{Roads
	{Sentiment

   The difference between Tactics & Strat[eg]y as defined by Drill
book is[?] Tactics when troops are in contact: Strat[eg]y before
contact.
This w^{d.} have to be amplified or rather rendered clearer to day:
Foch's troops are
everywhere in contact with E[nem]y. not strag[eg]y   goes on
behind the lines.

Rivers: mainly   for transport
Roads   "   for movement of troops
Sentiment   "   goes to provide aims[?], moral, in
                          civil pop[ulatio]ns. etc

   This lecture confined to strategical, geographical
information of : Paris, London, Königsberg.

London   = Sent River & Road Town
Paris   = Road & River Town
Königsberg = Sentimental Town

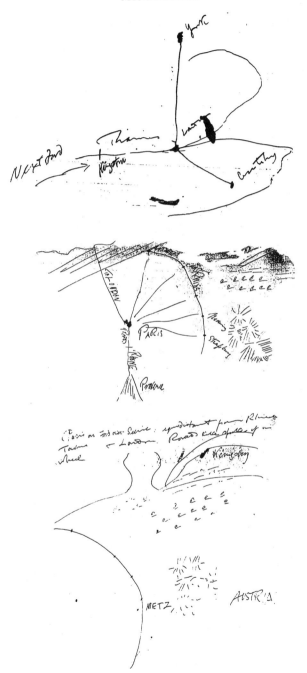

Paris on Ford over Seine: equidistant from Rhine Towns & London. Roads like spokes of a wheel.

London: <u>first</u> ford of the River

[c] Lecture on France

This lecture not about War but about Civilisations.

Main factor of <u>Frankish</u> Civ[ilisatio]n the fact that Rhine at every part of its course is exactly equidistant from Paris.

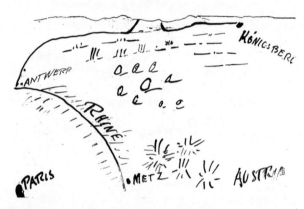

Trend of civilising influence always from S. E. to N. W.

<u>Troubadours.</u>

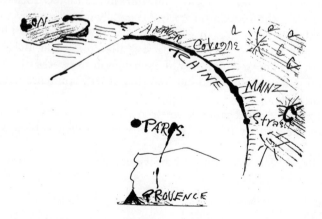

Bertran de Born.
Peire Vidal

If you had lashings of leave[19]
  Vie Parisienne

Marryatt

Mourir pour la France

From *A Mirror to France*, pp. 279–80.
Ford lectured between March and September 1918.

It was my sad fate towards the end of the late occurrences to be
ordered to lecture on history and the like to several thousand Other
Ranks – and twice a day! And twice a day I used to ask the question
– it was in our border country of raids and forays, a very northerly
north!

'If you had lashings of money: all the money you could ask for,
and if you had lashings of leave: all the leave in the world! what
would you do?'

According to the official records of attendance, before
completing that tour of duty I must have asked that question of
over 210,000 men and of several thousand officers. I never but once
got an answer beyond a usual gasp of agony at the image I had
raised. But, happening to lecture to my own regiment, which
regarded me, I suppose, as more amiable and less formidably
highbrow – for to other units I was generally introduced by a regimental sergeant-major, or sometimes even by a general! – I asked
that usual question. From the back of the dining-hall, 09 Evans,
Pte. D., the licensed humorist of the battalion, answered my 'What
would you do?' He called out bravely but with immense feeling:

'*Go mad!*'

It gave me the chance to answer myself better than usual, for
after many orderly rooms I knew 09 Evans as well as I knew any
man. And:

'Oh no, you would not,' I answered. 'With a white waistcoat

---

19 See the next excerpt.

and a Panama hat, with a fat cigar in your lips, three dozen of Veuve
Clicquot in the rumble, a tart in your arms, and a gramophone
braying beside the chauffeur, you'd be running down through the
South of France to make a hog of yourself in a white-and-gilt hotel
at Monte Carlo.'

And a dozen awestruck voices whispered:

'Gawd! Old 'Oof's struck it!'

They called me 'Old 'Oof' in that unit. But whether they were
disclosing their own secret thoughts or merely referring to the
known proclivities of 09 Evans, I don't know. A little of both, I
dare say.

From *Great Trade Route*, pp. 46–7.

When I was an officer of His Britannic Majesty's army I used to
make experiments, as far as was permitted by King's Regs., with
the men under my command. And I found that a sudden digression from the subject in hand would very much reawaken group
attentions that were beginning to wander. I would be lecturing on
the Ross rifle – which was a beast of a thing – or on the Causes of
the War or on any other department of the rag-bag of knowledge
that we had to inflict on the unfortunates committed to our charge.
And I found that if, suddenly, in the midst of a tiresome description of how to sight with the absurd gadget that was stuck on the
nose of that rifle or an even more tiresome disquisition on the
economic situation of the Central Empires, I suddenly introduced
a digression as to the best way those troops could spend their money
when next on leave in Rouen or as to my first ride in an automobile, those Tommies returned with a refreshed mind to the
consideration of how to get their bead-sight on VI o'clock of the
dummy provided for aiming at or to that of the depressed condition
of thirteen Rhenish-Westphalian basic trades at the beginning of
1914.

The physical effects are almost more striking. If you are in charge
of a company engaged on what is called 'jerks' and you find that
their actions are becoming slack – which means that their minds
are flagging – you should suddenly turn the men in another
direction. The comparative bliss of being able to take their eyes off
the blank barrack walls and to gaze instead at gasometers makes

them at once move precisely. Or again, frequently when marching
men along the desperately straight long roads of France, I have
suddenly right-wheeled them through a field gate and made them
form platoon in a field full of cows and scramble through or over
a hedge at the end of the field. The excitement of wondering
whether the officer has gone mad, or whether the Enemy have
suddenly turned up fifty miles behind the line, and the comparative bliss of looking at a bit of grass and some cows instead of the
long asphalt perspective of the road and the napes of the necks of
the files in front of them will, in spite of the fact that their journey
has actually been prolonged, make them fall in on the road again
with comparative cheerfulness and march much better for a long
time.

Immediate Effects on the Mind and on Literature

From 'Stocktaking'; 'I', *transatlantic review*, 1:1 (January 1924), pp. 75–6.[20]

During the late war, for instance, the aggressive and Intellectual classes used to ask unceasingly what purpose was served in 'trench' warfare by jumping to it on parade at home. The effect is psychological [...]

And the effect of imaginative culture on the natural mind engaged in human affairs is much that of drill on troops afterwards to be engaged in warfare. It affords and inspires confidence; it furnishes you with illustration in argument, knowledge of human nature, vicarious experience. It makes of the intelligent savage – a proper man!

From *Great Trade Route*, pp. 96–7.

Twenty odd years ago I was in a landscape of mud hills and old, empty food cans and cartridge-cases and old iron and rats and thistles and a corpse or two. It was disagreeable, and at times it grew to be worrying .... An intense worry that filled in all the world and the Huns and Army Headquarters. And when we were in support I used to get a horse and, on one pretext or another, ride for miles in search of a plot of ground that man had left undefiled. I would pretend to be looking for ferrets to destroy the rats with which our lines were infested; or straw for the transport; or better billets for our HQ who were always grumbling at their billets. If I had been able, as Divisional Billeting Officer, to have placed them in Leopold's Palace of Laeken they would have grumbled that the famous collection of musical instruments contained no saxophone.

---

20 Compare 'A Day of Battle', p. 36 above.

For their jazz.

Actually I would be searching for a patch of undefiled earth, with untrampled, unurinated grass, and unberagged hedges. I never found it. Beyond Steenwerck; beyond Locre; beyond Dranoutre; beyond Bailleul, to the Channel itself; every hedge corner had its turf fire with Tommies crouching over it – deserters, I dare say: its tank-depot; its aerodrome; its dead and distended mule.

I don't want you to think that I was unduly dispirited. It is not the horrors of war but the atrocities of peace that are impelling me to write this book in favour of pacifism. I – and most of my comrades of the trenches – have had much worse times since then than we had when a constant life in the open air and hard muscular work kept us insensitized fatalists.

From 'Preface' to *On Heaven* (London, 1918), pp. 7–8.

But I think that, in these sad days and years, we have got to believe in a Heaven – and we shall be all the happier if it is a materialist's Heaven. I know at least that I would not keep on going if I did not feel that Heaven will be something like Rumpelmayer's tea shop, with the nice boys in khaki, with the haze and glimmer of the bright buttons, and the nice girls in the fashions appropriate to the day, and the little orchestra playing, 'Let the Great Big World ....' For our dead wanted so badly their leave in a Blighty, which would have been like that – they wanted it so badly that they *must* have it. And they must have just that. For haven't we Infantry all seen that sort of shimmer and shine and heard the rustling and the music through all the turmoil and the mire and the horror? ... And dying so, those images assuredly are the last things that our eyes shall see: that imagination is stronger than death. For we *must* have some such Heaven to make up for the deep mud and the bitter weather and the long lasting fears and the cruel hunger for light, for graciousness and for grace! ...

From *Joseph Conrad*, p. 192.

A great many novelists have treated of the late war in terms solely of the war: in terms of pip-squeaks, trench-coats, wire-aprons, shells, mud, dust, and sending the bayonet home with a grunt. For that reason interest in the late war is said to have died. But, had you taken part actually in those hostilities, you would know how infinitely little part the actual fighting itself took in your mentality. You would be lying on your stomach, in a beast of a funk, with an immense, horrid German barrage going on over and round you and with hell and all let loose. But, apart from the occasional, petulant question: 'When the deuce will our fellows get going and shut 'em up?' your thoughts were really concentrated on something quite distant: on your daughter Millicent's hair, on the fall of the Asquith Ministry, on your financial predicament, on why your regimental ferrets kept dying, on whether Latin is really necessary to an education, or in what way really *ought* the Authorities to deal with certain diseases .... You were there, but great shafts of thought from the outside, distant and unattainable world infinitely for the greater part occupied your mind.

From 'Stocktaking: Towards a Revaluation of English Literature: VIII. The "Serious" Book', *transatlantic review*, **2:3 (September 1924), p. 281.**

I was standing, then, with three other officers in the mouth of a regimental dump in a disagreeable valley during the fighting on the Somme in July 1916 [....] It was a quite quiet evening, and we were waiting for dinner. In front of us, fifty yards away or so were four A[rmy] S[ervice] C[orps] men standing in a small circle, gossiping, each with the bridle reins of three mules looped through his elbows behind him. A German shell dropped and exploded in the very centre of that small circle. One man and three mules lay on the ground; the other three men after fighting for a moment with their animals let them go and bent over the man on the ground. The mules began to graze at once.

Being officers we naturally had to take charge, do what we could for the men, send to the Red Cross people whose station was in the wood just behind us, and so on. A piece of shell had gone right through that man.

Well, we went back into the dug out for our dinner and were eating and conversing very peaceably about the playing of a hand of bridge that we had lately finished. Then, the talk drifting, one of the young fellows began to talk of an operation for appendicitis he had had to undergo. We had to stop him: the mere talking of cutting flesh with a knife made us feel sick. Yet the sight of a man literally smashed into the dust had produced no emotions in us: certainly hardly more than I have put into the two paragraphs recording the affair. I know of no more striking tribute to the power of the word; at any rate I have come across none...

From 'Pure Literature', *Agenda*, **27:4/28:1 (Winter 1989/Spring 1990), p. 7.**

Pure Literature does not exist in order to excite moral emotions – every work of art may well have a profound moral purpose but the cause for its existence is not that moral purpose. If you had stumbled over one of the late battlefields of France, at night, just after a great strafe you must have had moral emotions aroused in you; but the battle did not exist for the purpose of stirring your emotions. Neither does the night, nor yet do the corpses. They are all profoundly indifferent to your existence.

After-Effects on the Mind, Literature and Society

From 'Just People'; unpublished typescript, Cornell, p. 1.

I wonder if such other writers as actually served in the front lines during the War have been affected like myself. For I find nowadays that almost all invented, thought out and worked up stories, by myself, or even those of great masters almost uninteresting. As if the life had gone out of them!

For, against the dispassionate, absolutely blind Destiny of 'over there' even the Fate that drove Madame Bovary to her death – even that malign and ingenious predestination seems an impotent collection of accidents: one can almost feel the author loading his dice against his character – his unfortunate victim. But the immensely wide, unseen densenesses of iron missiles, coming amongst the immense reverberations, all from one direction – that appeared to be the force of a Destiny so indisputable that no human mind could have invented it, directed it, or to be able to take it in.

At any rate I find my mind mostly dormant in the matter of inventions and my thoughts turning inwards to the recollection of real happenings in which Destiny seems to have played tricks on human beings who were just people, inscrutably and with a rather aimless finger.

From the Preface to *Transatlantic Stories*, pp. xxix–xxx.

We had, before the war too much hypocritical idealism, too much moral gasconnading, too much posturing in letters. And too much of it has survived.

Nevertheless the great benefit of the war was that it did make men search their hearts underneath the drum-beatings of the recruiting sergeants. You damn well had to. Whether you were a thorough-going militarist like myself who did it in unpleasant circumstances or whether you were the most German-born pacifist in the great wheat belt who did it in the sunlight driving a harvester over the great plains, you had to think what life was for – and what life was like. And men whose hearts have been searched not infrequently desire to write – and then they write with sincerity.

From *It Was the Nightingale*, pp. 48–9.

One had had [in the London of 1919] little sense of the values of life if indeed one had the sense that life had any values at all.

Now it was as if some of the darkness of nights of air-raids still hung in the shadows of the enormous city. Standing on the Hill that is high above that world of streets one had the sense that vast disaster stretched into those caverns of blackness. A social system had crumbled. Recklessness had taken the place of insouciance. In the old days we had seemed to have ourselves and our destinies well in hand. Now we were drifting towards a weir ....

You may say that everyone who had taken physical part in the war was then mad. No one could have come through that shattering experience and still view life and mankind with any normal vision. In those days you saw objects that the earlier mind labelled as *houses*. They had been used to seem cubic and solid permanences. But we had seen Ploegsteert where it had been revealed that men's dwellings were thin shells that could be crushed as walnuts are crushed. Man and even Beast ... all things that lived and moved and had volition and life might at any moment be resolved into a scarlet viscosity seeping into the earth of torn fields [....] Nay, it had been revealed to you that beneath Ordered Life itself was stretched, the merest film with, beneath it, the abysses of Chaos. One had come from the frail shelters of the Line to a world that was more frail than any canvas hut.

From *The Marsden Case*, pp. 143–4.

This is not a war novel. Heaven knows I, who saw something of that struggle, would willingly wipe out of my mind every sight that I saw, every sound that I heard, every memory in my brain. But it is impossible, though there are non-participants who demand it, to write the lives of people today aged thirty or so, and leave out all mention of the fact that whilst those young people were aged, say, twenty-two to twenty-eight, there existed – Armageddon. For the matter of that, it would be wicked to attempt it, since the eyes, the ears, the brain and the fibres of every soul today adult have been profoundly seared by those dreadful wickednesses of embattled humanity.

From It Was the Nightingale, pp. 54–5.

War-time England had been like a lunatic asylum. To go from London with its yells, posters, parades and exhortatory bean-feasts to Paris, dead, grey, silent, overshadowed, had been to go from a parrot-house in Coney Island to a Cathedral cloister. The reaction had to come in both cases. In Paris – even as in Berlin – the reaction must be against negationalism. That we shall witness. In London it had to be towards it.

From The March of Literature (London, 1939), p. 848.

The reason for the literary discredit that has fallen to the share of the realists in France, the country of their origin, is not a literary one. It arises from the depths of depression in which the war left the country of the lilies even in the hour of its triumph over the Nordic foe. In France, as in the rest of the world, the great words 'honour', 'chivalry', 'religion', 'self-sacrifice', 'loyalty' and the 'spirit of the forlorn hope' were dead. But in France alone was that extinction of the spirit of the past bitterly mourned and intensely regretted – more even by the young than the old. Thus, every nega-tional utterance will make the young French writer shiver as if you had touched in him an open wound. Even Flaubert whose pessimism was, as we have said, really a disillusioned optimism, is included in one ban with Anatole France who was a really Satanic denier of virtue.

From 'That Same Poor Man'; a revised typescript of an unpublished novel, otherwise titled 'Mr Croyd': Cornell; pp. 1–11.[21]

A dark young man in a blue suit and a vigorous old man, white-moustached and wearing a single eyeglass, sat, in July 1919, one at each end of a bench in Hyde Park. Each desired to speak to the other and so to open an acquaintance. But this had proved difficult; they had sat for twenty minutes and no opening had occurred.

The old man had served for four years in France and Germany. At first he had been a private soldier, then he had had the substantive rank of lance-corporal, though he had held various acting ranks. For four years on the Western Front the young man had behaved with conscience, valour and industry, so that, going out in 1914, in the ranks of the Honourable Artillery Company he had been speedily given a commission in the Special Reserve of his County Regiment.

To him fighting had been very terrible because of mental tortures rather than physical fear, though of course he had known fear. But he had been filled with acute dreads that his self-control might give way. It did at times give way even now after peace had been declared. It gave way whenever he was vividly reminded of the brown turmoil, the distorted limbs, the sweat and the clay that had coloured nearly a fifth part of his young life.

He had come originally from a comfortable home in a western county town and he had gone straight to France from the amenities and the formal life of a University where he had distinguished himself by industry and conscience in his studies; by regularity in his conduct and by alertness, soberness and loyalty to his side in the cricket field. Now he had no home and was afraid of himself.

The sights, sounds, psychologies and conditions of trench warfare had at first appalled, then disgusted and finally wearied him beyond the bounds of patience. The unceasing danger of the life; the great pain of two recoveries from wounds; the constant companionship of men less cultivated than himself and more avid of coarse distractions, had left him socially timid. He was now poor; he had only one very tenuous prospect of civilian employment and he fancied that the fact of his service in the field made him be looked

---

21 Compare 'From a Paris Quay', quoted in the Introduction, pp. 17–18, on the psychological effects of war.

at askance by such civilians as might have put work in his way, whilst the intense desire to marry a young woman of fortune and position who returned his love, but to whom he could hold out hardly any prospect at all of even the most modest competence, rendered him really miserable [....]

Dark, with a rather prominent forehead, a small moustache, eyes which when he was not smiling had a slightly distrustful expression, and with a marked jaw, he appeared to be just a young man of good station, clean, friendly and unnoticeable. He was actually merely the hollow receptacle for the potential nightmares of remembrance; for possible regrets, longings, uncertainties and loneliness.

[...] our young man desperately did not want to come into contact with mad, or even with highly excitable people. He had, for long, been too much afraid, himself, of going mad... Just a week before this interview he had consulted a mind specialist, as to whether he, as a conscientious gentleman, dare propose to marry a young girl to whom he was violently attached. The Specialist had said unhesitatingly that he could – after a long and meticulous examination of the young man who had laid bare his mind with extreme care ... What worried him was that he could not hear any at all vivid words concerning the late war without feeling a desperate desire to burst something – as it were an iron hoop – . It was a desire; and you had to control it.

The Specialist had said:

'Then keep out of the way of what you call vivid words about the late war... You won't have to come across many of them... We are all sick of them; you will find no one wants to utter them or listen to them... It will die out altogether in a year or two; get married; keep happy. Have a family. You are all right... You may have dreads for a year or two. That will be unpleasant for you; it won't hurt your wife or children. That's all.' He had waved the young man out of his consulting room.

From 'That Same Poor Man'; pp. 57–60, 172–6, and 184–7.

As if from immeasurable tranquilities the Corporal's voice came, saying that he knew how it was! He said indeed, that he knew not only how, but what it was – to be overdrawn at his bank and to have his next quarter's income annexed by the banker. But he said there was generally a way out; and leaning back on his seat he assumed more and more the air of a friendly omnipotent deity...

The young man gradually reassumed control of his mind, though his limbs seemed still to remain shaken and not very controllable. It seemed to him perfectly right and proper that an unknown corporal should promise him valuable advice and even assistance. He, Captain Humphry Pilcer, DSO, MC now had a backer... And he was not ashamed. He had been through too many strains to feel ashamed of anything he could pick up in the way of wisdom, help, or mental assistance when his hysterical fit was on him... For it had not been easy to find in this aching city any one who could be at once sympathetic as to his sorrows and instructed as to their nature.

It was like letting out the juices of an old abscess. This fellow was in the family; he had no doubt been batman to many troubled officers... He began to talk artlessly:

He, he said: He, Captain Humphry Pilcer and the rest of it, twenty-six years of age, had not where [sic] to lay his head... Foxes had holes, if they weren't stopped. He hadn't... He said it seemed funny, laughing sardonically... An officer and a gentleman – nowhere to sleep that night...

Clara Sophia [Podmore] had helped him – tremendously... But she wanted him to take rooms. Somewhere with 'SW' at the tail of the address... But you can't swindle boarding house keepers! You cannot.

'Hang it all!' he exclaimed, 'A little overdraft... Yes! But the boarding house keepers; with white gas-globes and children in the basement... Officers' widows most of them!'

He said he would rather make a hole in the water than that.

He found that, for some reason or other, he had tears in his eyes! A simple and inexperienced soul, he thought it horrible that the widows of his brothers who had died, as he knew, in circumstances of horrible agony, should be reduced to making menial livings and be exposed to the peculations of needy swindlers. He reflected bitterly that the mind doctor had told him that he would be all right if he avoided vivid pictures of the 'late struggle'. This, the doctor said, he would find easy since the Civil Population were sick of the war... But how were you, Pilcer, of the Duke's Own, to avoid seeing pictures of the 'late struggle'?

'*You had* to see vivid pictures,' he said to the Lance-Corporal. He said it by way of apology – for you do not actually apologise to a Lance-Corporal if – as he had just done – you call him a —! You explain your state of mind .... And, shamefacedly, at last, he said he truly believed that his late agitation had been because the night before he had seen the rain-soaked figure of a sergeant that they both remembered as once so splendid and resourceful... Rain soaked and begging!

'I don't believe,' he phrased it, 'That I should have let out so if it had been just my own funeral... I hope not... But there seem such Army Corps of hard cases... All over the shop!'

The Lance-Corporal's voice came through to him queerly for his agitation was beginning again at the thought of dishonoured thousands. It said:

'Come and stay with me till you can turn round. I am one of the oldest friends of your family... I was at Oxford just before your father... With your uncle!'...

The young man just said:

'Good God! I knew you would try to do something for me... you're a poor man probably... But...' He was going to say something about getting his own foot in the stirrup... He could not however trust himself to speak any more... The sudden presentation of this last glimpse was too much for the muscles round his eyes and his jaws... For he considered it as a last glimpse of the tremendous solidarity which had made so many lay down, not so much their lives – that was a little matter and soon over – but their thoughts, their services, their infinite solicitudes, their entire industries and their deep love, for days, for months, for years, the one for another... Now those divine and ephemeral friendships dissolved, – after having glorified the world... [...]

'It was the frozen circle of the Divina Commedia,' Mr Croyd said deferentially towards Miss Podmore. 'Then it thawed... our office was a Connaught Hut; the furniture was bully-beef cases; in eternal twilight. The floor was mud. A bucket filled with light coke and pierced with holes... The fumes made us all cry...'

Humphry maintained silence; as if he were obstinate.

'Round the Connaught Hut was an immense plain... Or, no, it was a hillside... An infinite jelly of mud. And we had 2,900 men... Heavens what spavined, muddy men!... And more work than you can imagine. And chilblains, bleeding on all my finger-joints... Chilblains – at my age!'

Humphry Pilcer gulped:

'Isn't that enough?...

'One afternoon,' Mr Croyd went on, 'We were beaten to a standstill. There were 14,500 papers to be filled in .... And we had only one candle. We all came to a standstill – I just as much as the officers!'

There wavered before Humphrey Pilcer's eyes, the slants of an infinite plain of mud nacreous in the twilight; there returned to him the atmosphere of unceasing pain, infinite lassitude, unending confusion and simultaneously the insupportable, the almost irresistible impulse to burst by some – by any – made force the invisible bonds that held him in space and time .... By some – by any – final action .... Any action that ended .... that ended anything.

The old diabolical man in khaki was telling an anecdote of himself that he remembered with hatred and mortification .... He had burst out suddenly on poor Major Augustine Howells, telling him that he intended to refuse duty: that he had had enough. After two years of it! What for? Why? What purpose did it serve? He had indeed asked what he was going to do when he came out of the Army? How was he going to earn even a crust of bread? [...]

'But,' Mr Croyd continued his own train of thought, 'what I want you to get into your head is this... I gave you those details because that is how, in the mud, a great Army is moved and docketed and its accounts kept, its characters and healths recorded, its Wills executed – and its burial crosses provided with details. I told it you prolixly. This is why. One day you will write a War novel... Every writer now living will one day write a war novel... In that day little fragments of those prolix details will remain in your mind and, out of them, you will mould your whole effect – of immense columns moving off in the rain, with little figures crouching over candles doing their accounts... That is what writing is!' [...]

The boy never afterwards knew how he came to be on the upper floor talking to John Grimsdick about his revolver .... Grimsdick was kneeling on a rug unpacking the old battered valise and Humphry just vaguely remembered that he had told Mr Croyd that he was horribly upset about Sergeant Tommy Brown whom he had seen selling matches to a theatre queue ....

At that Mr Croyd had said something that had at once maddened him and brought tears of pity to his eyes. He had tried to re-

construct that speech afterwards for his own comfort; for it had
seemed to him beautiful in the midst of the trembling agony that
came upon him. Once, later, he tried to write it down. It began
something like this, in the note that Humphry made... Clara Sophia
had said that they were vile – all of them who had slept in beds.
And Mr Croyd had said that vile was not the right word. She must
think more exactly...

He had gone on to say that this war had been a great misfortune
for good, fat men – and for others. They stayed at home and
increased their substance. For the rest of their lives, after it was all
over, they would regret that they had not 'gone'. It was a dreadful
thing for a good, fat man to have to nurse regrets and to consider
that it was his duty to relinquish material advantage. So he would
hate the other fellow. He would ruin him to the best of his abilities
– which would be many. He would do this so that there might be
fewer manifest reminders. A man in the workhouse or selling
matches is as good as dead. He does not attract much attention.
That was what the good fat man – and others – desired.

They wanted not to be reminded; they wanted the remembrances swept up and burned as their gardeners were ordered to
sweep up and burn last year's leaves that had fallen on their gravel
walks... But that was not vileness; it was the instinct of self-preservation. No man who is haunted by phantoms can live and propagate
his species. The wolf is not vile; the rat is not vile; nor yet is the
louse... Why then should men uniting in themselves the instincts
of the wolf, the rat and the louse, be called vile?

The context of those speeches remained in Humphry's mind.
They were what had finally driven him up into the loft.
Nevertheless, before he went the old man had uttered one speech
that was like the words out of a book .... That was the reason why
he afterwards tried to write it down. It gave him something to look
at and to calm himself by when these fits were on him, though at
the moment it had driven him away.

And, in the end – Mr Croyd had said – what did it matter? These
men, now starving, were now giving their lives most fully,
honourably and consummately. They had not calculated when they
had gone; now they were paying the price. That was just. Fine,
uncalculating actions must be carried through to the end and paid
for!

'And so, what does it matter? That is life; that is the whole of
life... The leaves that were beautiful and gracious are swept up and

burned; the men that were gallant and splendid, starve; the memories that were sacred are defiled; the great family that passed the torch from hand to hand sees its noblest and its best selling matches in the rain – but never so noble and never so good as then they are ....' Mr Croyd had dropped his voice to say: 'And that is the lot of the human race ....'

Humphry had felt himself on the unbearable point of tears... And suddenly Mr Croyd, looking hard at him, had sent him to ask Grimsdick to put him on the phone into communication with Scotland Yard so as to get figures - as nearly exact as might be – of the precise number of returned BEF men who were actually in the workhouses of the metropolis at the moment or had slept in casual wards the night before. Mr Croyd had said that Scotland Yard would get him the figures in a minute if they knew it was for the gutter press they were to work ....

Grimsdick, stolid, brown like a block of wood, was kneeling in the loft over the battered valise from which there appeared to pour a stream of sour-smelling, brown and distasteful, woollen, leather and metal detritus... Unmoved Grimsdick plunged his hands amongst these foul things that the boy hated for their memories... And slowly Grimsdick disentangled the mildewed strap, the triangular leather pouch with the distended nose...

Pilcer stretched out his hand and stood looking down at the nape of the heavy man's neck. There was, above the collar a firm roll of flesh, brown and with short silver hairs... If the holster had not been closed!... the impulse was unbearable; irresistible, atrocious! ....

All the while he heard his own voice, quite calm, giving his message about telephoning. Yet there was an iron hoop that must... that must be burst!

For a hundred years the brown square man was rolling himself onto his feet. He said something about cleaning the revolver... He had saved his life by getting onto his feet. Humphry was breathing again. It appeared that the telephone was in another stable. God after all was good. He was to be alone for a little.

At the top of a little green painted platform from which green steps led down to cobbles, Humphry suddenly found himself emerging into bright sunshine; a profuse sweat poured down his face; his lips thanking God and going on thanking God .... Because Mr Grimsdick was descending the green steps swinging the holster at the end of the strap ....

From 'Appry la Gair', *Piccadilly Review* **(23 October 1919), 5.**
[This anonymous letter from a 'distinguished man of letters' to a
review which Ford was writing for at the time, sounds very Fordian:
not just for its ironic Tory feudalism, but its allusions to the Welch
Regiment.]

There are two classes in the State that should be respected – those
who produce and those who administer. All others are parasitic.

Begin with the Working Man. I do not say with the Labour
Party. Let us stop cheap gibes at men wanting high wages. I want
all I can get. So do you. Our side has far too long occupied itself
with the woes of the suburban shopkeeper. Whistle him down the
wind.

Let us then stop cheap gibes at Working Men who desire a good
time – for it is our sacred duty to give them a good time. We have
no other duty. Let me tell you.

My regiment was called the Suicide Club during the late war. It
issued in August, 1914, posters saying that the — Bn. — Regiment
was the shortest road to France. We recruited, in a mining district,
sixty per cent of the mining population by December, 1914. Then
the Government forbade us to recruit any more. My regiment
raised twenty-eight battalions of miners, and there were other
regiments recruiting in the same area.

And you will not tell me that I – as a Conservative, or Unionist,
or Coalitionist – am to subscribe to cheap gibes at these men
because they want a good time. I would rather cut off my right
hand. I *promised* them a good time '*appry la gair finny*'. I trained them
in this country to confront death. I used, in France, all my personal
prestige as an officer to induce them to confront death and bear
anguish with composure. I would rather starve than take a profit
on their labour.

From *Provence*, **pp. 304-06.**

You cannot, however, have vast organizations without faith – and
Christianity as a faith died a few days after the 4th of August 1914
... the only sign of protest against that reign of crime and assassina-
tion having been the death, as soon as the effects of war manifested
themselves, of Benedict X... Of a broken heart on August 19, 1914

.... I like to think that the poor old Church, thus before our common faith died, should, alone of all its derivatives, have achieved that tribute to the Saviour ....

And so the whole Western world once the war was finished plunged into a sort of Albigensism .... What else could it do, the parallel being so very exact? ... For the appalled soldiery saw all the churches of the world plunge into that hellish struggle with the enthusiasm of schoolboys at a rat hunt. Not a pulpit thundered that if you slay your fellow man your forehead will bear the brand of Cain. Great lights of the churches plunged into the whirlpool itself – and not armed only with maces, either .... I saw, in 1917, an Anglican dignitary emerging in Rouen from the street in which was the house presided over by Mlle Suzanne. With a revolver at his belt and the full insignia of an infantry field officer – not of a chaplain! At dawn! I was marching a number of men in a garrison fatigue .... I said to him in mess afterwards that he had been very matútinal .... He said: 'You mean, ah, matutaïnal .... All Latin-derived words with the termination *inal* are pronounced *aïnal*,' in his best Balliol voice. I said: As for instance uraïnal! ... which even deans pronounce otherwise, and he cursed me up and down, using language that would have shocked the regimental sergeant-major ....

I don't of course blame him .... Why shouldn't the clergy of a national church be Englishmen too? ... But I had been marching over a hundred men – most of them Nonconformists of his battalion to whom he was well known.

And there is worse than that. I mean the performance of their sacred duties by the clergy on the battlefield .... Before the great attack on Wytschaete in the Salient I was given, along with such Catholics as there were in my battalion, the holy communion by Father Butler, our admirable, cultured and heroic chaplain. It was a touching and primitive ceremony, we kneeling in the straw of a barn whilst the pigs moved among our feet, the shells went overhead and Father Butler preached a sermon on the more abstruse aspects of the doctrine of the Immaculate Conception. He did that very properly and humanely so that our minds should be taken off our surroundings .... Or there is the story, that in those days the French found touching, of the Jewish Rabbi who was killed in No Man's Land whilst holding a crucifix before the eyes of dying men – incurring no doubt damnation for himself .... The Christian dead, however, were credited with having died duly fortified by the sacraments of the Church of Rome ....

But even whilst we were taking the communion the thought occurred to me that it would have been better for the poor reeling world if the Church of which Father Butler was the servant had ordered him to refuse to us the sacred elements, since we knelt there with the purpose of murder in our hearts ...

Memorialising the War

From *It Was the Nightingale*, pp. 52–3.

England had paid a terrible toll of the most English of its youth. In Notre Dame there was – there still is – a small tablet not much larger than a sheet of *The Times* of New York or London. It was surmounted by the pretty royal arms of England and her Dominions and announced that it was there to the glory of God and to the memory of more than a million British dead who lay for the most part in the fields of France .... It is a fine piece of English swank that that solitary tribute should be so small and so restrained. It is the fitting tailpiece to the Scrap of Paper speech,[22] and if England had compassed nothing else she would be justified of her national and emotional rectitude. For myself I never come in the shadows on that lettering and those symbols in gold, azure and vermilion without feeling more emotion than – even in shadows – my British upbringing will let me express ....

'Years After' (1929); unpublished typescript: Cornell.

On Sunday afternoons – and at this time of year mostly at sunset and in the light falling through the great inimitable rose-windows to the West – I see a little pretty tablet on a column of Notre Dame. It is little and pretty – no other adjectives will describe it, for it is not very much larger than a pocket handkerchief and it is in bright reds, blues, yellows, gilding, with pretty lions, leopards, harps and lettering. It commemorates... 'One Million British Dead' who lie 'for the most part in France'.

And that, as far as I know, is the only memorial in Paris, which is in the heart of France, to all those million who died and to all

---

22 The German Chancellor, Bethmann Hollweg, referred to the treaty of 1839 guaranteeing Belgian neutrality as a 'scrap of paper' when he responded to the British ultimatum of 4 August 1914.

the labours and heart searchings of the six or seven million of the rest of us who did not die but suffered 'for the most part in France'.

And somehow, oddly, it is good that that memorial should be obscure and little and pretty and mostly ignored. Because, if it were an immense, vainglorious mass of stone, it would be less a symbol of the better world that those deaths and those unchronicled heart-searchings and sufferings have given us. For us who voluntarily fought the war was one to end what was called jackbooting in the world. And jackbooting is ended. There is no potentate or head of a nation now who thinks that the rattle of the sabre or a gesture indicating heavy artillery parked in hundreds of thousands can advantage himself or his peoples. Enormous gestures, swank, vast expenditures on ostentation have mostly gone and for a million victorious dead you affix to a dark wall – a little, pretty tablet. I do not think that those dead who are now all-wise would have it altered.

And I wish that that consciousness that – whatever the material depression of today – the moral advantage that we have gained is enormous and possibly even eternal – I wish that that proud consciousness might be more the note of England today and that it might be the dominant thought in the minds of those who in London will devote their couple of minutes' silence to those memories.

I cannot afford to commit myself to this apparently vainglorious utterance because my contacts with England are now practically non-existent and because I have thought of little else for, let us say, sixteen years now... for the most part in a France which is safe through our efforts. The action of England on that day of a fifteen years ago August was the proudest and finest action that, on the large scale, History has to record and it has been justified of itself, if only because it, by that, achieved the right to affix its totally inadequate and yet so tremendously fitting, small, glowing object in the shadowy recesses of a foreign and oblivious shrine. It was Gambetta who said: 'N'en parlez jamais; pensez y toujours.'[23]

---

23 Léon Michel Gambetta (1838–82), republican politician who led the attempt to defend France against Prussia in 1870: 'Speak of it never, think of it always.'